International Political Economy Series

General Editor: **Timothy M. Shaw**, Professor of Political Science and International Development Studies, and Director of the Centre for Foreign Policy Studies, Dalhousie University, Halifax, Nova Scotia

Titles include:

Francis Adams, Satya Dev Gupta and Kidane Mengisteab (*editors*)
GLOBALIZATION AND THE DILEMMAS OF THE STATE IN THE SOUTH

Preet S. Aulakh and Michael G. Schechter (*editors*)
RETHINKING GLOBALIZATION(S)
From Corporate Transnationalism to Local Interventions

Elizabeth De Boer-Ashworth
THE GLOBAL POLITICAL ECONOMY AND POST-1989 CHANGE
The Place of the Central European Transition

Edward A. Comor (*editor*)
THE GLOBAL POLITICAL ECONOMY OF COMMUNICATION

Randall D. Germain (*editor*)
GLOBALIZATION AND ITS CRITICS
Perspectives from Political Economy

Barry K. Gills (*editor*)
GLOBALIZATION AND THE POLITICS OF RESISTANCE

Stephen D. McDowell
GLOBALIZATION, LIBERALIZATION AND POLICY CHANGE
A Political Economy of India's Communications Sector

Ronaldo Munck and Peter Waterman (*editors*)
LABOUR WORLDWIDE IN THE ERA OF GLOBALIZATION
Alternative Union Models in the New World Order

Michael Niemann
A SPATIAL APPROACH TO REGIONALISM IN THE GLOBAL ECONOMY

Ted Schrecker (*editor*)
SURVIVING GLOBALISM
The Social and Environmental Challenges

Kendall Stiles (*editor*)
GLOBAL INSTITUTIONS AND LOCAL EMPOWERMENT
Competing Theoretical Perspectives

Caroline Thomas and Peter Wilkin (*editors*)
GLOBALIZATION AND THE SOUTH

Kenneth P. Thomas
CAPITAL BEYOND BORDERS
States and Firms in the Auto Industry, 1960–94

Geoffrey R. D. Underhill (*editor*)
THE NEW WORLD ORDER IN INTERNATIONAL FINANCE

Amy Verdun
EUROPEAN RESPONSES TO GLOBALIZATION AND FINANCIAL MARKET INTEGRATION
Perceptions of Economic and Monetary Union in Britain, France and Germany

Robert Wolfe
FARM WARS
The Political Economy of Agriculture and the International Trade Regime

International Political Economy Series
Series Standing Order ISBN 0–333–71708–2 hardcover
Series Standing Order ISBN 0–333–71110–6 paperback
(*outside North America only*)

You can receive future titles in this series as they are published by placing a standing order. Please contact your bookseller or, in case of difficulty, write to us at the address below with your name and address, the title of the series and one of the ISBNs quoted above.

Customer Services Department, Macmillan Distribution Ltd, Houndmills, Basingstoke, Hampshire RG21 6XS, England

The Global Political Economy and Post-1989 Change

The Place of the Central European Transition

Elizabeth De Boer-Ashworth
Associate (Research)
Centre for Governance and Public Management
University of Limerick
Ireland

First published in Great Britain 2000 by
MACMILLAN PRESS LTD
Houndmills, Basingstoke, Hampshire RG21 6XS and London
Companies and representatives throughout the world

A catalogue record for this book is available from the British Library.

ISBN 0–333–65125–1

First published in the United States of America 2000 by
ST. MARTIN'S PRESS, LLC,
Scholarly and Reference Division,
175 Fifth Avenue, New York, N.Y. 10010

ISBN 0–312–23463–5

Library of Congress Cataloging-in-Publication Data
Boer-Ashworth, Elizabeth de, 1962–
The global political economy and post-1989 change : the place of the Central European transition / Elizabeth De Boer-Ashworth.
p. cm.
Includes bibliographical references and index.
ISBN 0–312–23463–5 (cloth)
1. Poland—Economic policy—1990– 2. Poland—Economic conditions—1990– 3. Czech Republic—Economic policy. 4. Czech Republic—Economic conditions. 5. Hungary—Economic policy—1989– 6. Hungary—Economic conditions—1989– 7. Poland—Foreign economic relations. 8. Czech Republic—Foreign economic relations. 9. Hungary—Foreign economic relations. I. Title.

HC340.3 .B625 2000
338.943—dc21

00–023345

This book is printed on paper suitable for recycling and made from fully managed and sustained forest sources.

10 9 8 7 6 5 4 3 2 1
09 08 07 06 05 04 03 02 01 00

Printed and bound in Great Britain by
Antony Rowe Ltd, Chippenham, Wiltshire

With love for my husband, Dr Luke Ashworth,
who sets the standard to which I aspire

Contents

List of Tables

Acknowledgements

I would like to pay sincere thanks to Nabil Adawy, without whose decisive and professional help I would not have been able to complete this project. I would also like to thank Brian Keary for his comments. A special thanks to Peter Carey whose work with this manuscript substantially improved its content and presentation.

I would also like to give my appreciation to Dominic Murray and Tracey Gleeson of the Centre for Peace and Development Studies for the use of the centre's facilities and their friendly support.

Finally I would like to thank all those people in Central Europe who offered help and supplied me with statistics, research materials and/or consented to personal interviews. I list below those I wish to particularly thank:

Dr Ingeborg Nemcova
Department of Economic Policy, Faculty of Macroeconomics and Public Administration
University of Economics in Prague

Professor Dr Ludek
Urban Institute of Economic Studies, Faculty of Social Sciences
Charles University, Prague

Dr Frantisek Turnovec
Director CERGE, Centre for Economic Research and Graduate Education
Charles University, Economics Institute, Prague
Academy of Sciences of the Czech Republic

Mr Stavinoha
Vice Director
Department for Political Relations to the EU
Ministry of Foreign Affairs, Czech Republic

Mr Jiri Zukal
Department of the European Communities
Ministry of Foreign Affairs, Czech Republic

Dr Laszlo Varadi
Center for Public Affairs Studies
Budapest University of Economic Sciences, Hungary

List of Abbreviations

AFD	Alliance of Free Democrats
AMA	Agricultural Market Agency
ARMA	Agency for Restructuring and Modernization of Agriculture
CAP	Common Agricultural Policy of the EU
CDP	Civic Democratic Party
CEECs	Central and East European Countries
COMECON/ CMEA	Council for Mutual Economic Assistance: trade agreement for inter-Soviet bloc trade
CSE	Consumer Subsidy Equivalent
CSSD	Czech Social Democratic Party
EC	European Community
EBRD	European Bank for Reconstruction and Development
EFTA	European Free Trade Area
EU	European Union
FDI	Foreign Direct Investment
FYD	Federation of Young Democrats
GATT	General Agreement on Tariffs and Trade
GDP	Gross Domestic Product
GNP	Gross National Product
G7	Group of Seven: USA, UK, Canada, Japan, Italy, Germany and France
HDF	Hungarian Democratic Forum
HSP	Hungarian Socialist Party
HWP	Hungarian Workers' Party
IFIs	International Financial Institutions
IMF	International Monetary Fund
KOR	Workers' Defence Committee
MFN	Most Favoured Nation
MOF	Ministry of Finance
MOI	Ministry of Industry
MOP	Ministry of Privatization
NAFTA	North American Trade Agreement
NEM	New Economic Mechanism
NIF	National Investment Funds
NIS	Newly Independent States
NATO	North Atlantic Treaty Organization

OECD	Organization for Economic Co-operation and Development
OPEC	Organization of Petroleum Exporting Countries
PHARE	EU funding body for aid and support programmes for Central and Eastern Europe
PPF	Patriotic People's Front
PSE	Producer Subsidy Equivalent
R&D	Research and Development
SPA	State Property Agency
UNCTAD	United Nations Conference on Trade and Development
UNICEF	United Nations International Children's Emergency Fund
USSR	Union of Soviet Socialist Republics (Soviet Union)
WB	World Bank
WTO	World Trade Organization
WZ-WZZ	Foundation Committee for Free Trade Unions

1
Introduction*

During September 1998 *Newsweek*[1] was published with a cover emblazoned with a cartoon graphic of an ill globe. In large letters the cover sported the following: 'Sick and Tired: Is the World Growing Weary of Market Capitalism?'. Eight years after the collapse of Soviet communism, the triumphalism of the West has given way to worry. Issues of global financial stability, flight of foreign investment and increasingly ineffectual national governments have become a concern for all countries. The widening and deepening of the capitalist project, to become more global, has not brought the stability and prosperity expected.

The main contention of this study claims that the manner in which the Group of Seven (G7) countries and international organizations such as the International Monetary Fund (IMF) have dealt with the transition of the former Soviet Union, and its satellites, would be crucial to the way the West would confront all subsequent crises of global capitalism. Theory, especially Western theories towards economic development, had become more prominent and widespread throughout the Cold War. With the disappearance of Soviet communism, there was no other serious theoretical contender other than liberal capitalism, from which to create developmental policies. Nevertheless, assumptions of linear progress that are often found intertwined with theories of liberalism and/or capitalism have been called into question in light of the marked growth of global and regional inequality. Current market-driven economic and developmental solutions, even though they are

* Throughout this study academic disciplines and schools of thought such as International Relations, International Political Economy, Realism and Modernization theory have been capitalized to differentiate them from the common use of these terms.

now largely uncontested from an ideological point of view, do not have impressive results. Its seems that in our technological age we have become more adept at transmitting existing ideas at an ever increasing speed, but not at fashioning new ideas. Moreover, the late twentieth century seems rife with a confusion between the Enlightenment's project of human emancipation and the capitalist ideology of 'improvement' which is tied to production and profit. We seem to be moving more quickly in a direction of which we have only a limited comprehension. Ultimately, this study is interested in the influence of economic power. However, developments in global governance, and late twentieth-century capitalism make it difficult to get at the heart of recent trends in a way which would allow us to gain at least some level of understanding of what is happening to the world around us.

This study attempts to highlight the importance of certain changes to the global political economy, using the transition in Central Europe as an example. It begins by concentrating on the macro/global level. In the following sections it examines the pivotal role played by Western norms and values and how their transmission since the age of empire to the present day has shaped our current system. In this introduction an attempt is made to explain how intensification of the transmission of Western norms combined with structural changes to the global financial sector have had an enormous impact on how policy-makers deal with financial and economic crisis. This section also highlights why the Central European countries of Poland, the Czech Republic and Hungary have been chosen as examples. The transition projects that transformed these countries from communism to capitalism were very ambitious. It was also the most invasive package put together by the IMF, International Financial Institutions (IFIs) and members of the G7 countries. The transition in Central Europe (similar to other parts of the former Soviet Union) would see loan conditionality encompass not only economic behaviour but also public and private institutions and legislation on an unprecedented scale. After the post-communist transition project the West would make these invasive measures standard practice in overcoming any economic crisis, whether Mexico in 1994 or Asia in 1997–98.

Moving onto the micro/local level, this book attempts to reveal how Central Europe would play a lynchpin role as the experimental policy laboratory in which procedures, now standard, would be shaped. As a result of their proximity to the European Union, Poland, the Czech Republic and Hungary are being considered as case studies. Of all the countries in transition, these countries were to be the showcase examples of what could be achieved when retooling a country in the image of a Western liberal capitalist state. It is hoped that this study will illustrate how the transfer of Western norms was to prove more problematic than had originally been expected. The transition in Central Europe would reveal as much about the weaknesses of Western thinking and assumptions as it would the problems of installing an alien system over a failed one.

Over the course of the coming chapters major trends and flaws in our current global system have been examined and discussed. Moreover, this examination illustrates how these trends have impacted upon Central Europe. Furthermore, the behaviour of the West during the transition in Central Europe would change the standard operating procedures of financial institutions involved in a variety of forms of global governance. Using Central Europe as a starting point it is hoped that a level of insight can be achieved with regards to where our current global system is heading.

1.1 Scope and aim of research

The main aim of this book is to examine major trends in the Global Political Economy. There have been considerable changes since the fall of Soviet communism after 1989 and this work endeavours to place these changes in a theoretical and historical context. This book focuses its research on two main areas: (1) issues of global governance, with a particular concentration on IFIs and (2) specific examples of the effect of policies prescribed by international organizations to the area of Central Europe during its transition from communism to capitalism.

The specific case study countries of Poland, the Czech Republic and Hungary are discussed in detail. Empirical data is employed in an attempt to provide a grounding for the main argument of this work, that the developmental approaches used by the West during the post-Soviet transition would shape the way the West would deal with future economic global crises.

The topic of the global political economy is intensely complex. As a result the literature and sources used in this research work span a variety of social science disciplines. Works of mainstream international relations and international political economy make up the majority of the research. However, an important contribution is made by history, sociology, economic and law sources. Core statistics were supplied by the central statistical offices of each of the case study countries as well as from organizations such as the Organization for Economic Co-operation and Development (OECD), the European Community (EU) and the

IMF. In addition to this standard research, information was gathered through direct research in Central Europe and academic contact with a variety of university and research centres in the EU and Central Europe.

Chapter 1 hopes to provide the reader with a solid background as to the structure of the global system and the theoretical thinking that has gone into its construction. These issues are discussed at length in Section 1.2: 'The power of Western norms'. In Section 1.3 the study moves on to look at more recent structural changes in the global political economy. This section suggests that policies suggested by international financial organizations such as the IMF would have a significant impact on the international economic system. This chapter also provides a discussion of the role of the Soviet Union in the economic life of Central Europe prior to 1989.

In Chapter 2 the study examines how theories of development have been applied to Central Europe. A demarcation is made between developmental approaches to Central Europe before the fall of Soviet Communism in 1989 and policies applied after this time.

Chapter 3 provides an introduction to the case studies. It concentrates on Western policies toward Central Europe during the 1990–93 period of the transition. The chapter looks specifically at policies that were applied to all three countries in this study.

Chapter 4 provides an overview of Polish history and describes the problems encountered during its communist period. The chapter also provides a detailed account of the collapse of communism as well as discussing the policies put in place during the transition. The last section in the chapter looks at the results of the policies put in place during the transition.

Similar to Chapter 4 on Poland, Chapter 5 concentrates on the Czech Republic. The chapter begins with a discussion of the history of Czechoslovakia and its ultimate disintegration. The remainder of the chapter concentrates specifically on the Czech Republic and its experience during the transition.

Chapter 6 concentrates on Hungary. It begins with a short history of Hungary and then continues on to detail the collapse of communism and the transition process. As with the other case study chapters, there is an examination of the results of the policies that were put into place during the transition.

Chapter 7 concentrates on the growing relationship between Central Europe and the European Union. It explores the EU's motivation behind its acceptance of Poland, the Czech Republic and Hungary as applicant countries to its organization. To illustrate possible problems and benefits with regards to enlargement, this chapter also provides a detailed examination of post-1989 changes to Central Europe's agricultural sector.

Chapter 8 provides a summary with conclusions. It is hoped that the main themes of this book are brought together in such a way as to provide a certain level of understanding with respect to where the current Global Political System is heading.

1.2 The power of Western norms

There are two common populist misconceptions with regards to the relationship between Europe (and now, by extension North America and the other members of the G7[2]) and the rest of the world. One notion holds that the technological revolution of the 1970s and 1980s has been responsible for an unprecedented level of globalization and this can be used as an explanation of the ability, by the West, to exercise political/economic control worldwide. Presuming, therefore that technologically led globalization has radically altered our global system. The other argument runs counter to the one above. Largely Realist in its conception, this argument assumes that the domination by the most powerful of the less powerful, has been occurring since the beginning of the last millennia. This argument is based on the traditional Realist concern regarding the excercise of power. Using this as a starting point it could be argued that the exercise of political/economic power by the G7, over the non-Western world, is little different in its intent, for instance, than the conquest of North America in the fifteenth and sixteenth centuries. Obviously, we have oversimplified the arguments here, but there has been a tendency in both popular opinion and academic work to draw on one of these two streams of thought. While it is true that the current state system had its birth with the Treaty of Westphalia in 1648, the development of the present-day divisions between the developed and the less-developed world has its roots in neither the far distant past nor recent history. Its development can be traced directly to the great age of Imperialism that existed between 1870 and 1914.

The capitalist countries of Europe (particularly Great Britain, France, Germany, Belgium and later the United States) had enjoyed increased wealth and influence throughout the late eighteenth and nineteenth centuries. However, with the exception of the conquest of North America, there was no systematic movement to convert informal trade ties and the influence of wealth into formal imperialism (Hobsbawm, 1987: 57). This would change in the later part of the nineteenth century. Within a period of 20 years the globe would be carved up into territories under the direct rule or effective political domination of a small number of wealthy states. Before this period there were large parts of the world that had political independence and cultural autonomy, even if it did have trade ties with the European world. By 1900 the Pacific and Africa would be almost completely divided among the European powers. Hobsbawm points out that: 'between 1876 and 1915 about one-quarter of the globe's land surface was distributed or redistributed as colonies among a half-dozen states' (Hobsbawm, 1987: 59). Britain alone, increased its territory by over 4 million square miles (ibid.). This process would create the twentieth-century phenomenon where the globe would be divided between the 'First World' and the 'Third World', the 'North' and the 'South', and the 'Developed' and the 'Less-Developed'. Whichever terms are used, the resultant meaning is the same. It is the recognition, despite the end to formal colonialism, that we still live in a world in which a small group of countries have considerably greater access to wealth and power than do the majority of countries, and this divide fits closely along the lines of late-nineteenth-century imperialism.

There has, of course, been significant change since the end of the First World War. However, we must ask ourselves whether this change can actually be heralded as the progress it is often suggested to be. The age of Imperialism was, at its worst, characterized by unpalatable attitudes towards race and religion, which often resulted in mass cruelty or even genocide. At its best, it remained a highly paternalistic form of governance bent on the transmission of European/Western values to all parts of the world. Nevertheless, there is an important difference between the policies executed in the non-Western world today at the behest of the IMF or the World Bank (WB) and the formal colonialism of the late nineteenth century. Today, very few Westerners need live with, or be concerned by, the results of the structural adjustment programmes of IFIs for developing countries. A rather unfortunate claim can be made that Western governments during the Age of Empire exhibited a greater sense of responsibility for those not living in the Western world than exists today.

Nineteenth-century political concepts, which translated into a sense of responsibility toward the developing world, have seldom been discussed during the last half of this century. The waning of interest in the philosophy of the 'moral imperative' associated with the 'Age of Empire' is understandable. The language is both starkly racist and elitist. The paternalism of colonization was intimately associated with the phenomenon of massive 'white' settlement. In Northern Africa alone over a million and a half settlers from the northern Mediterranean moved to the region between 1820 and 1910 (Hobsbawm, 1987: 354). South America absorbed 3.6 million European settlers during the same period (ibid.). Although nineteenth-century European emigration often meant the misuse or abuse of local populations, it did mean that settlers had to physically live in the system they had created. We must ask ourselves if there were, for instance, a million recent American or European immigrants settled in Central Europe, would this have reduced the harshness of the 'Shock Therapy' or Structural Adjustment Programmes forced upon these countries after 1989. The answer would probably be yes. The large American Jewish population living in Israel, for example, has had a considerable effect on the treatment of that country by the rest of the West. This argument does not attempt to place nineteenth-century colonialism in a positive light, but rather illustrate to what extent the bigoted attitudes of the period remain imbedded in the policies of present-day global economic institutions and the governments of the West.

During the height of Imperialism (a word not in common usage until the 1890s), the European 'civilizing mission' was understood to encompass the development of the rest of the world. If the non-Western world was not doing well it was seen as a failure of the West. The onus of responsibility for success of the system was assumed to lie with those in the wealthy parts of the world. It was the 'moral imperative' of the colonizing powers to recreate their territories in their own image. Before the First World War, many leaders and industrialists were proud to call themselves 'Imperialists'. However, the racist language of the day became increasingly unacceptable. By the early 1940s the term 'Imperialist' had become largely pejorative. Although the term fell out of favour, the outcomes of future international economic development policies would not have dissimilar results to its early twentieth-century counterparts.

After the Second World War, formal colonialism was gradually abandoned and the physical holding of foreign territory became unattractive to policy-makers in the West. Nevertheless, developed countries continued to assume that they had some responsibility with regards to helping countries in the rest of the world to modernize. Although misguided, often with disastrous results, Modernization Theory (a discussion of Rostow's theory can be found in Chapter 2) was a hangover of the nineteenth-century assumption that the success of the development of the Less Developed World was the obligation of the West. Even though the language of imperialism had become politically unfashionable, much of the West's policy prescriptions would remain hauntingly similar. The whole argument, for instance, of the need for comparative advantage, in which developing countries were encouraged to specialize in producing 'what they were good at' usually a primary agricultural product, was never to lose its popularity. There was a belief in linear progress in which developed countries showed developing countries the future path. This was coupled with lip service towards liberal economics (despite the fact that protectionism remained a part of both North American and European national policy-making) was as much part of 1950s economic development rhetoric as it was at the turn of the century.

Somehow, the late twentieth century brought with it a curious change in philosophy, in which the non-Western world would continue to be pressurized into adopting Western prescriptions with regard to economic development. The twist, however, was that if Western theoretical prescriptions failed in their practical application, it was no longer those who had conceived of the policies that were to blame, but those who were forced to accept them. It is now up to the rest of the world to adopt the values of the Western world. If the adoption is unsuccessful then the failure is the problem and the fault of those outside the West. Therefore, the August 1998 economic crisis in Russia is not due to IMF prescribed loan conditionality, but Russia's presumed laxness in converting these conditions into policy. Using this line of reasoning it becomes easy to chastise many of the Central and Eastern Europe Countries (CEECs) for the poverty they experienced during the transition depression of 1990–93. The fault lay not with Western prescription, but with the CEECs inability to translate the policy into economic prosperity.

The theory behind the IMF's loan conditionality is strongly neo-classical and neo-liberal, what is often associated with new-right forms of policies. These approaches all have an antipathy towards government interference and a deep belief in market capitalism. In interviews with officials of the American Federal Reserve bank, the following was the response to dealing with problems in the international financial market: 'When you don't understand what's happening, but you have a bedrock belief in the market, you simply make sure it functions properly . . . let it do its work and it will scrub away your problems' (Klee and Thomas, 1998: 27). Rooted in ideas such as Adam Smith's 'Invisible hand', the market is assumed to work along natural laws and as a result neo-liberal economics developed the conceit of being a science. This view has encouraged a certain brand of 'liberalism' which in turn is tied to a late-twentieth-century faith in those who can successfully engineer or manage science in whatever form. Meaning that to every problem a solution must be able to be found: 'To someone with faith in science, poverty must be seen as a consequence of our ignorance or more likely, of the ignorant practices of the poor' (Augelli and Murphy, 1998: 79). This argument makes the poor and vulnerable in the global society responsible for their own poverty.

Immanuel Wallerstein, in his work on Eurocentrism in the social sciences, expresses considerable concern with regards to the continuing strength of belief in nineteenth-century concepts of liner progress (Wallerstein, 1997). He points out how even International Political Economy critics of capitalism and globalization seem to have fallen into the trap of relying on eurocentric universalist theories of development. Wallerstein seems unclear regarding what is exactly meant by 'Eurocentric'. Much of his discussion seems to be levelled more at American-style social science. It is perhaps, more accurate, therefore, to talk about Amerocentric social science or even transatlantic Western-centrism. Nevertheless, the saliency of Wallerstein's argument maintains a certain resonance. There remains a conviction that progress is linear and that developing countries ultimately should follow the example of the West. Even though much writing on globalization is critical it still uses the presumptions that are in evidence in nineteenth-century theorizing with regards to extending 'civilization'. Wallerstein admits that the term 'civilization' is a loaded one and that it has a variety of meanings attached to it. His basic line of argument is that those who support the extension of Western norms further into the wider world are relying on a nineteenth-century 'Whig' (liberal) explanation of the past in which the present is the best of times and that the past has led inevitably to the future (Wallerstein, 19997: 96). If we refer to Butterfield's classic on the Whig interpretation of history, he points out that:

> It is part and parcel of the Whig interpretation of history that it studies the past with reference to the present ... it has often been an obstruction to historical understanding because it has been taken to mean the study of the past with direct reference to present. ... The total result of this method is to impose a certain form upon the whole historical story, and to produce a scheme of general history which is bound to converge beautifully upon the present – all demonstrating throughout the ages the workings of an obvious principle of progress.
>
> Butterfield, 1931 (this edition 1965): pp. 11–12

With this belief in linear historical progress the spreading of, for instance, Western types of accounting methods to Asian banks is simply one more chapter in the march of progress. These concepts tie-up with terms such as modernity and civilization, and support the view that the transmission of Western-centric norms is not only permsissible but natural. However, Wallerstein makes an invaluable point in his questioning of those who criticize the spread of Western norms tied to capitalism. A common argument is that during colonization the West interrupted the indigenous development of non-Western systems. Wallerstein cautions that this illustrates that progress, and non-Western forms of capitalism, are as assumed by those studying the developing world as those who supported its existence in the West. It is worth taking note of these concerns, as there is a continuing confusion between the achievement of human organizational systems which have moved away from blatant cruelty, and the development of modern capitalism. The enlightenment and modernity did bring with it the concept of progress, which is usually taken to mean material progress, but there was also the development of the concept of human emancipation that was not particularly linear, but sought to explore the idea of envisioning a life without fear or pain. The West's 'civilization' of the non-Western world could be said to have concentrated much more on the former rather than the later.

However, it must be conceded that the late-twentieth-century version of the 'civilizing' mission has not only been confined to economic systems. Similar to Africa and Latin America during the 1970s and 1980s, Central Europe was also strongly encouraged to adopt Western forms of political organization. This was especially true with regards to the promotion of democracy in Central Europe. Often, the transmission of 'capitalism' took priority, assuming markets would pave the way for political change. Within the case study chapters of this study we discussed why Central Europe was willing to adopt both 'democracy' and 'capitalism' from the West. Why, however, does the West continue to feel the need to transmit its norms and ideas to the wider world. The desire for security is one popular argument, however, George Lichtheim in his discussion of Imperialism, makes the prudent observation that in the past Western prescriptions for change, based upon the transmission of modernizing theories of economic development, does not always have the desired result: 'There is no guarantee that modernization will produce political stability, democracy, socialism or anything else' (Lichtheim, 1977: 150).

Radical historians have suggested that the spread of Western norms during the 'Age of Empire' was largely driven by the needs of Western capital. This was definitely Hobson's argument in his 1902 study of Imperialism. He saw Europe and America's need for controlling territory as being strongly tied to the West's need to export its capital without which it would be unable to expand its wealth (Hobson, 1902). Hobson felt that imperialism resulted from under-consumption in the home market. This in turn was tied to the failure to redistribute wealth at home. As a result imperialism did not benefit the population at large. Hobsbawm, however, had a different but related view to that of Hobson's and suggested that the driving force behind imperial expansion lay not in the need to export capital, but in the need to export goods. To Hobsbawm colonization was an ever intensifying search for markets. The British economy was reliant on the export of textiles and a full 60 per cent of her textile exports went to India and the Far East (Hobsbawm, 1987: 69).

While the structure of early-twentieth-century empire may seem unrelated to the study of Central Europe, there are some striking similarities that deserve to be considered. During the 'Age of Empire' colonies were encouraged to specialize in the production of a tradeable good, usually a commodity. Using the argument of comparative advantage as a theoretical underpinning many colonies specialized in exporting a limited range of goods. In Canada for instance wood and fish products would remain the staple of their export trade well into the twentieth century. After the Second World War, these mono-product economies were shown to be exceedingly vulnerable to the vagrancies of the international market. Despite this, the initial policy prescriptions after 1989, laid down by the IFIs during the early years of the Central European economic transitions, would follow a model of economic development and modernization not dissimilar to that of the former European colonies. The Polish, Czech and Hungarian governments were informed of the need to specialize, but the process was to begin with the capping, or lowering of wages, to encourage the development of labour intensive, low-tech industries. In tandem with this development, Central European countries were told to lower their trade barriers, which immediately caused a huge influx of imported finished products from the West, mostly from the European Union (see case-study chapters for details). Despite the end of colonialism and the failure of the modernization projects in areas such as Africa, the same policies continue to be transmitted from the wealthy to the poorer countries of the globe. In this sense, the transition in Central Europe is following a well-established pattern that has been replaying itself for a hundred years.

One of the major differences in the transmission of Western values and norms in the late twentieth century as opposed to the early part of this century, is the attempt to disseminate the bicameral model of political democracy. Although the concept of 'imperialism' was to become tainted, the same cannot be said of the concept of 'democracy' which continues to be one of the few political ideas that remains largely untarnished. As a form of political governance, democratic systems continue to have a strong level of acceptance and widespread support as a mechanism embodying genuine legitimacy. As a result, organizations such as the IMF will often combine unpalatable economic reforms in tandem with suggestions for the adoption or strengthening of democratic systems of governance. It can be said that the unattractive elements of capitalism are often introduced on the back of the good name of liberal democracy.

Even though democracy is often welcomed or fought for, it must not be forgotten that it is as much a part of the spread of Western norms as is the IMF's stipulation of neo-classical economic policies for development. As a political phenomenon it originates within Europe. The various struggles from the sixteenth through to the nineteenth centuries saw the organic (often violent) development of present-day forms of parliamentary democracy. The spread of democracy today is very different; countries that have had little or no history of democratic development may within the space of a few months undergo a wholesale adoption of a Western style liberal democracy. This was the case with Poland, whose pre-1989 era of democracy was confined to the years of 1919 to 1939. Nodia's discussion on post-communist transitions goes as far to say that liberal democracy has become the Western model to which most countries aspire (Nodia, 1996). He, like Susan Strange, believes in the primacy of ideas. Nodia discusses how elites in Central Europe, as with other parts of the non-Western world, are heavily influenced by what is popular with elites in the West. The supporting of the philosophy of liberal democracy has almost become an intellectual fashion accessory. The depth and pervasiveness of Western norms can be seen in terms like 'transition'. Nodia points out that there are no longer democratic 'revolutions' (Nodia, 1996: 20). Democracy has become the accepted ideal, therefore countries who now become democratic are not 'revolting' away from the norm, but are rather in 'transit' towards it.

Commonly influenced by Western educations or Western elites, those governing Central Europe 'crafted' their new democracies. Bottom-up democracy gave way to top-down democratic movements. Democracy, as a political concept, remains one of the West's most popular political exports. Nevertheless, there have been criticisms that Western democratic models are often incompatible with the cultural traditions in other parts of the world and is simply part of an ever widening 'cultural imperialism'. The only part of the globe that is seen as offering any serious threat to the spread of Western norms and values is the Muslim world. Huntington makes much of this in his much debated *Foreign Affairs* article 'The Clash of Civilizations' (Huntington, 1993). His main argument is that global cultural differences will be the locus of future conflict. Unfortunately, his conception of culture, as opposed to ideology, seems underdeveloped. His assumption that it is the strangeness of a foreign culture that causes conflict leaves academics with little to explain most ethnic conflicts and civil wars in which the populations are often intermarried and share the same space and political institutions. For instance, the violence in Northern Ireland would be difficult to explain by employing Huntington's view of the world. Huntington's work is extremely useful, however, as a guide to preconceptions of American policy-makers, and one suspects many within the G7 as well. His division of the globe seems to have less to do with culture than it does with dividing the European and North American world from the rest. He is very worried about the threat (the 'clash') of the Islamic world with the Western world. However, the Arab world, similar to either Latin America and South East Asia, was heavily tied into the global expansion of the 'Age of Empire'. It is not an untouched part of the world which offers a unique challenge to the West. It is just reflecting a different set of values, some of which are indigenous, while others have their origin in the long historical connection between Europe and the Arab world. Although the G7 countries continue to have greater influence, than do other states, in the international organizations constructed after the Second World War, this does not mean that they have complete control of the Western norms they continue to transmit. During the inter-war years, it was the adoption of European conceptions of the nation, freedom and self-determination that would serve as a catalyst strengthening Arab nationalism (Kinder and Hilgemann, 1978: 168).

There continues to be a long line of political ironies associated with the relationship between Western Europe (and later the West in general) and the wider world. Tsar Nicholas II (1894–1917), in an attempt to emulate his West European contemporaries, would attempt to force various forms of modernization onto the people of Russia. In reaction to Nicholas' clumsy attempts at modernization without representation, a new force would emerge. However, this new force would be as foreign as its predecessor. The philosophy of the Bolsheviks, would have its roots in the works of Marx, a German who conducted much of his research in the British Museum. Similarly, what many today think of as a lynchpin Islamic revolution owes much to the treatment of Iranians under the Shah of Iran. What few realize is that the Ayatollah Khomeini had spent years in the capital of modern ideological revolution, Paris (Nodia, 1996: 23). It is important to point out this inter-connection. Although it is possible to discuss the Western world as opposed to the non-Western world, this does not mean that these two areas are hermetically sealed. Even though the relationship can be asymmetrical in terms of influence this does not mean that a cross-fertilization of ideas will not take place.

This book illustrates how the Soviet period in Central Europe was dominated by a desire to meet Western industrial production standards. The mismanagement and over-borrowing engendered by the Soviet version of Modernization Theory would see the entire area turn, again, to Western Europe and the other G7 countries. It would do this in an attempt to rid itself of a system that had, in actuality, been a crude attempt to adopt Western forms of industrialization. The sheer power and often lack of success of Western norms, entwined with the influence of its economic might, cannot be over-emphasized.

Part of the difficulty in the transmission of values and ideas, is that during the cross-over certain philosophies and approaches can be over-emphasized, or their importance exaggerated. Amsden *et al.* (1994: 1) suggest that the danger for CEECs is that, just as promises made about the benefits of communism were inflated, so it may be again with the proposed benefits of capitalism. Amsden's worry is that the region has moved from 'pseudo-socialism' to 'pseudo-capitalism' (ibid.). The highly selective version of capitalist development presented to Central Europe through the conditionality of loans was a parody of existing national capitalist economies. The ultimate outcome, was an economic performance in Poland, the Czech Republic and Hungary that was below their collective potentials. The capitalism that was encouraged would see a capitalist economy dominated by small companies and an increasingly weak state. Amsden *et al.* (1994: 16) highlight the problem where: 'a complete tableau of transition economics was never fully specified, and precisely what policy instruments were supposed to achieve which specific growth targets was not made absolutely clear'. This difficulty grew out of an enormous reticence, on the part of the Western advisers to the transition, to discuss institutions. Levels of currency devaluation, interest rates and so on where discussed frequently, but the forms and function of institutional controls needed by governments was avoided. The failure of communism was often crudely interpreted as a failure of government, not a failure of legitimacy combined with poor management. Therefore, the Western norms that were pushed were those in which state institutions played a minor role. Irony, would again have its part to play, for while the philosophy of the free-market was the predominant message, the only body which could ensure its existence was the state. In this regard, the early period of transition was not dissimilar to what Karl Polanyi (1994: 140) observed about Western Europe: 'The road to the free market was opened and kept open by an enormous increase in continuous, centrally organized and controlled interventionism'.

The situation with regards to the transmission of Western norms in Central Europe was thus twofold. On the one hand they were forced, through the medium of loan conditionality, to adopt Western norms. On the other hand the norms that were transmitted were, particularly in the beginning of the process, only a narrow aspect of the Western experience. Walter Weisskopf in his work on alienation and economics gives a detailed account of how the profit motive is only part of capitalist development:

> In the social legislation regulating child labour, the working day, working conditions, health insurance, workmen's compensation, and so forth, the pursuit of profit was restricted to protect the interests of certain disadvantaged groups... in other words, capitalist society rested, from its very beginnings, on two normative principles which were in dialectical juxtaposition: the acquisitive attitude in the free market on the one hand, and social protectionism for the sake of the common good on the other hand.
>
> Weisskopf, 1973: 143

The importance of social legislation in all Western liberal-democracies was not given sufficient attention. The image presented to Central Europe was a collection of Western societies in which economic transaction was the dominant theme. James Mayall's work on globalization and international relations takes up this point by suggesting that there seems to be a weakness *vis-à-vis* understanding the role of law and what it represents. He raises the important question: 'What ultimately is jurisprudence, the theory of law, but the attempt to construct a plausible human structure to limit the potentially destructive effects of human will and wilfulness?' (Mayall, 1998: 243). Much of what was transmitted to Central Europe was connected to economic theory, rather than studying the institutional structures of the Western countries they hoped to emulate. By looking at the volume of social legislation needed to make capitalism stable, the Central European analysts of the early transition could have received a fuller understanding of the project they were undertaking. In effect the difference between neo-classical economic theory and existing social legislation in Western liberal-democracies, is the difference between what we say capitalism does, and how it is actually dealt with in practice.

With regards to post-communist transitions the failure to examine the complex social and institutional components of capitalism has often led economic thinking to view economic development in a narrow way. Jean-Paul Fitoussi suggests that after the collapse of the East, the Western solution was that they should adopt the West's system. However, in Fitoussi's words: 'all we had as the dominant representation of our system was its theoretical descriptive categories' (Fitoussi, 1997: 148). In practice, none of the Western economies had become totally capitalist, in the sense of a completely unfettered free-market. This being the case, it becomes difficult to talk about 'capitalism' as a concept because it means so many different things to different groups. American-style capitalism is popularly conceived as relying on market forces to a greater degree than the more managed capitalism of the European Union. Nevertheless, it is very difficult to extricate exactly what capitalism is within any society. Despite the growing ambiguity of the term 'capitalism', this did not halt the attempt to transmit an ideal form of it to Central Europe. The neo-classical economic model of capitalism, whose transmission was attempted, relied heavily on the economic assumption that the market always runs toward equilibrium. This is curious because, as a discipline, economics models itself on the hard sciences. In the hard sciences there is one underlying principle of the entire universe, that everything runs toward entropy *not* equilibrium. All things naturally destabilize not stabilize. It would seem that if economics did not want to accept this basic scientific principle then the subject should accept human agency and therefore the societal influence on markets. This is not the case, and the neo-classical model, still in its theoretical form was one of the most powerful Western ideas to be ingested by policy-makers in Central Europe.

In recent years, the transmission of Western norms to Central Europe have become less simplistic and stylized. Since around 1994 Central European policy-makers have acquired a more sophisticated view of the Western world, just as organizations such as the EU and the other G7 members are acquiring a less one dimensional view of CEECs. During the Cold War, the Western world tended to view the Soviet Union and its satellites as a monolithic block. In the immediate post-1989 period there was a tendency to prescribe identical policies to small countries such as Latvia and large countries such as Hungary. Quickly, however the West, and the EU in particular, began to differentiate the CEECs and the former Soviet Republics. This may have less to do with mutual understanding, however, and more to do with the European Commission's attempt to digest and control the prospect of the EU's enlargement. In this process of categorizing, Poland, the Czech Republic and Hungary were considered suitable candidates because of their geographical proximity to the EU and their respective levels of development. This process has been difficult for many Eastern European countries, such as Bulgaria and Romania, whose governments' find it difficult to be judged by an organization that seems reticent to accept them as members.

Ultimately, the discussion of Western Norms and their transmission to the wider world remains an intellectually unsatisfying one. Although few would dispute that there were impediments to Western influence towards Central Europe during the Cold War, it remains very difficult to pinpoint the exact nature or depth of the spread of Western norms since 1990. Of course, empirical evidence can be found with regards to loan conditionality, and suggestions of a political nature, found in the European Agreements. In terms of economic development the spread of neo-classical ideas in economic policy seems quite evident. Nevertheless, the overall transformation of Central Europe suggests that the process has gone deeper than the mere enacting of a series of legislation based upon signed agreements with Western institutions.

There has come to be a pervading acceptance of the idea of 'liberalism'. The political philosophy of liberalism was conceived in the seventeenth and eighteenth centuries. Its main focus is on the liberty of the individual, accomplished through a minimal, nightwatchman state. Traditionally, a *laissez-faire* government would ensure law and order but otherwise refrain from intervening in the business of its citizens. This reticence on the part of a *laissez-faire* state, to interfere in the activities of others, is particularly true in the case of economic markets. Therefore, both nationally and internationally, liberalism suggests a commitment to free-market principles, usually without government intervention, and an advocacy of international free-trade policies.[3]

The philosophy of 'liberalism' in the late twentieth century has become embedded to the point of invisibility in most Western institutions. Enrico Augelli and Craig Murphy, discuss 'liberalism' as both an ideology and a political force. Much of their analysis relies on the work of Gramsci, and it is during their discussion of ideology that they offer the argument that Gramsci's concept of this phenomenon is more satisfying than Marx's in that it broadens the meaning beyond the material. Here we enter the realms of ideas where Augelli and Murphy, explore a similar line of thought to Nodia. The main thrust of their argument is that: 'When ideas become widely-held convictions they play a prominent role in social history' (Augelli and Murphy, 1988: 14). And so it has become with the concept of 'liberalism' in both its economic and political forms. It has become so much the norm in both North America and Europe that debate within these countries centres around how to distribute resources within a liberal-economic, liberal-democratic state, but rarely questions the right of either to exist. Augelli and Murphy underline the depth of acceptance of this ideology by pointing out that:

> this is exactly what happened in industrial societies when liberalism became the ubiquitous ideology of traditional intellectual centers as well as the doctrine of organized political parties. Schools and parties began to disseminate an atomistic conception of society and glorify the individual pursuit of wealth and power. . . . Liberalism does not encourage critical reflection or lead to the identification of new common interests or to new forms of collective action.
>
> Augelli and Murphy, 1988: 29

This is not to say that 'liberalism' is fundamentally negative. On the contrary, as a political movement and ideology it has often served as a springboard for human emancipation. The problem with 'liberalism' in so far as it has been transmitted to Central Europe is that the ideological vacuum left after the failure of Soviet communism has also created a situation in which there seems to be little else other than 'liberalism'.

Naturally there are a number of important theories that are part of the academic landscape. Critical theory, French post-structuralism and post-modernism are all twentieth-century theoretical contributions to a wide variety of social sciences. However, if we look at policy-making, we find that despite the rich diversity of approaches that are available, it is the traditional liberal agenda that remains popular with its parsimonious conceptions of democracy and capitalism. Why has this orthodox view had such a long ideological 'shelf-life'? This entire chapter has been trying to offer an explanation beyond the simple one of the domination of one area of the world by the other. Although differences in access to wealth and power exist, there is a cross-fertilization of ideas between the West and the non-West. Economic and political power structures continue to reveal the privileging of the wealthier countries over the less wealthy, but all this does not fully explain the continuing reach of Western influence.

Stephen Gill, in his contribution to Murphy and Tooze's (1991) book on international political economy, tries to explain the continued existence of hegemony. Using Gramsci, he points out the social nature of our reality and the way in which how we think about the world determines the shape and construction of our organizational structures (Gill, 1991: 51). If we accept Gill's interpretation of Gramsci, we are left with the conundrum of why there has been so little resistance to the spread of Western influence into areas such as the CEECs. Western norms were at best welcomed and at worst tolerated. The explanation that the desire to jettison their communist past had a large part to play is valid, but this cannot be the total explanation because the spread of Western norms continues in parts of the world that have had no connection with the Soviet system. The process of the transmission of ideology and political norms must be more complex than the unadorned outcome of domination. Stephen Gill suggests that: 'Hegemony, in other words, can never be the simple product of the preponderance of a single state or grouping of states' (Gill, 1991: 72). Gill is trying to illustrate that there has to be some form of social free will (within the bounds of the possible), including the presence of some form of social legitimacy and agreement for a hegemony to exist (ibid.). Considering the less than perfect record of Western norms with regards to economic development it is important to examine its attraction more closely.

A key work in unravelling the theoretical tangle involved in current pieces on Western hegemony has to be that of E. M. Wood's work on modernity, post-modernity and capitalism. She is unhappy with the concept of 'modernity' and, as a result, critical of present-day theorizing which uses successor terms such as post-modernity and globalization (Wood, 1997: 539). Wood feels that the periodization of history from the nineteenth century to the modern and post-modern is misguided. She believes that many people have confused the Enlightenment[4] project with the development of capitalism. The way in which capitalism has become identified with modernity creates a paradox, according to Wood, in which capitalism and bureaucratic domination are just natural extensions of the progress of reason and freedom (Wood, 1997: 543). Her argument asks us to question current theorists who would have us jettison what is best in the Enlightenment project, such as a commitment to universal human emancipation. In Wood's opinion, the values of the Enlightenment project are being blamed for destructive effects we should, in fact, be ascribing to capitalism (ibid.: 544).

Wood grounds her study in the development of Enlightenment values as opposed to industrial production. She reveals how the home of modernity, eighteenth-century France, was approximately 85–90 per cent rural (Wood, 1997: 545). France's internal market was limited and still largely agricultural. The main actors in the development of the Enlightenment were professionals, writers and thinkers not industrialists. She suggests that: 'Their quarrel with the aristocracy had little to do with liberating capitalism from the fetters of feudalism' (ibid.). The Enlightenment project, according to Wood, had at its very heart a programme for civil equality and the attack on privilege. Universality was not developed as a tool of domination, but rather was conceived as an antidote to aristocratic particularism. She suggests that the continental philosophy of the Enlightenment was quite different from the ideology of improvement that was developing during this time period in England. The English concentration was on the improvement of productivity, profit, and science. The English population at this time were more urbanized than its French counterpart. Wood goes as far to say that ideas of modernity that encompasses a fascination with technocentrism and economic 'improvement' can largely be traced to the early development of English urbanization and industrialization (Wood, 1997: 548–9). Ultimately, She feels that much of the Enlightenment project owes its origins to a non-capitalist society. Wood very clearly states that by this she does *not* mean *pre*-capitalist but *non*-capitalist. In other words she sees the Enlightenment as: 'not just a transitional point on the way to capitalism but an alternative route out of feudalism' (Wood, 1997: 545). Using this line of thought Wood suggests that we are not actually in a post-modern era, but are actually seeing the maturity of capitalism that has its roots in the ideology of industrial improvement. Globalization and technological change have not assisted the Enlightenment project, but rather simply seen the extension of the logic of the old mass production economy to all areas of life (ibid.: 550). She sees the Enlightenment project of human emancipation as being side-lined, with the logic of the economic overtaking the logic of the political. Her fear is that we are not seeing epochal shifts from the modern to the postmodern. Wood sees no discontinuity of capitalism:

> on the contrary, capitalism itself is reaching maturity. It may be that we are seeing the first real effects of capitalism as a comprehensive system. We are seeing the consequences of capitalism as a system not

> only without effective rivals but also with no real escape routes. . . . So this is not just a phase of capitalism. This is capitalism. If 'modernity' has anything at all to do with it, then modernity is well and truly over, not created but destroyed by capitalism. The Enlightenment is dead.
>
> Wood, 1997: 558–9

Wood's suggestion that the Enlightenment is dead is, perhaps, premature. The anti-capitalist nature of the Enlightenment has spawned such movements as socialism, anarchism and social liberalism. However, her analysis of the confusion between the project of human emancipation and the growing pervasiveness of capitalism is most useful. The way in which these two concepts have been presented in tandem, goes a long way to explaining the continued acceptance of Western norms and values. Western hegemony, does not exist only because of its economic power. If we refer back to Gill's reading of Gramsci, there has to be some form of tacit acceptance of the values being transmitted in order for a hegemony to exist. This helps illuminate why Poland, the Czech Republic and Hungary were so willing to become part of the European Union and the wider Western world in general. Activists against communism in Central Europe (many of whom were part of the governing structure) were attracted to the ideal of 'civil equality' and the attack on particularist privilege. The political movements in this region, therefore, tended to be pro-democracy rather than pro-capitalist. The confusion between values of liberal-democracy and the methods of capitalism would eventually result in considerable disappointment with the transition. Central European policy-makers who basically attempted to design a political system based upon Western ideals of human emancipation, were jaundiced with the reality of the economic experience in the form of capitalism. It could be argued that the confusion detailed by Wood's article, is not the result of pure accident. Those who support market capitalism often use the language of the Enlightenment to justify the spread and effects of market capitalism. And the principles of the Enlightenment *are* appealing. Concepts that embrace fair treatment, equality before the law, freedom of speech, and criticism of the privileged are all based upon the idea of a human existence without cruelty or fear. The students who risked their lives and personal freedom in the 1989 Tianamen Square massacre in Beijing, did so in an attempt to introduce democratic and emancipatory issues into the political forum, even if it was done at the expense of their own safety. It is undoubtedly a project that was influenced by Western examples of working liberal democracies. However, one suspects that demonstrations of this kind have little to do with a non-Western desire to join Western-style consumerism. Unfortunately, now at the end of the twentieth century it is next to impossible to conduct a project of human emancipation (in whatever form that may take) and not be immediately influenced into adopting the wider trappings of a globalized Western capitalist economy. This was definitely the case in Poland, the Czech Republic and Hungary. In order for them to be successful in their pursuit of a freer way of life they were left with little option but to install the kind of capitalism suggested by those who would lend them the money to make their dream of a system based upon political legitimacy come true.

A worrying development within the last 15 years has been the way in which the acceptable face of Western influence, in the form of democratic principles, has been increasingly sidelined in favour of an increasingly integrated global capitalist system. Often the language of emancipation is used as a vanguard for systems that increasingly contain strong elements of Western control. In the following chapter we wish to take this argument, of the power and nature of Western norms, and discuss how this is related to the role of the international financial sector.

1.3 Structural change and the global political economy: the role of the financial sector

Concern about global financial stability, has been at the very heart of the international organizations created in the twentieth century. The financial shocks of the 1920s and 1930s were a main contributor to the international depression that laid the groundwork for the violence of the Second World War. Problems began in the mid-1920s when exceptional instabilities in the money markets led to a boom in short speculation on the stock market. This in turn would see an over-extension of global financial markets. In the US the volume of loans taken on by stock brokers for speculative use mushroomed. Brokers' loans in the early 1920s stood at about US$1 billion. By 1926 this had more than doubled and by the end of 1927 the amount reach almost US$3.5 billion. On 1 June 1928 the figure had grown to US$5 billion and by November of that year it had reached almost US$6 billion. World financial markets had never before experienced this phenomenon. The level of over-extension can be appreciated if it is remembered that when the IMF was created in 1944 its entire fund (made-up of contributions by 126 countries) was 8 billion (Galbraith, 1973).

Price fluctuations occurred in commodity markets, and this began to effect the price of gold, upon which the financial system rested. National governments in 1927 did not think that fluctuations in the price of gold would become serious and concentrated mainly on tariff and other trade restrictions. When gold began to fluctuate it exacerbated the problem of repaying the First World War reparations and debts. Countries such as Britain and the US gave loans to help other countries make their debt and reparation payments (France and Germany). However, reparations were not allowed to be paid in goods, therefore, Europe saw a depletion of its gold reserves. Money borrowed did not go into the improvement and investment of economic activity but rather went to servicing debt.

The general vacillation in prices and currencies meant that speculation on the money markets was primarily short term and further intensified the instability. Major financial institutions were reticent to continue giving loans to countries who were losing their ability to repay debt. In May 1931 the Creditanstalt of Austria was in difficulties. German banks were also in a weakened position. Domestic and international runs on the banks followed. On 13 July 1931 the Danat Bank was closed and the next day all Berlin Banks (except the Reichsbank) were closed by decree (Hasib, 1957–58: 9).

London was in a precarious position because it had borrowed short-term capital only to lend it to Germany on a long-term basis. As a result all German assets in major English houses were frozen which precipitated a run on London banks. Huge amounts were borrowed from France and the US but still confidence was lacking. On 21 September 1931 Great Britain left the gold standard. By the end of October British Dominions (except South Africa), the rest of the Empire, three Scandinavian countries as well as Portugal, Egypt, and Bolivia had departed from the gold standard (Kindleberger, 1973). This was a most profound development and meant the end of the existing world economic order. It was the shadow of this financial collapse and subsequent global depression that encouraged international co-operation after the war.

A solution to unexpected financial instability was seen as crucial, when the allies began to construct the post-war order. Stability was to be achieved through the creation of appropriate international organizations and through the rebuilding of Europe through the Marshall Plan.[5] The Marshall Plan was to give the United States enormous influence over the shape of post-war Europe. It was America's commitment to multilateralism that ultimately would see the rise of the EC. The US funds dispersed through the Marshall Plan required European countries to co-operate and for states to put forward joint proposals for the dispersal of funds. This distribution was done through the Organization for European Economic Co-operation. The purpose of the plan was to restore Europe, but also to recreate the region in such a way that would make it compatible with the new economic order. Western Europe was encouraged to liberalize trade and move towards exchange convertibility. Nevertheless, the process was difficult and would take 12 years, from 1946 to 1958. In 1958 Western governments finally made their currencies convertible. During that same year France, Germany, Italy and the Benelux countries brought the European Economic Community into existence, based upon the Treaty of Rome they had signed earlier in March 1957. The dispersing body for the Marshall Plan was to be reorganized and renamed as the OECD and was joined by the US, Canada and Japan (Cox, 1987: 215–16). All these countries were committed to the post-war new world order. In effect the United States had sponsored the new world order. During the Marshall Plan years (1947–58), the US consistently tolerated balance-of-payments deficits to allow Europe to recover. By 1960, most of the world was part of the this new economic order with the notable exception of the Soviet Union.

In tandem with the re-development of Western Europe was the creation of the international organizations that would embody the liberal principles of the new order. At the 1944 Bretton Woods conference, the allies conceived of a series of organisations to ensure global security and prosperity. At least that was the original intention of these organizations. The International Trading Organization would not be ratified, but the initial General Agreement on Tariffs and Trade (GATT) would act as the international body which would cope with trade-liberalizing negotiations. The United Nations was designed as a forum to deal with security issues. The WB[6] as a development bank that would lend to those countries unable to acquire credit elsewhere and the IMF was to promote international monetary co-operation and exchange rate stability. In the WB and the IMF voting was weighted according to the financial contributions made by each countries. This translated into considerable American influence. In 1946, the US contributed over a third of the IMF's funding and as result had 33 per cent of the vote (Russett and Starr, 1996: 429). Even though its percentage vote has decreased over the years, it continues to strongly influence the decisions made by the IMF.

These financial organizations of the Bretton Woods system originally had only limited agenda and most of their programmes were of short duration. Much of the IMF's work dealt with the monitoring of currencies under the system of fixed exchange rates that operated until Nixon unilaterally took the United States out of this system after August 1971. During the post-war years the IMF helped countries, both developed and under-developed, which suffered from temporary economic crises. This would change. By the mid-1970s the developed countries would rarely use the IMF, and with the abolition of the system of fixed exchange rates the IMF was in need of a new role.[7]

It is this new role that the IMF has cast for itself, more than any other international organizational development, that would see the intensification of the spread of Western norms and practice. Moreover, the type of norms that were transmitted would concentrate heavily on the neoliberal form of capitalist development. It began with Africa in the late 1970s and 1980s, when a plethora of IMF programmes would be implemented. The conditions of the loans were often rooted in neo-classical economics, where the concentration tended to be on the economic and often ignoring the realities of deep-seated political and social problems. Not surprisingly, the IMF programmes in Africa had limited success. The Fund was heavily criticized for its blinkered concentration on only economic indicators. It seems that the IMF's response to this criticism was to make its prescriptions more elaborate and encompass issues of governance such as social or military spending. Strangely, despite the Fund's own development towards greater institutional pervasiveness, it started to advise even weak states to pare down government and to put greater faith in free market forces to solve their economic deficiencies.

The Latin American debt crisis in 1982 had a big impact on how the IMF would conceive of its future programmes. It also coincided with a range of new-right governments in the United States, Canada and Britain. The rise of the new-right in the developed world was linked to the types of monetarist policies that would be encouraged in the developing world. It revolved around a continuing fear of debt. Because debt was held by national governments the problem was taken to be that of 'too much' government, and quickly following behind this logic was a growing belief that the 'free market' could solve problems that had frustrated governments.

Part of the move to 'free markets' was not just the encouragement of freer trade in goods, but a deep confusion became apparent with regard to markets in goods and finance. In terms of policy prescription it seemed as if these very different aspects of capitalist life were to be treated as the same thing. Therefore, while the GATT (now the World Trade Organization or WTO) concentrated on greater trade liberalization during the Uruguay Round (1986–93), the IMF would encourage greater liberalization in global financial markets. In addition to the WTO and the IMF, leaders of commercial lending banks would also encourage financial deregulation. In December 1997 a WTO deal on opening banking, insurance and security markets was signed by more than 70 countries. According to Wade and Veneroso: 'executive groups including Barclays, Germany's Dresdner Bank, Société Générale of France and Chubb Insurance, Citicorp, and Ford Financial Services of the US, agreed discreetly to impress on finance ministers around the world the benefits of a WTO deal' (Wade and Veneroso, 1998: 19). Many see the liberalization of financial markets as simply a natural extension of the liberalization of trade in goods. However, the effect of financial deregulation is profoundly more invasive than the agreed removal of border tariffs or non-tariff barriers. It is not only the act of financial deregulation that is often problematic but also the knock-on effects of pursuing these types of policies.

The effects of financial deregulation can afflict Western and non-Western countries alike. Nevertheless, there seems to be an emerging pattern which reveals that in times of crises in the non-Western world, Western capital benefits, particularly in terms of gaining control of foreign assets. However, the split cannot be made purely on West versus non-Western lines. In Pontusson's study of changes to Swedish capitalism, he points out how the Swedish domestic markets were deregulated in 1985–86 in an attempt to deal with a problem of growing national debt. All exchange controls were phased out in the late 1980s, and in 1992 all restriction on foreign ownership of corporate equity was lifted (Pontusson, 1997: 59). Following on the heels of market deregulation, the Swedish government was faced with a serious recession. Pontusson, believes that radical deregulation of markets, and of financial markets in particular, has made Sweden very susceptible to the threat of hostile takeovers by foreign interests (ibid.: 69). The Swedish example is of a wealthy Western country adopting voguish policies of the day in an attempt to solve a debt problem. In countries classified as 'developing' or in 'transition', the effect of financial deregulation would have a similar but more extreme effect.

In the case of Central Europe, market and financial deregulation put enormous pressures on already weak states. The economic policies that encouraged the unilateral freeing of Central European markets, particularly in terms of encouraging greater international competition, caused widespread recession. Deregulation and recession were exacerbated by problems left over from the communist era. Many state-owned enterprises needed restructuring, but due to loan conditionality Central European governments were encouraged to sell the companies as they were. This resulted in these state owned enterprises being sold for very low prices. This occurred in tandem with deregulation in financial markets and regulations allowing various degrees of foreign ownership (see case study chapters for details). This resulted in many Western companies being able to purchase entire sectors of Central Europe's industries, especially in areas of utilities, pharmaceuticals, and the automobile industry.

The spiral of deregulation, followed by recession, resulting in takeovers by foreign capital, is not a phenomenon confined to Central Europe. It has become the hallmark of crisis management by international organizations such as the IMF. With the demise of the Soviet Union and its satellites, all things socialist appear to have been discredited, and solutions to economic problems have become an ever tightening circle of neo-liberal prescriptions. If these policies are unsuccessful the response seems to be to offer a stronger, 'purer' form of capitalism. The assumption being that if a policy does not work it is not by reason of a flaw in the policy, but because it was not implemented properly. In other words, if the developmental policies suggested by the leading IFIs fail to offer results, the solution is to encourage local governments to adopt more of the same. More worrying is the trend in which, if Western neo-liberal economic prescriptions are in trouble, then the rest of a host country's governing apparatus must be brought in line with Western practice. Present IMF loan conditionality often requires changes to government structures, taxation policies and public accountancy practice.

This study attempts to show the power of neo-liberal Western influence on the way in which the transition in Poland, the Czech Republic and Hungary was undertaken. The most striking neo-liberal economic policies were encouraged during the period of 1989–93. After this time, Central Europe's relationship with the EU would, in effect, shield it from the worst pressures of international capital and the prescriptions of the IMF. Obviously, protection by the EU is an observable form of the spread of Western norms and values. However, it was in some sense a way in which Central Europe could become the 'West'. Bartlett and Seleny show how auto-sector multinationals in Hungary were unable to bargain for the kinds of concessions expected by multinationals in non-Western host countries. The exploitation by companies offering foreign direct investment of weaker states was short-circuited by the European Agreements in Central Europe. According to Bartlett and Seleny:

> And so in a reverse twist on traditional theories of FDI, the EU's eastward extension of liberalism simultaneously levelled the playing

> field between foreign investors and noninvestors and strengthened the bargaining hand of post-communist states. Although Hungary and the other East European states remained in a weak position vis-à-vis the European Union itself, their convergence toward EU norms rendered credible the claims of local authorities that they could not provide specific concessions to individual multinationals.
>
> Bartlett and Seleny, 1998: 335

Nevertheless, simply because Central Europe would soon join the EU and so be buffered from the direct influence of the IMF does not diminish the importance of the aforementioned trend, it just means that Central Europe's geographical location allowed it to escape from a situation that many other countries cannot.

The Central European case, however, has fundamentally changed the way in which the IMF deals with economic problems. Before the collapse of the Soviet Union, loan conditionality was largely economic. During the former Soviet Union's transition from communism to capitalism the IMF broadened its mandate to suggesting forms of government control and private sector institutions. This appears to have become a standard operating procedure. The IMF now appears to use the method of complete transition to all forms of crises, even if the countries in question are not in need of it. A case in point is the Mexican peso crisis of 1994. Since the North American Free Trade Agreement (NAFTA) signed by Canada, Mexico and the United States in 1992, successive Mexican governments have been dismantling an economy that in the past was built upon a philosophy of government control and import substitution. Driven by a need for debt reduction, Mexico had cut government spending, privatized state-owned companies and opened itself up to foreign direct investment. In short, it had adopted the IMF model of economic development. The problem, however, was that rather than providing economic stability these reforms actually engendered a financial crises and in December of 1994 the peso began to go into free fall. The IMF, Wall Street and IFIs in general were shocked by the unexpected crisis. Not dissimilar to Central Europe, Mexico's geographical proximity to the United States would stimulate the IMF to furnish a huge US$40 billion financial package to stabilize the crisis (Kapur, 1998: 120). However, the prescription for Mexico's crises was to suggest a further opening up of its economy to global financial markets. Unfortunately, it was a problem of a flight of foreign capital that exacerbated the peso crisis to begin with. By encouraging a further unfettering of global financial markets, the IMF has actually increased the likelihood of further sudden financial crises. Rather than considering some form of regulation of international markets, the IMF insisted that what was needed was more 'transparency' regarding the affairs of developing countries and has insisted that more national financial information be made available to the IMF (Kapur, 1998: 120). It can be argued that the IMF has missed a serious element to this development. It is allowing private capital ever greater freedom to take market risks. The risks are high, but so often is the gain. However, when financial markets turn sour it is often national governments that are left with the task of bailing out companies and banks in times of crisis (Hutton, 1996: 154–68). A situation has developed in which financial gain benefits private capital, but financial liabilities lie at the door of national governments. Private risk-taking often leads to public debt. Private capital reaps the benefits/profit of institutional instability in the financial sector, but it is governments which bear the debt/cost of instability.[8] It would seem that governments would have a case against the profiteers on the grounds that they bear the burden of responsibility when a system goes into crisis.

In Wade and Veneroso's (1998) article on the Asian financial crisis of 1997, they point out that the IMF is often blind to problems in the private sector. Freeing global financial markets encourages private firms to borrow more heavily abroad. An example of which can be found in the creation of Thailand's offshore banking facility in 1992. The Asian crisis was not caused by government debt, which had been the albatross of most Central European countries and Mexico. In fact most of the Asian countries in question, had very stable economic indicators. The problem lay with private corporate debt. Korea's corporate debt to GDP ratio, for instance, was 30–50 per cent higher than the comparative ratio in the United States (Wade and Veneroso, 1998: 8). With the freeing up of financial markets, Asian companies with high capital leverage found they could borrow more cheaply abroad. Wade and Veneroso point out that: 'In Korea, foreign debt incurred by banks and companies that borrowed from them exploded from very little in early 1990s to roughly \$160 billion by late 1997' (Wade and Veneroso, 1998: 10). Foreign lenders continued to give loans to private firms in Asia despite the fact that their debt ratios were far above the prudential limits that were normally adhered to in Western markets. When Asian currencies became overvalued by their pegging of local currencies to the American dollar (then in decline against the yen), export markets dried-up and Asian firms entered a crisis, as did the international institutions that had lent them money.

The IMF's response to the crisis, was illuminating. The first order of business was to suggest to the governments of the affected economies that they should narrow their current account deficit and keep inflation low. Furthermore, the IMF asked Korea to make serious structural and institutional reforms. Despite, the fact that the crisis was to do with the mismanagement of private capital, the solution was to control government spending and reform government institutions. In effect it was a public solution for a private problem.

The case of Central Europe and the former Soviet Union is pivotal to the way in which the IMF would attempt to solve all post-1990 crises. The precedent had been set. The Fund had the mandate to change not only the actions of governments, but the very form of these governments themselves. During the 1970s, the conditions put upon a recipient of an IMF loan would usually number less than 12. Usually these requirements would be guidelines on government spending. The number and invasiveness of loan conditions was to mushroom during the 1989–94 transition period, especially in the context of the former Soviet Union. By the time of the 1997 Asian financial crisis, recipients of the IMF bailout would have to adhere to anywhere from 50 to 80 detailed conditions (Kapur, 1998: 123). According to Kapur's *Foreign Policy* article, loan conditions encompassed issues as disparate as deregulation of garlic monopolies to taxes on cattle feed and new environmental laws (ibid.). In addition to the above, the IMF required Southeast Asian financial institutions to adopt Western financial prudential limits and Western accounting standards which would facilitate international accountancy firms in their auditing of Asian Banks (Wade and Veneroso, 1998: 12). The core of this policy was to destroy government-directed lending and to facilitate the monitoring of these countries financial policies by outside institutions.

The growing intrusiveness of IMF conditionality is but one aspect of a recent growing trend. The other trend is the 'debt for equity' swaps that were used during the Latin American debt crisis in the 1980s. Using this practice as a starting point, Jeffery Sachs in 1990 suggested that foreign direct investment could take the place of a 'Marshall Plan' for Central Europe's transition. The encouragement of direct investment, over the lending of money to governments, stimulated the foreign buyouts of Central European state-owned enterprises. While, the phenomenon of selling to foreign buyers may offer short-term relief it does give foreign capital an opportunity to increase its influence. This trend was to be followed in the Asian crisis where debt-to-equity swaps would see a great increase in Japanese and American ownership of Southeast Asian firms.[9] The media in Korea (and in Southeast Asia generally) has started to discuss the current crisis with its Western-influenced solutions as the 'Second Opium War' a clear example of US/IMF imperialism (Wade and Veneroso, 1998: 14). However, despite criticism of the IMF and Western-style policies, its prescriptions tend to be tolerated by recipient countries.

Whatever the intentions of the IMF and other international financial institutions, the outcome of their current loan policies ultimately seems to result in an increase in Western ownership of companies in recipient countries. The role of the financial sector, particularly the way it has been shaped by IMF policies, has appeared to have accelerated not only the spread of Western norms and practice but also the direct control by G7 companies, of non-Western assets. Whether this trend will prove to have a stabilizing or destabilizing effect on the global system remains to be seen.

1.4 The place of the Soviet Union

The Second World War could not have been won without the aid of the Soviet Union and as one of the victorious allies it stood poised to help create the post-war order. Although the Soviet system was not democratic, it was as much a part of Enlightenment thinking as its Western counterparts. There was a great emphasis placed upon rational linear progress. Unfortunately, this did not concentrate on the progress of human emancipation, but focused on championing the advancement of industrialization. Moreover, this form of industrialization was to take place in an environment in which the state had ultimate control over production. It was the incompatibility of the Soviet economic system with the rest of the world, combined with its military aspirations, that would sour its relationship with its other wartime allies.

The Cold War and the Soviet Union's largely closed economic system would separate it from the Bretton Woods post-war international economic order. The very basis of Marx and Engels' political theory was the critique of capitalism. A fundamental aspect of this ideology was control over the means of production. As a result, the Soviet system was based on economic management that was the very antithesis of a market system based upon private entrepreneurship. There was a firm belief that industrial production could be used to organize society along rational lines and create a world of material abundance rather than poverty or want. Ultimately, the Soviet system hoped to employ resources in a rational way so as to serve society's needs rather than having to constantly pander to the profit motive of the capitalist (Hill, 1985: 145).

In practice, the Soviet economic system worked through a series of five-year plans. During the inter-war period the Soviets concentrated on collectivizing entire sectors of industry and agriculture. It attempted, through mammoth bureaucratic structures, to supervise the economic management of all sectors while implementing production targets set out in the five-year plans. Naturally, the ideal of complete centralized control proved unworkable and by the 1940s economic management had gone over to a complex system in which a host of different ministries developed their own industrial empires. This caused considerable duplication and resulted in a large amount of wasted resources. The only area of economic activity that was not controlled by a ministry were certain services (i.e. watch repair, hair dressing) which were organized in small private co-operatives. Small plot, private farming also continued (Hill, 1985: 148). In all other aspects of production, state ministries would have absolute control. It was into this system that Poland, the Czech Republic and Hungary would be incorporated after the war.

After the Second World War the Soviets were concerned about the American Marshall Aid Plan for Western Europe's post-war recovery. In response, they created their own organization. In 1949 the Soviets established the Council for Mutual Economic Assistance (CMEA, better known as Comecon) (Hill, 1985: 205). Comecon was to be the chief mechanism for controlling intra-bloc trade. Its trading partners would also become members of the Warsaw Treaty Organization established in 1955. Because of the nature of the Soviet state, Comecon was more than a trading organization. It was an instrument by which the Soviet Union could co-ordinate economic development between the member states. By the 1970s, Comecon was supervising the harmonization of the economic plans of member states. Even though membership of both the Warsaw pact and Comecon would encompass most of the Soviet satellite states and its allies, its main trading partners were East Germany, Poland, Czechoslovakia, Hungary and Bulgaria (Hill, 1985: 206).

The Soviet Union's economic system was fundamentally anti-capitalist. The absorption of the CEECs after the Second World War pulled these countries into a system that would limit their access to the international liberal economic order. It was the heritage of state planning and Soviet control that the countries of Central Europe were keen to move away from after 1989. The transition in these countries was, therefore, a transition from the system that the Soviet's had created, but could not maintain, to a system whose spread and control had been very successful. They joined the Western-dominated international political economy. It was not until the fall of the Soviet Union that the international political economy truly became a global political economy.

2
Western Developmental Approaches

Looking at theory as it has been applied to Central Europe tells us a great deal about the specific political and economic concerns of the day. Twenty years ago Western developmental approaches concentrated heavily on the 'Third World'. Today, developmental literature, in the West, devotes considerable space to those countries in 'transition', that is former communist countries. Change in theoretical approaches can be heavily influenced by a given political environment. Therefore, it is not necessarily the most inventive or nuanced theories that become adopted as policy. The well-developed arguments of authors of critical theory, radical International Political Economy and post-modernism, have not been able to make a substantive impact on mainstream economic development policies. The Western developmental approaches applied to CEECs have tended, it seems, to be dominated by some form of orthodoxy. This, however, does not mean that the approaches applied have always been the same. Indeed they have changed dramatically over time. The thread that links approaches in this geographical region is an unfortunate one. All Western orthodox developmental theories, whether Realist or neo-liberal have either marginalized this area or exploited it. For scholars of economic development, particularly as it pertains to Africa, the above supposition would not be a new one. In the following section we hope to show how Western developmental approaches were strongly dominated by political Realism when applied to CEECs before 1989 and how this was exchanged for economically liberal approaches after the fall of communism. Moreover, the second part of this chapter attempts to establish how the theories which failed in Africa, such as modernization theory, structural adjustment, etc. have been applied to CEECs despite the fact that these theories' to date have delivered a poor performance. The power of

Western norms has already been examined in Section 1.2 of this study. The purpose of the next section will be to give an historical overview of its application.

2.1 Western developmental approaches towards Central Europe: pre-1989

The bipolar nature of the international system after the Second World War coloured not only security concerns but also all international theories including approaches to economic development. This was the era when Realism, as a theoretical approach, was at the apex of its popularity in the West. Political Realism is grounded in a belief that there are certain laws of politics and that these are ultimately based upon human nature. Realism has a pessimistic view of human nature seeing it as ultimately power seeking. In terms of international politics the Realist would concentrate on foreign policy and use the state as the predominant unit of analysis. The international political sphere, according to the traditional Realism of E. H. Carr or Hans Morgenthau, would be characterized by anarchy, meaning the lack of a world government (Pettman, 1991: 56). Therefore, politics in the international sphere would be based on the maximization of an individual state's power. Ideas based on a balance of power between great nations held a certain resonance for those living during those post-war years. While the Realist perspective seemed very sensible during this time, it did seriously blind many Western scholars to the complexity of the international system. It fostered a very narrow view of the world in which the actions of the superpowers were paramount.

Realism did perform the function of explaining, to a certain degree, the foreign policy behaviour of the United States and the former Soviet Union. However, it left a gaping hole when it came to explaining the behaviour of small states, non-aligned states, nationalism, ethnic conflict and religious fundamentalism. Despite the prevalence of these types of variants to the international system, most theory in the West continued to concentrate on superpower politics.

The strength of this manifestation is clearly illustrated in a 1969 article by Annette Baker Fox on 'The Small State in the International System'. Fox examines some of the attitudes towards the study of smaller countries. At the beginning of her article she quotes Hedley Bull who had completed a review of a book examining small states (Fox, 1969: 751). Bull pondered: 'whether, however viable the small state might be in international politics, it really presents a viable subject of study'.[1] He was voicing a commonly held view that studying small states in the context of International Relations theory was not very pertinent. This conclusion was reached by basing Realist theories on power politics. The less power, in terms of force, a country had the less relevant it was. This approach can be largely traced back to the works of Hans J. Morgenthau whose book, *Politics Among Nations: The Struggle for Power and Peace*, was to be a standard text for Western scholars throughout the post-war era (Morgenthau, 1948). Morgenthau's tenet that international relations are about states pursuing interests defined in terms of power, assumes that the role of small states is that of a nuisance or a pawn in the great game of superpower politics.

Were the Realists on the mark, regarding small states, during the post-war period? There were many supporters of the Realist position in the West during the Cold War because the bipolar nature of the international system seemed to confirm their approach. One suspects, however, that the traditional Realists may have underestimated the role that small states can play as catalysts for international conflict. Despite the research concentration on the superpowers, the majority of conflicts up to the late 1960s did not involve either the United States or the Soviet Union. Fox points out that up until 1969:

> the most interesting aspect of the incidence of violence following World War II is that great powers were involved, even indirectly through military aid, in relatively fewer cases than in the pre-World War II period. The Soviet Union and the United States were each connected with only four to six.
>
> Fox, 1969: 759

Of course, the above quote could be brushed aside by pointing out that this period coincided with rapid de-colonization, therefore, Britain, France as well as the United Nations may have found themselves in non-Superpower conflicts or peacekeeping roles. A further attack, by employing a Realist position, could suggest that the superpowers would have been reluctant to become involved in conflicts of any kind for fear of escalation and the possible use of nuclear weapons. This argument against the study of small states and peripheral conflicts seemed both plausible and powerful until the outbreak of the Vietnam War (1961–73). In the end, this conflict caused no nuclear war, and the fall of Saigon in April 1975 somewhat dented the belief that a superpower (in this case the United States) could effectively harness its power to successfully achieve its goals.

Western theory in the post-war era, whether that of International Political Economy or International Relations, remained strongly dominated by the Western allies' perspective on the world. As a result Britain was seen as a large state, whereas the Netherlands was labelled as a small state, as was India (Fox, 1969: 751). The idea of placing the Netherlands in the same size category as India seems, to a present-day reader, somewhat nonsensical. However, work done during this period in international studies concentrated heavily on security concerns. It becomes clear, therefore, that 'small' and 'large' refers less to size and more to a country's respective role in international security arrangements.

This fixation on security was to completely engulf the West's view towards CEECs prior to 1989. During President Truman's administration (1945–53) Congress passed the Mutual Security Act of 1951, which stipulated that all kinds of American foreign aid – military, economy or technical should be oriented to:

> strengthening the free world in its resistance to Communism. The act, in force until 1961, required that no country was to be considered eligible to receive aid if it were not aligned to the West.
>
> Augelli, 1988: 84

Eligible candidate countries that were less developed were to be exposed to a sort of evangelicalism designed to spread the 'American way' in terms of economic development. This was combined with the West's sophisticated level of influence over financial institutions such as the IMF and the WB. The Realist approach may have over-estimated America's ability to use force or the show of force to acquire its goals, but the United States' influence on the structure of the international monetary system after 1945 was profound.

As a result of America's unique position after the war a succession of US administrations from Truman up to Reagan would be responsible for setting the tone and substance of many economic aid and development projects among the poorer countries in the international system. It is interesting to note that the main thrust of developmental approaches during the Truman administration would be almost identical to those thrust upon Poland, the Czech Republic and Hungary after 1989. There was a strong feeling during the 1940s and 1950s that the only way to attain economic development was to keep the state/government from interfering with the market. This was also the belief behind the IMF's loan conditionality in Central Europe during the 1990s. Throughout the post-war era it was assumed that trade liberalization and a conservative monetary policy would create an appropriate climate for foreign investors. It was thought that if developing countries stuck to these policies economic growth would follow. These policies would also benefit American financial interests abroad (Augelli and Murphy, 1988: 82).

When, however, economic development was truly needed to bolster the strength of an ally, the above principles were not applied. As mentioned in Section 1.2 of this study, in order to help Western Europe recover after the war the Marshall Plan, beginning in 1948, infused much needed capital into war-torn European economies representing 6.25 per cent of US Gross Domestic Product (GDP). Credit was given on very favourable terms. No country in Europe had a convertible currency until 1958 and the United States permitted Europe to maintain trade barriers to allow for a post-war economic recovery. The harsher version of economic development was to be reserved and practised on the globe's poorer countries in the Third World.

The anti-Communist element of international aid-conditionality was to soften somewhat during President Eisenhower's administration (1953–61). The Eisenhower doctrine allowed some aid to go to non-aligned states. There was a general feeling that the threat of communism was perhaps not necessarily America's top international interest. A move was afoot to increase American influence abroad with a wider range of political and economic policies. This American attitude towards developing countries was to be carried through to John F. Kennedy's Presidency (1961–63). Intellectuals working for the Kennedy administration formally recognized that poverty was a leading cause of the attraction towards communism. They believed that this attraction to communism was doomed to failure and disappointment, but a danger nonetheless. This began a change in tack with regards to the West's approach to development policies. Projects were designed to deliberately target poor countries in an attempt to stimulate growth and alleviate poverty. This was not done in the interests of international wealth redistribution as called for by many Third World countries. Instead, the method chosen was loans supplied through IFIs and the organizations created by the Bretton Woods agreement, namely the IMF and the WB. Loans, however, would not be given without some form of conditionality. The policies created through the medium of loan conditionality was based on Modernization theory. A crucial assumption in Modernization theory believes that if a state is given the physical accoutrements of a modern industrialized state such as transport facilities, it would then be or quickly become a modern state. Dam and highway projects, for example were particularly popular. Money was to be made available for these large projects, particularly infrastructure. The ability of the recipient country to pay back the loan and adhere to its terms was intended to inspire the confidence of foreign investors. This, it was assumed, would create economic growth which would undercut poverty. The most popular intellectual blueprint of Modernization theory used at this time was W. W. Rostow's theory of the stages of economic development. Rostow's theory was strongly determinist and saw all countries going through an evolution from a traditionalist society to reaching a point of 'take-off', followed by the development of a society of high-mass consumption which he categorized as 'modern'. He did not concentrate on the West alone and felt that the Union of Soviet Socialist Republics (USSR)/Russia had reached 'take-off' before the First World War. He was not only an academic, but was very influential in both the Kennedy and Johnson Presidential administrations, and acted as an official American adviser to Vietnam. The main thrust of Rostow's version of Modernization theory was to attempt to see countries reach the 'take-off' stage which would then lead, according to his theory, to a period of self-sustaining growth like that experienced in the West. This economic development was to remove poverty by seeing wealth 'trickle-down' through all classes providing some form of benefit to all. Rostowian Modernization theory was to remain the theoretical mainstay of American, and Western developmental approaches in general, throughout the 1960s and 1970s (Rostow, 1960/Augelli and Murphy, 1988: 87–8).

How did the post-war fear of communism and the popularity of Modernization theory affect the CEECs? For many theoreticians and policy-makers, the socialist nature of Poland, Hungary and Czechoslovakia was to blind them to the similarities between these countries and non-communist countries particularly which had experienced similar economic policies and problems. In Malcolm Grieve's 1995 article he highlights this tunnel vision by quoting Joan Spero from her 1981 work:

> While some members of the Eastern bloc may join Western institutions ... there will be no re-integration of the world economy and of its management systems ... separation will remain the major characteristic of East–West economic relations.
>
> Grieve, 1995: 81, quoting Spero, 1981: 327–8

The question is: to what extent was this split assumed as opposed to actual? Were the countries of Central Europe truly isolated from the global political economy? If we take the case of Poland we see that interaction between East and West was stronger than one might presume.

After the Second World War, despite Poland's position as a satellite state of the Soviet Union, it was an original signatory to the Bretton Woods agreement (Bjork, 1995: 90). Poland had asked the WB for a loan of $600 million to help with post-war reconstruction. In the end the Polish government was to receive only $45 million. Poland's request coincided with Harry S. Truman's administration which to the view that strong conditionality should be attached to aid given to any country particularly those in the socialist camp. The ideological convictions of the West were married with a strong belief in the power technology and science to solve problems. Truman had great faith in science, American technological achievement, and industrial progress (Augelli, 1988: 83). He believed that technical assistance implemented through advisory missions would illustrate not only the benefit of following in the footsteps of the West but that it would also quickly improve the standard of living of the recipient countries. As a result Poland could only use the WB loan it received for very specific types of developmental assistance. The attitude of the West toward Poland, *vis-à-vis* loan conditionality caused strained relations. During the 1950s Poland, by way of protest, withdrew its membership from both the IMF and the WB.

Despite the strong influence exerted by the Soviets over Central Europe with regards to military matters, their control over the various economies was not strong. Polish agriculture, for instance, was never properly collectivized. Most of the food produced in Poland was grown on privately owned farms. Trade in all of the Central European countries was also not totally isolated. While it is true that the lion's share of imports and exports from Poland, Czechoslovakia and Hungary went to the USSR, at least a third of their trade in the pre-1989 era was with the EC and the European Free Trade Area (EFTA) countries (Messerlin, 1995: 204).

There was, in terms of trade, a general recognition that goods coming from the communist bloc were likely being sold for under their production cost value. Suspicion of product dumping saw many countries in the West apply some form of quantitative restriction on trade originating from the CEECs. Despite these forms of closely administered trade arrangements, trade and economic relations did exist. During the post-war period Japan and the EC concluded a series of comprehensive arrangements, which included a system of quotas, bilateral agreements and quantitative restrictions, with Central Europe (Smolik, 1995: 244). The US had denied GATT's Most Favoured Nation (MFN) status to the CEECs after the war. However, during the 1970s it granted MFN status to both Poland (1970) and Hungary (1978). The Hungarian New Economic Mechanism (NEM), implemented in January 1968 was a move away from total government control of the economy (Richet, 1981: 26). Similarly economic reforms in Poland during the 1970s saw an increase of total investments of 18.4 per cent annually between 1971 and 1975. The development strategy that was being followed in Central Europe in the 1970s seemed to be one of trying to attain Western standards of wealth without introducing democracy or privatization. While not willing to adopt a Western style political system there was a recognition that foreign capital through trade could increase the aggregate wealth of these countries. The CEECs tended to have very similar theories, beliefs and policies with regards to creating economic development. This period was to mark the beginning of the heavy borrowing by many of the CEECs. Despite their centrally planned state apparatus they were to be effected by, and take part in, the global economy. This is particularly true with regards to credit and international financial arrangements. Stagnation in the late 1970s and early 1980s was to signal the failure of many Central European countries who tried to modernize without significant political/government reforms. By 1980 Poland's debt had reached a remarkable US$24 billion, with 96 per cent of its total export earnings going to debt servicing (Prust, 1988: 3–12; WB, 1987: 17). The only country that had managed to control its debt was Czechoslovakia, but more specifically that part of the former Czechoslovkia which would later become the Czech Republic post-January 1993. The culture of fiscal conservatism in the Czech Republic would serve it well during the transition when, unlike its neighbours, its comparative lack of debt gave it a certain amount of independence when dealing with international financial organizations.

It is perhaps dangerous to over-emphasize the links that Central Europe had with the West. However, it is worth pointing out the connections that did exist, as it somewhat weakens much of the Realist/neo-Realist work done during the Cold War period. Although the political tensions between the East–West superpower blocks are well documented, the economic isolation was not as stark as many, such as Spero, have suggested. In part this can be explained by the dominance in the West of Realist theory and its blindness to activities that were not part of the formal relations between states. A Realist approach would assume that countries operate in their own self-interests and that politics is a struggle for power. This view is supplemented by a belief in the importance of sovereignty as the most essential characteristic of an international state. The term strongly implies political independence from any higher authority and also suggests at least theoretical equality. However, for the CEECs the situation did not fit neatly into a textbook description of International Relations where independent countries relate to each other in an anarchical global system. They were militarily dominated by the Soviet Union a fact which most foreign policy analysts of the day were happy to concede. However, the CEECs were also being pulled into the Western system of global capitalism through their international borrowing and adherence to western models of industrial progress. Much of Central Europe's bilateral relationships with Western countries was overlooked by contemporary analysts. The concentration on state foreign policy focused contemporary research on relations between governments. As a result economic relations, particularly private transactions remained under-analysed.

Had more economic and developmental research been done on Central Europe after the Second World War it would have revealed that the developmental approaches employed would not have been widely different from those of either the Truman or Eiesenhower administration towards Latin America or Europe's developmental strategies toward Africa. Most of the developmental approaches of the time had some form of political/security motivation, but the economic development component relied heavily on faith in industrial progress, large infrastructure projects and a belief in the power of science through technological assistance. Bjorn Hettne in his 1994 article highlights this phenomenon with regards to socialist development strategy. Marxist theory itself does not discuss development as such. Hettne suggests that instead Stalin's five-year plans were to become the development model for most socialist countries. As the decades progressed many socialist countries attempted to have dual goals of creating better socialism combined with greater economic development (not so different from the West's belief in the dual development of industrialized wealth and democracy). However, as time went on the socialist countries increasingly began to use the most developed Western countries as a benchmark for their own industrial performance. Eventually, any kind of move toward a civil society model was abandoned in favour of a non-capitalist version of development. In the end 'socialism', as Hettne says: 'became more or less a transition ideology for "late-comers"'. In terms of economic development 'communism' created policies that would ultimately encourage a transition to, rather than from, capitalism (Hettne, 1994: 40).

The failure of the modernization approach to development in Central Europe was very evident by the 1980s. The conditionality imposed upon them by IFIs placed many of the authoritarian-style governments under pressure to institute wage and price reform. The lack of legitimacy of the political systems in Poland, Czechoslovakia and Hungary had laid the ground work for popular uprisings against the unpopular governments who were beginning to cap wages and raise prices. The spiral of debt and economic stagnation was, in the final analysis, what would bring down the communist regimes in Central Europe in 1989–91.

The collapse of the Soviet Union and its various socialist allies was largely ascribed to the failure of the communist system. Fingers were pointed at the inflexibility of the central planning model. Lack of both political freedom and the ability to accrue private capital were also considered explanations for its rapid fall. Without a doubt, bureaucratic inefficiency and political repression in Central Europe played a leading role in the downfall of the various communist governments. The question is whether the economic situation these countries found themselves in was peculiar to the Socialist bloc or whether developing countries around the world were faring differently?

The election of Reagan to the American Presidency in 1980, was to herald a new era for Modernization theory and its application as a Western developmental tool in the Third World. Like Truman before him, Reagan felt comfortable with the concepts of progress, human (American) destiny and scientific achievement. But the use of American foreign aid and its influence over the WB and IMF was not only to promote the cause of industrial progress but it was also to support American 'common sense' ideas and material interests, in the Third World (Augelli and Murphy, 1988). However, the liberal political economy model was not to prove a panacea to the problem of Third World development. Many developing countries had economies that were not diversified. Exports from these countries tended to be commodities or in highly competitive areas of manufacturing such as textile and steel production. The countries of Latin America and Africa suffered in the early 1980s as the world market offered no relief for their stagnating economies. All countries had taken loans from the West and, in the wake of the commodity price slump, most countries simply did not have the foreign exchange to meet their borrowing commitments. High interest rates in the mid-1980s were to exacerbate the situation. Murphy and Augelli, point out that: 'Annual interest payments on the medium and long-term loans of all the developing countries grew a further 14% to $58 billion in 1984' (Augelli and Murphy, 1988: 174). Quoting a 1985 WB report, they summarize the effect of the 'modernization' model coupled with liberal economic policies:

> Growth has slowed in most developing countries ... average per capita real incomes in Africa are no higher than they were in 1970; in much

> of Latin America they are back to the levels of the mid-1970s. Dozens of countries have lost a decade or more of development.
>
> Augelli and Murphy, 1988: 175

Although there was an ideological divide between many of the countries of Central Europe, Africa and Latin America, the outcome of each areas' own developmental strategy was to have virtually identical economic effects. What lessons can be learnt from this comparison? From a purely 'dependency' analysis viewpoint, it could be easily argued that as Central Europe was the periphery of the Soviet Union it was not surprising that it was treated similarly to Western peripheral states. The connection, however, seems somewhat deeper than this. Obviously many past governments of Central Europe, Africa and Latin America have been guilty of gross mismanagement of public resources. In Central Europe the mismanagement was done under the guise of socialism and in parts of the Third World it was often done under the name of *laissez-faire* liberalism or national independence. The link seems to have been created during that period of the 1970s when their respective failures in growth and development caused the indigenous governments of these countries to turn to international financial institutions. Once upon the path of foreign borrowing the CEECs and the Third World would have had to have met specific internal conditions in order to qualify for loans. Consequently, over a decade later states in the 'East' or 'South' found themselves in a situation of fiscal crisis. International debt and loan conditionality, which promotes a very specific Western approach to development, seems to be the thread connecting the fate of most developing countries whether its origin was in the socialist camp or outside.

2.2 Western developmental approaches towards Central Europe: post-1989

During the later part of 1989 and the beginning of 1990, the mood in many CEECs was euphoric. The spell of political repression was lifted and a chance to create a fair and legitimate society seemed to lie open. The philosophical void created by the collapse of communism was substantial. There was a general move away from that which was, or had been, associated with socialism. At a certain level, Central Europe's ideological move to the West was a question of faith. There was a general belief in the triumph of capitalism after the fall of communism. It was an example of binary thinking in which the assumption was, if the

Soviet system had been harmful then the West's system must be beneficial. The irony that the collapse of communist Central Europe had in part been caused by over-borrowing from the West was lost on the new governments.

In Poland the first elections were held during June 1989, with presidential elections held in November 1990. However, free parliamentary elections were not held until October 1991. Many of the decisions, regarding the character of the transition, occurred while the 1989 provisional government held power. The situation was slightly different in Hungary. This country had already made a number of liberalizing reforms before 1989. A referendum was held in November 1989 to decide on whether parliamentary or presidential elections should be held first. As a result of this referendum parliamentary elections were held during March–April of 1990. These early elections gave their government added legitimacy during the transition process. Even during the early days of the transition there was apprehension with regard to the wealth and power of the West. Central European governments were walking a political tightrope. They would need western capital, but could not be seen to be 'selling out' to the West. There tended to be a hierarchy of Western influence in each of the three countries examined in this study. Czechoslovakia (Czech Republic after 1 January 1993), was to be the least influenced of the three countries. A caretaker government was established in December 1989 with free elections held by June 1990. Despite the similarities between these three countries in transition, their vulnerability to the West differed. Czechoslovakia had always been fiscally conservative and more successful at public resource management than many of its neighbours. Czechoslovak debt service ratio at the beginning of the transition was at the World Bank approved level of approximately 19 per cent (Nesporova, 1995: 181). As a result they were not so willing to be dictated to with regard to the adoption Western approaches to capitalist development during the transition. This is not to say that both the caretaker government of 1989 or the elected government after June 1990 was not committed to substantial reform. The 'shock therapy' model, however, was not embraced by the Czechs in the way it was in Poland. Policy-makers in Hungary, were also not totally convinced by the idea of a rapid transition process. It had the least amount of foreign consultants of all the Central European countries and attempted to come up with a more indigenous form of the process of moving from communism to capitalism. However, it did have a debt problem and was committed to making repayments to its creditors. Although Hungary's per capita debt was four times that of

Czechoslovakia it did manage to keep to its repayment schedule due to strict fiscal management. This caused austerity and curiously also meant that the Western financial institutions were inclined to approve of their policies, despite the gradualism inherent in Hungary's transition. This left Poland as the most suitable country for neo-liberal developmental experimentation. During the beginning of the transition period, Poland was unreservedly pro-Western. Added to this was Poland's deep dependence on foreign borrowing. It was here that the 'shock-therapy' model was to be initiated in its least unadulterated form. Nevertheless in all three countries the project was the same: a transition to Western capitalism through the policies of membership to major international organizations (i.e. WB, IMF), removal of trade barriers/barriers to foreign investment, the creation of a convertible currency and the establishment of private ownership.

A full discussion of how 'shock therapy' was conceived and applied to Poland is discussed at length in the case-study chapter, however, in this section it is important to examine the thinking behind the liberal capitalist project as it was applied to Central Europe. All the new governments, especially Poland, were keen to turn their backs on the Soviet-influenced past through embracing Western ideas. With hindsight it could be argued that Central Europe's willingness to jump towards capitalism was likely to have been a born of a desire to be accepted once again by its former hegemon, Western Europe. It was less a leap towards capitalism than a leap towards Europe. There was a general acceptance in Central Europe of the strongly liberal capitalist blueprint policies of privatization and transition. There was little interest in Central Europe of using anything other than the prescribed liberal policies in the transition process. There was an alternative literature to the largely neo-classical economic works used by policy-makers during the transition. Considerable work had been done during the 1980s by International Political Economy scholars. Works by authors such as Stephen Gill, Craig Murphy, Roger Tooze, Susan Strange and Bjorn Hettne had all discussed, in one form or another, the power of hegemonic ideas/structures on groups lacking in influence. During the early years of the transition, CEEC ideas based on the recognition of knowledge structures, societal transition, or the need for some sort of entrenched civil society, never really materialized. Indeed, there seemed to be a lack of self-awareness of what was being asked of these countries.

This is not because alternatives to 'shock therapy'[2] were not available. A fortnight before Jeffery Sachs' plans for the former Soviet Union were articulated in *The Economist* on 13 January 1990 (Sachs, 1990), President

Mitterrand of France had given a New Year's Eve address stating his vision of transition. Mitterrand saw a confederation of allied states stretching from the Atlantic to the Urals. His vision saw the Eastern bloc remaining connected through trade and other ties but in alliance with Europe. Much of this would have been accomplished through guidance from the French-dominated European Bank for Reconstruction and Development (EBRD). This would have negated the need to destroy Comecon. Similarly, Chancellor Kohl as the president of the Deutsche Bank had suggested a plan which would have developed Central Europe and the former Soviet Union as a unified bloc (Gowan, 1995: 18).

Such policies would have left a certain amount of economic integrity to the former Soviet Union offering a better economy of scale of similarly industrialized countries. It would also have likely forestalled the serious recession caused by suddenly switching Central European trade away from Russia. At present, Central Europe is currently recovering from the sharp liberal policies adopted during the transition, but the same cannot be said of Russia. Central Europe had been one of Russia's major industrial trading regions. There is speculation that it is unlikely that Russia will be able to recover truly from its current economic malaise without re-establishing its trade ties with Central Europe. In part, this is because of the curious nature of post-war Russian economic development. The Soviets encouraged Central Europe to develop heavy industry. This was done in part because it meant that Poland, Czechoslovakia and Hungary would be in a position to purchase raw materials from the Soviet republics. The outcome of this policy was that much of the Soviet bloc's industrial capacity was located in its Central European periphery. With the break up of Comecon and the redirection of Central European trade, Russia lost not only a traditional trading partner but also its allied industries. Complex economic policies have been employed to justify a peculiarly invasive form of political intervention whose outcome may have damaged the development of an entire region. Perhaps it was an unintentional outcome of the transition. But, the transition process in Central Europe would be done in such a way as to truly diminish the economic strength, and hence political stability, of Russia.

In terms of Western developmental approaches, international financial organisations have considerable leverage by which to make recipient countries comply with loan conditionality. Evidence for this is overwhelming. Institutions, from the WB to the GATT (now the WTO) continue to be the cornerstones upon which the international economic system is structured. The importance of this is often forgotten. Many scholars of the global political economy have concentrated on regime theory as it pertains to trade. By concentrating on trade and GATT/WTO negotiations it is possible to come up with a rational choice model with each individual state actor making their negotiated moves in a free system. Much work on regime theory concentrates on the liberal aspect of the international trading regime and the struggle to increase the rules of liberalism while maintaining legitimacy in the system. There remains the question, however, as to whether studying formal trade flows gives an analyst a full view of the global economy. Chris Brown estimates that increasingly 'intra-firm' trade is eroding the former importance of national trade flows. He estimates that the 'intra-firm' trade of global companies accounts for 'between a quarter and a third by value of the trade by the industrial countries' (Brown, 1997: 168). Critical International Political Economists would not find it surprising that many conservative theorists chose to study the GATT/WTO. If we examine all the management structures of the international system from the United Nations to the IMF it is the GATT/WTO that is the only international institution left over from the post-war/Bretton Woods era that does not have weighted voting. The weight of the votes in all other Bretton Woods institutions are directly linked to the post-war power structure. This has translated into continued influence by industrialized countries over certain crucial areas in particular access to international credit. Voting rights by the WB are based on the extent of each country's shares in the capital stock of the WB. In the IMF it is based on a quota system. These shares and quotas are based upon a country's total economic performance measured in US dollars (Rotte, 1997: 48). This translates into a unique position for most industrialized countries who then virtually dominate the transfer of money to poorer states. We begin to grasp the significance of this with regard to the CEECs when it is realized that the WB and the IMF supplied 69 per cent of borrowed capital going into that area between 1991 and 1993 (of US$11.6 billion, only US$3.6 billion came from sources other than the WB and the IMF) (ibid.: 47–8). This was to give the West a powerful leverage over the types of developmental policies that would be adopted by Central Europe during its transition.

The influence of the West and the tendency for many scholars to ignore the inherent illiberal character of the system fits well with Susan Strange's analysis of the nature of influence in the international political economy. In her analysis of the 'financial structure' she is mainly concerned with the way in which 'credit is created, allocated and put to use' (Strange, 1991: 35). The way in which credit was employed with regard to conditionality towards loans received by Central Europe is striking. It also falls in line with Strange's notions of a security structure, a production structure and a knowledge structure. These were all intertwined with regard to their influence over the transition countries. Financial influence obviously plays a role in influencing developmental policy outcomes. However, one must not underestimate the part played by the knowledge structure. Strange sees the power of the knowledge structure as effecting outcomes on an abstract level where there are belief systems which are associated with value preferences 'that inhibit or validate some kinds of action rather than others' (Strange, 1991: 37). Strange's argument ties in with this study's discussion in Section 1.1 regarding the power of Western norms. There was a strong urge by Central European policy-makers to opt for a strict liberal economic blueprint for the communist-to-capitalist transition. The neo-classical economist and Harvard professor, Jeffery Sachs, was to play a significant role as privatization adviser to the Polish government during the transition process. Moreover, Western approaches to development had already been introduced to the Central European elite as many had taken economic degrees in the West and returned home with a commitment to putting their knowledge into practice.

Central Europe's acceptance and attempted adherence to liberal economic policies can also be explained by the theoretical background that both the 'East' and the 'West' shared. A belief in linear progress existed on both sides of the ideological divide. In both the West and the Soviet Union, approaches to economic development were characterized by the dominance of abstract (ahistorical) modelling over contingent (historical) analysis. The model of development used by the Soviet Union was a Marxist form of modernization theory. This could explain why more gradual approaches to the transition were rejected at the local level. In the past, national development approaches under communism were very invasive and tended to cause huge structural changes in a short-span of time. In post-war Czechoslovakia, for instance, the economy was completely transformed from producing items in a high-quality light industry to producing heavy industrial goods. This was accomplished by a Stalinist five-year plan (1949–53). As a result their net material production (based upon units manufactured) increased by 10 per cent a year (Dyba and Svejnar, 1994: 97).

The connection between Marxist and Liberal economics is that both have a certain parsimony to them. These theories share an abstract quality and can be understood and transplanted throughout space and time. This may have been a factor in the willing adoption by many

Central European economists of the policy prescriptions of advisers such as Sachs and organizations like the G7 and the IMF. CEECs have had a long history of central government-controlled, universalist, modernization development plans imposed upon them. It is not surprising, therefore, that when the communist developmental model failed, scholars from that region went looking for a replacement model which would give the 'correct' blueprint for success in as short a time as possible.

The developmental blueprint chosen, however, was problematic. Alice Amsden[3] *et al.* (1994: 1) produced a detailed study of the transition process in 1994 which seriously called into question the types of policies encouraged by the West. These authors worry that the benefits of developmental approaches suggested by the West to Central and Eastern Europe have been overstated. Part of the difficulty experienced by Central Europe can be ascribed to the crisis of confidence experienced by many industrialized countries during the 1980s. The rise of the new right and the resentment of the newly industrialized Asian countries caused the US and international financial institutions to exaggerate the benefits that a completely free-market approach would have regarding development. Unfortunately, those engineering the IMF loan conditionality neglected to point out to the transition countries that gains from protectionism are always concentrated whereas the benefits of free trade are always dispersed. Similarly protectionism exacts its costs from the population at large, whereas the costs of free trade tend to be levelled at the most vulnerable groups of the population (Brown, 1997: 156). In any case, the subsequent tailoring of conditionality of Central European loans meant that these countries' ability to choose from a series of developmental policies became very circumscribed. The whole project seemed infused with a strong belief in the economics of Say's Law – that: 'supply creates its own demand and that markets automatically maintain equilibrium if wages are low enough' (Amsden *et al.*, 1994: 6). Moving on from this premise, there was a belief that keeping wages down was one of the lynchpins of the privatization process. However, the complete realisation of the ideal remained out of reach. All types of conditionality imposed or encouraged by the West were based on a *laissez-faire* model that dated from the eighteenth century. Historically this model had grown to replace a very peculiar kind of mercantilist cottage-industry, embedded in the societies of Northwest Europe. It was a curious choice of blueprint, considering that so many modern examples of late transition to industrialization abound. Choosing eighteenth-century England, for instance, as opposed to twentieth-century Singapore remains an interesting omission. This neo-liberal philosophy, when combined with a latter-day version of Rostow's modernization theory, was to have little more success in Central Europe than it did in Africa in the previous decade.

The capitalist model used by countries such as South Korea, Japan, Taiwan and parts of China is one in which the state plays a strong role. Their democratic credentials are often suspect, but their model of economic development has had more success than those applied by the West in Latin America and Africa. Central Europe was not given the opportunity to choose a model other than one that was strictly liberal and economically neo-classical. The difficulty with this model is that it leaves much to the private market. However, this was primarily what most Central European economies lacked. In effect, there was an expectation that these countries' problems could be solved by employing a market mechanism in a context where there was no historical background for this kind of policy. Where a strong business class should have been there was a void. The closest thing Central Europe had to a middle-class bourgeois was the educated class of professionals. Flaws in the strategy became apparent when Poland, Czechoslovakia and Hungary moved to full currency convertibility during the early 1990s. At the same time their repayment commitments also demanded hard currency. In the space of about 10 months these Central European countries saw trade with their largest trading partner, Russia, plummet. The former Soviet Union did not have the ability to purchase Central European goods in a convertible currency. This spelt the death of Comecon and local trading arrangements. Countries in transition, such as Hungary, demanded that external trade should be done in American dollars in an attempt to keep up with its own loan repayments. This was to engender a 40 per cent drop in trade between the former Soviet Union and Hungary between 1990 and 1993 (Bossanyi, 1995). This, in turn, caused the economy to suffer as investment in the national economy also fell by 23 per cent during the same period (Bossanyi, 1995). This scenario was common among all the Central European countries between 1989 and 1993. In an attempt to stem the tide of economic collapse many of these countries were advised to open their economies further to foreign trade. This further eroded their financial situation as their current accounts became seriously depleted. In the Czech Republic exports declined by 25 per cent in 1992, but imports grew by 40 per cent (WIIW, 1996: 245). The main argument for trade liberalization was that it would attract foreign investment. However, the more serious and unstable the fiscal crisis became the less foreign investors were interested in Central Europe. Despite Central Europe's attempted adherence to the developmental agenda suggested by the IMF and other international financial institutions, investors were not impressed with the results and took their money elsewhere. Between 1989 and 1993 China, an unrepentant communist country whose developmental strategy continued to give a strong role to central government, was to receive US$25.9 billion in foreign direct investment (FDI) (United Nations Conference on Trade and Development, UNCTAD, 1994). All of Eastern Europe and the Newly Independent States, on the other hand, were to receive only US$11 billion in FDI for the same period (Commission for the EC, 1994). In addition to a lack of foreign investment a succession of wage capping had decreased the buying power of those living in the Central European countries. As a result the domestic economy also began to show signs of serious decline. As Amsden points out:

> The industrial strategy in the first years of the transition implicitly amounted to 'getting the prices right' (i.e. reducing real wages and increasing capital and raw material costs) and specialising according to 'comparative advantage' or manufacturing a bundle of goods whose production techniques favoured the relatively cheapest available domestic factor inputs (land, labour, or capital).
>
> Amsden *et al.*, 1994: 8

The problem with the above strategy was that it was theoretically designed for countries with a very low industrial base. Lowering wages and liberalizing imports would give labour intensive industries, such as textiles, some form of competitive advantage. However, this policy ignored that much of Central Europe was rich in mid-tech industries particularly in the sciences which employed a highly educated workforce (Amsden *et al.*, 1994: 8–9). Little attempt was made to restructure the state industries before they were sold. As a result many were sold to foreign investors who were interested in exploiting low wages or maintaining a global market share rather than investing money for the long-term reform and sustainability of these companies. FDI was intended to modernize these economies, but the figures have not been encouraging. While it is true that all Central European countries have been recovering from the 1990–93 recession, increased trade or GDP figures does not, itself, mean that these economies have actually managed to change their industrial structure. In Poland, for instance there has been a marked growth of exports to Germany. However, this increase has been done through the selling of raw or semi-processed goods at very low prices. As a developmental approach it is unlikely that this type of economic activity will help Poland become a modern technologically based economy. It illustrates, as it did in Latin America and Africa, how careful Western policy-makers must be in transplanting foreign ideologies and methods.

The entire 1989 to 1994 transition process had a surreal quality. This can, perhaps, be explained through a recognition that the real transition in the early 1990s represented the collapse of the Soviet Union not the triumph of capitalism. However, many perceived it as such. Ghia Nodia,[4] suggests that many countries became convinced that democracy and capitalism were the only things left to make a transition to (Nodia, 1996: 15). The phenomenon of the 'designer democracy' was to make its appearance. Unlike the strongly ideological French Revolution of the late eighteenth century, the transition in Central Europe was not based on an indigenous revolutionary project. Ideological revolutions tend to be very violent. What happened in Central Europe does not really qualify. The whole project was principally engineered by liberal elites in Poland, Hungary and Czechoslovakia. These elites often sought to implement Western-derived democratic and macroeconomic models. Most of the Central Europeans involved had some form of degree in law, politics or economics. In Hungary, one group instrumental in the 1989 collapse of communism was the Forum of Independent Lawyers, which had worked with eight other opposition groups to bring down the communist government. The passion of the founding fathers of American independence or the fire of Leon Trotsky, was missing. Nodia refers to the transition as the: 'cold-blooded crafting of democracies along ready-made lines' (Nodia, 1996: 23). Neither the economic nor the political transition in Central Europe was based on indigenous ideology or organic transition. Democracy was not something that grew naturally out of the region's past. For most countries in Central Europe, democracy had only been a brief experience from the Treaty of Versailles (1919–20) to the Nazi invasion of 1939. In some case the democratic experience was even shorter, such as in Poland where a *coup d'état* in 1935 put the country under the control of the Polish Generals.[5] Democracy as a political objective after 1989, was chosen because, with the fall of communism, it seemed the only reasonable course of action. For Nodia, this makes for an underlying cynicism to the process as a whole with the only benefit being that 'unimpassioned democrats seem to be faced similarly with lukewarm antidemocrats' (Nodia, 1996: 22). There was, of course, a reaction against the democratically elected governments once the economic harshness of the transition process set in after

1990. However, the politicians who were elected in Central Europe between 1994 and 1996, most of whom belong to socialist or retooled communist political movements, are as technocratic and as committed to the 'liberal democratic capitalist' movement as their predecessors. In fact, many campaigned on a platform of being able to complete the transition process more successfully then the incumbent governments.

What Poland, Hungary and Czechoslovakia wanted out of the transition was multifarious. A European identity, a desire for political justice, hopes for a better way of life, security from fear, all these aspirations motivated the transition process. Moreover, their respective governments were willing to accommodate Western forms of economic development in order to appease international financial institutions and foreign direct investors thereby ensuring that they would be able to continue with their transition project. What, however, did the major industrialized countries want out of the transition? They were all involved in one way or another through either financial or political organizations. Western developmental approaches to Central Europe were more invasive in their influence after 1989 than during the pre-1989 period because of the Cold War. Nevertheless, an argument could be made that the purpose was the same. Since the end of the Second World War, the international order established by the Western World has been increasingly trying to extend its influence in such a way as to make the system fully global. With the collapse of the Soviet Union, an opportunity was presented to the West to remake an entire region in its own image.

3

Central Europe: Introduction to the Case-Studies*

The following chapters will give a detailed examination of the transition in Poland, the Czech Republic and Hungary. Why have these three examples been chosen and how does their experience tally with historical and international trends in the spread of Western norms and values? First, the three countries in this study are natural choices both because of their relative economic development in Central and Eastern Europe, and their physical border with the European Union. Their level of development and proximity made them early targets for trade agreements and transition funding. Secondly, from the point of view of the G7 leaders, the collapse of the Soviet Union had left a power vacuum. Western aid and advice offered to Central Europe was designed to ensure its transition to Western capitalism and thereby ensure stability in the area. This transition, however, would not be immune to the problems that have been faced by other countries attempting to reach a level of sustainable development. The connection between the experience of Central Europe and other parts of the developing world rests upon the nature of economic development theory. As mentioned earlier (see Chapter 2), developing countries and countries in transition need investment capital in order to maintain or introduce structural changes.

---

* The terms, 'Central' and 'Eastern' Europe, can cause confusion. Often first-wave EU applicant countries are termed Central European, however, this puts Estonia and Slovenia with Poland, the Czech Republic and Hungary. Similarly countries referred to as East European may contain Slovakia because it is unlikely to join the EU with the first wave of applicants. For the purpose of clarity in this book, Central Europe refers to Poland, Hungary, the Czech Republic and Slovakia. The term Eastern Europe refers to Estonia, Latvia, Lithuania, Romania, Bulgaria and Slovenia. When Central and Eastern Europe are referred to together the reference is to all 10 countries.

Investment usually comes in the form of aid or loans from the West and this leads ultimately to the implementation of neo-classical economic development[1] policies.

The discipline of economics performs an important role in the governance of all Western countries. What is often forgotten is that economic activity represents only one part of a state's functioning and responsibilities. Where the experience of the past, *vis-à-vis* the spread of Western norms and values, connects with the transition in Central Europe is the tendency of development policy to concentrate strongly on economic policies.

In the following case-study chapters transition policy is shown, in large part, to be economic policy. What this meant for Poland, the Czech Republic and Hungary was that a thin sliver of human experience (economic exchange) was to be used to construct policies that would act as a template upon which to transform the entire society. Indeed, the term 'transition' in Central Europe was often interchangeable with 'economic transition'. The most dramatic case of the three countries in this study is Poland, which implemented the most neo-classical economic policies in the name of its transition. The process of economic transition it could be argued often overshadowed the other project of democratization. In the case-study chapters, E. M. Wood's argument regarding the confusion between the project of the 'enlightenment' and the spread of 'capitalism' (see above, Chapter 1) is apparent. As mentioned earlier, Wood pointed to the confusion between the project of human emancipation, often embodied in democratization, and the spread of capitalism which seeks to facilitate global economic exchange. During the late 1980s the dissidents in Central Europe were calling for democracy. After the collapse of the communism in 1989 the project of the transition changed from a project concentrating specifically on human emancipation to one strongly concerned with the installation of capitalism. The development of a working democracy remained important to those living within the three countries studied. In terms of Central Europe's relationship with the West, however, democracy was a necessary initial condition which then allowed for the economic transition. In the following chapters, it is clear that Western aid and investment would focus heavily on the economic transition.

The development of policy toward Central Europe was a complex affair. There were bilateral and multilateral discussions between the governments of the G7 and Central Europe. There would also be confidential negotiations between the governments of Central Europe and international financial organizations such as the WB and IMF. Despite the complexity of the negotiations the policy prescriptions suggested by Western governments and institutions would be based strongly on neo-classical economics.

Examining a phenomenon as large and elaborate as the transition in Central Europe makes it difficult to select a specific example to show the transmission of neo-classical economic policy. Nevertheless, it is useful when trying to highlight a the nature of hegemony to chose an aspect of this transmission. A Gramscian analysis can be used here to help illustrate the way in which hegemonic ideas, in this case Western ideas, are transmitted. Stephen Gill has done considerable work on the Italian political philosopher, Antonio Gramsci, who wrote during the beginning of this century. Gill points out that a crucial element of Gramsci's notion of hegemony was the concept of the 'organic intellectual' (Gill, 1993: 24). 'Organic intellectuals' are people who effectively mediate between the population and the hegemony. They market the ideology that allows the hegemony to exist and reproduce itself. In this sense intellectual reproduction is directly linked to processes of historical change. An 'organic intellectual' is involved in research and policy prescription which offers a social explanation of the world, but at the same time is linked to a larger political strategy. It is possible for an 'organic intellectual' to be totally unaware of the role he/she is playing in terms of perpetuating a specific set of conditions that allows a hegemony to exist. This is especially the case with economic theorists. Within this discipline there is a strong assumption that you can separate the subject and the object of study and thereby create an unbiased, scientific appraisal of the human condition. Gill's interpretation of Gramsci, however, suggests that this is in fact not possible and therefore knowledge, identity and interests always impact on each other. This means that all theory 'is for someone and for some purpose' (Gill, 1993: 24). 'Organic intellectuals' are vital for the existence of any hegemonic system, according to Gill, because they have the ability to 'theorise the conditions of existence of the system as a whole, suggest policies and justifications for such policies, and if need be to apply them' (Gill, 1993: 110).

For the purpose of this study, Dr Jeffrey Sachs will be used as an example of an 'organic intellectual' to show one of the ways Western values are transferred from the West to non-Western countries. Although this study concentrates specifically on Central Europe, Sachs' role as an 'organic intellectual' has been world wide. He is a career academic and by 1983 was full Professor at Harvard University before the age of 30. During the early part of his career (1986–90) he gave economic and financial reform advice to the governments of Bolivia, Argentina, Brazil, Ecuador and Venezuela. After 1990 he would advise the Polish government during its transition, and from 1991 to 1994 he led a team of economic advisers who worked with the Russian President, Boris Yeltsin (Sachs, 1999: 1). The advice given by Sachs would be neo-classical in nature and facilitate policies that would further integrate the host country into the wider capitalist world. Ultimately, Sachs is only one man and his importance should not be overstated. He does, however, represent a very powerful school of thought and his role in Poland's transition gives an insight into the way in which Western norms are transferred.

After the fall of communism in 1989, CEECs were left with the difficult task of creating free democratic states. The task was made more difficult as all their economies were suffering with debt. The speed of the communist collapse had caught policy makers in the West off guard and as a result limited work had been done on strategic policies to be adopted by the OECD in such an event. The result was a general scramble for policy ideas during January 1990. An influential article during this uncertain time was Jeffrey Sachs' article of 13 January 1990 in the *The Economist*, entitled 'What is to be done?'. His article focused predominantly on the economic aspects of transition, and argued for quick and total decollectivization. His policy suggestions were based on a very particular type of Anglo-American economic liberal approach. Sachs' ideas were based on neo-classical economics, and his own work in particular was referred to as 'The Economic Theory of Transition'. Sachs reputation as a policy adviser in Latin America was well known and as a result American and British policy-makers, in search of a cohesive plan, were attracted to Sachs' proposals. Sachs' American-style developmental policies would later be adopted by the G7 countries. This was not because Sachs ideas were unique, but rather because his ideas conformed to the dominant paradigm of capitalism. As a result Sachs' policy suggestions in his 1990 article was representative of those which were applied to all countries of the former Soviet Union. Strict neo-classical policies were supported by financial institutions and G7 governments, although there was some dissent. The French and German politicians attempted to put forward an alternative approach which would have seen the former Eastern bloc countries retain their trade ties with the former Soviet Union and allow for a gradual change to a market economy. This was rejected in favour of the now well-known policy of 'shock therapy'.

Sachs' main transition argument in 1990 was not only for privatization, but also for the West to supply large amounts of private investment into Central Europe. The opening-up of these economies resulted in an initial 'bidding war'. The EC was concerned about the region of Central and Eastern Europe because it was their own economic backyard. To this end they supplied US$660 million in economic assistance followed closely by the US who under the Bush Administration (1989–93), offered US$146 million in emergency aid (Bjork, 1995: 95). The disbursement of these funds were usually carried out through industry or academic partnerships with the West. Western consultants and policy experts also played a role in deciding which projects or sectors would be supported. As a result, economic assistance from the West often came attached with a neo-classical economic philosophy.

The general approach to the transition can be characterized under the following objectives mentioned in Peter Gowan's (1995) article:

(1) Breaking-up the Comecon region and above all, breaking East–Central European countries from the USSR;
(2) Making a root-and-branch switch (to a particular form of capitalist institutional structure in each state) a precondition for normalising relations with that state;
(3) Imposing, therefore, a hub-and-spoke structure on the relationship between the West and East–Central Europe, with each target state in the region relating to the others principally via its relationship with the Western hub;
(4) Starting the process of regional transformation in the states with the most politically sympathetic governments and then using both negative and positive incentives to extend the required mix of domestic policies across the region as a whole;
(5) The entire process would be carried forward by the capacity and will of Western States to provide, in the main via their multilateral organisations, the necessary positive incentives for co-operative government and constraints for uncooperative governments;
(6) The revival of economic activity in co-operative target states would take the form of trade-led growth toward Western Europe, compensating for Comecon's collapse;
(7) Co-operative states would gain full access to the market of the EC (partly through radically changing some of its key institutional pillars, such as its trade regime and Common Agricultural Policy),

> very substantial economic assistance and eventual membership of a greatly enlarge EC.
>
> Gowan, 1995: 6–7

Although not completely realized this was the initial plan for the transition particularly as conceived by American policy-makers in their talks with the G7. Although the European Community was interested in the entire region, it was particularly interested in the Central European countries of Poland, the Czech Republic and Hungary. The process was an attempt to integrate Central Europe into the West and capitalism. Sachs played a visible role in the transferring of Western economic norms. He had been advising the Yugoslav government in 1989, but changed his focus to concentrate specifically on Poland in 1990. Sachs suggested that if Central European countries were to be truly integrated with the West they would have to seek membership of the IMF, WB and GATT/WTO. All these international organizations are committed to the further liberalization of markets. It was expected therefore that transition countries would open their economies to foreign investment and international trade as well as making their national currencies fully convertible. The introduction of these policies, it was assumed, would lead to the establishment of private ownership as the 'engine of growth' (Sachs, 1995). It was hoped that this would form the mainstay of the fledgling capitalist economies in Central Europe.

Admittedly, the early years of the Central European transition neoclassical prescriptive policies would prove damaging and a serious recession occurred between 1990 and 1993. When the IMF sanctioned the 'Shock Therapy' approach to development it was done in the expectation that countries which adopted this model would attract fairly large amounts of FDI. There were problems with the logical consistency of arguments made by Westerners or Central Europeans educated in the West. Basically Central European governments were told that they did not need a Marshall Aid package because the transition would be financed by foreign capital. The issue of control was never really addressed. In practice when 'Shock Therapy' had been put into place, the economic slump it caused actually deterred, as opposed to attracted, foreign investment. The claim that FDI was the only vehicle for technological change was only true to the extent that the G7 countries and the IMF told the Central European governments that this was the case, and pressured all countries to open their economies to FDI. In Poland, for instance, the 'transformed' economy found it difficult to attract the kind of necessary investment to stimulate growth. It is interesting to

Table 3.1 FDI Flows into the Visegrad Countries, 1990–93 (net inflows in US$ millions)

	1990	1991	1992	1993
Czechoslovakia (pre-Jan. 1993)	199	594	1,054	–
Czech Republic (post-Jan. 1993)			983	561
Slovak Republic (post-Jan. 1993)			71	100
Poland	88	117	284	850
Hungary	377	1,459	1,471	1,200
China			11,100	25,900
All Eastern Europe and Newly Independent States (NIS) 1989–93				11,000

Sources: Commission of the EC, *European Economy*, Supplement A, no. 3, Mar. 1994, Directorate-General for Economic and Financial Affairs, Mar. 1994, and for China, UNCTAD, 1994: 13.

note that China has resisted IMF prescriptions. Unfortunately, it has also ignored pressure to heed internal demands for democracy. In terms of capitalism, however, it has opted for a slower 'third' kind of transition to market-socialism,[2] not dissimilar to the suggestions put forward by the French and Germans as a possible template for Central/Eastern Europe back in 1990. A slow transition was rejected by the other G7 countries, predominantly by the US and the UK, on the grounds that it would discourage FDI. However, in 1992 alone China attracted more FDI than that acquired by the whole of the former Soviet bloc between 1989 and 1993 (Gowan, 1995: 40). Indeed China's FDI investment more than doubled between 1992 and 1993 (see Table 3.1).

If Central Europe is to develop into a prosperous European region it will need the kind of attention that Western Europe received after the Second World War. It is worth noting that the Marshall Aid package was not given to Europe until July 1948 after it had become patently obvious that it would not recover properly without massive US help. One hopes that the CEECs may be treated better in years to come, particularly on the issue of allowing them to develop their own domestic economies as opposed to encouraging a specific type of export-led growth which only work in times of international economic expansion.

When looking at the case-study chapters the reader must understand that there is a clear demarcation between the performance of Central Europe in 1998 and its performance in 1993. The strong American-style neo-classical economic policies that were supported through IMF-loan conditionality in the early part of the transition were substantially modified after the 1994 European Agreements came into effect. In preparation for future EU membership, Central European economic and social policy was expected to follow that of social democratic EU states. In this way the principles of the 'enlightenment' and the concentration on solidifying the democratization project was strengthened. This is not to say the EU was acting as a selfless agent, although, the Central European adoption of EU legislation forced them to take on social, workplace, and competition legislation which had been built up within the EU in order to make capitalism function. The stability created by these legislative changes and Central European access to the EU would also act as a magnet for FDI. The important issue to remember is that the IMF 'shock therapy' model of economic development was as unsuccessful in Central Europe in the 1990s as it had been in Africa in the 1980s. It only has the illusion of success because of Central Europe's relationship with the EU. The EU approach to development is still a form of Western capitalism, but the criteria laid down by the EU revealed an intense awareness of the social ramifications of the transition. Moreover, this organization has targeted considerable funds towards the region in the form of aid rather than loans. In its plenary session of 9–10 September 1998 the EU's influential Economic and Social Committee supported a motion to supply additional funding to EU candidate countries (EU 1998: V, 1). This funding will be substantial. For the 10 candidate CEECs to comply with EU environmental regulations alone will require an EU investment of over a 100 billion ecu (US$85.86 billion) (ibid.). It could be argued that the IMF and the OECD's unwillingness to construct a 'Marshall Aid' plan for Central Europe ultimately left the EU with this responsibility.

Central Europe's current economic success has bred a dangerous misunderstanding. The liberal economic policies applied to Central Europe during the early years of the transition were very invasive and were based on a very narrow view of what constituted capitalism. These types of neo-classical economic policies continue to be prescribed by the IMF to other countries in economic crisis. Encouraging strong free market principles in vulnerable states which suffer from debt appears to cultivate political and financial instability. There seems to be little appreciation that Central Europe's current stability has more to do with EU aid, and the adoption process of relevant EU legislation, than with the policies of the IMF.

When reading the following chapters, which contain a detailed account of the transition process in Poland, the Czech Republic and Hungary, be aware of the part played by the West in the transition process during 1990–93. Notice the heavy concentration on the transmission of economic capitalism. The case-study chapters reveal how the initial attraction to 'shock therapy' or at least a quick transition became reconsidered in the face of a serious recession in all three countries. After 1993, the hard work of establishing a capitalist yet liberal democracy would be continued in a more complex, but ultimately more successful way through Central Europe's commitments to the EU. Regardless of the type of transition, whether fast or slow, the desired outcome by the West was to pull Central Europe into the wider global political economy. Although this process is not complete, all three countries in this study are now as dependent on the West as they were on the Soviet Union before 1989.

4
Poland

The purpose of this chapter is to offer a background case-study. This chapter provides an analysis of events that have led Poland to where it is today. As a result of its geographical location, Poland has always been in the 'squeeze' area between Russia and Germany, a position that has often proven difficult. The following sections looks briefly at Poland's early history, especially its turbulent twentieth-century experience. The decades leading up to the 1989 transition are covered in detail in an endeavour to explain Poland's problem of debt and the nature of the Polish dissident movement which brought down its single-party communist rule. An examination of the policies of transformation follow in order to illustrate the difficulties associated with moving from a command to a market-driven economy.

4.1 Brief history of Poland

Many Westerners would admit to thinking of Poland as a small and peripheral power. However, Poland has a long and rich history much of which shows it to have been a regional power with considerable influence. In terms of Polish national identity its long history and status as a former power in the region is intensely significant. This is particularly true if we look at its relationship with Lithuania, Belarus and the Ukraine. Early on, even when these countries were sometimes under the rule of a single monarch, it was Polish culture that tended to dominate. An example of this was the dynastic marriage, on 18 February 1386 between Poland's Queen Jadwiga and Lithuania's Grand Duke Jogaila (Jagiello), whose lands included most of the Ukraine and Belarus (Burant, 1993: 396). As a result Poles, Lithuanians, Belarussians and Ukrainians came under common rule through marriage. This period commonly known as the Jagiellonian period has become, in Poland's national mythology, one that is romanticized as a time of great Polish power and culture. Polish influence in the area remained and in 1569 the Polish–Lithuanian Commonwealth came into existence (ibid.). Amazingly the predominant nature of Polish culture in this area was largely uncontested for centuries among the elites who became Roman Catholic and adopted Polish culture as their own. The same did not happen, however, to the peasants who maintained their own ethnic identity.

Polish elites saw themselves as the legitimate transmitters of Western European culture to the east. This belief or self-identity of Poland as a lynchpin between the west and the east remains to the present. However, the assumption was that the cultural transmission would always go from west to east. It was during the sixteenth century that Poland reached its height as a European power. Indeed, it was at one stage in this century one of the largest continental powers. Its national territory ran from the Black Sea in the south to the Baltic in the north, from the Ukraine in the east to the rich plains that ran next to the Vistula river in the West (a further discussion on the rise and decline of Polish power can be found in Tausch and Prager, 1993). Poland's inclusion in the world economic system at this stage, although important, was in its capacity as a supplier of commodities, not finished goods. Its wealth remained agricultural.

The social system in place during what Polish historians refer to as the 'long sixteenth century' was one of feudalism. While landowners made up less than 5 per cent of the population, indentured serfs (peasants) accounted for over 70 per cent, the balance being made-up of clergy, small landowners, the urban middle class and Jews (Rotworowksi, 1979: 338). Polish grain was the main export during this period. Despite Poland's agricultural wealth, the inflexible nature of its social system meant that even though demand for grain increased in the sixteenth and seventeenth century, Poland was slow to respond. Productivity was low on large aristocratic estates, and this, combined with other factors such as continuous war, pushed Poland into decline (Brenner, 1977: 70).

The lack of a bourgeoisie and limited purchasing power on the part of disenfranchised peasants, meant that Poland had no internal market for goods (with the exception of luxury trade for the wealthy landed gentry). The result was economic stagnation. Poland went from being a major regional power to a mere shadow of it former self. By the end of the eighteenth century, Poland's neighbours, (the kingdoms in what are present day Russia, Germany and Austria in particular) had become increasingly powerful. The upshot of this situation culminated with the First Partition of Poland in 1772. By the end of the eighteenth century Poland had been divided between the great empires of Austria, Russia and the Kingdom of Prussia.

Despite its temporary revival as a Grand-Duchy of Warsaw by Napoleon (1806–12), by 1815 Poland had ceased to exist as a separate country. With the Congress of Vienna Poland came under direct Russian control. The collapse of Poland meant that Russia, Austria and Prussia now all shared a common border. Many Poles felt anger and resentment at the great European powers for their division of Poland. In 1794, after the 2nd partition of Poland (1793), a general uprising occurred in both Vilnas and Warsaw, under the national hero Tadeusz Kosciuszko[1] (Kinder and Hilgemann, 1979: 285). Both of these uprisings were put down with force by Prussian and Russian troops. The recurrence of Polish nationalism was a continual source of irritation and conflict to the large powers. With a series of uprisings taking place thoughout the nineteenth century, the result was an irrepressible nationalist movement that kept resurfacing.

The great powers had done themselves a disservice by partitioning a country as long-established as Poland. It would make exiles of people such as the composer Chopin (1809–49). The result was to reinforce claims of submerged nationalities throughout Central and Eastern Europe (Macartney and Palmer, 1972: 6). Russia dealt with Polish dissidence in two ways: (1) violent repression in times of revolt; and (2) the introduction of the doctrine of panslavism in which the Russian language was forced upon minorities in an attempt to wipe out ethnic differences. The Poles, however, continued their fight for independence during the mid-to-late 19th century aiming for the complete reinstatement of their Polish–Lithuania Commonwealth borders. The Prussians were also plagued by Polish nationalism. During the first part of the century many Germans were not unsympathetic to the plight of the Polish state, however, by 1860 Prussia like Russia had decided that the only way to deal with Poles was through military action and the repression of everything Polish.

The Austrian-Hapsburg Monarchy, unlike the other two Eastern European monarchies, found it easier to deal with Polish nationalism without frequent recourse to violence. This can be attributed to the large number of ethnic minorities found in the Austro-Hungarian Empire. The Hapsburg Monarchy was adept at playing one group of minorities off against the other. Therefore, as Poles, Czechs, Ruthenes, Serbs and Croats argued over who should or should not have certain rights in the empire, the imperial government in Vienna remained secure and unchallenged. Moreover, the Polish aristocracy formed a large part of the ruling elite in the eastern part of the Hapsburg Empire with both the Hapsburgs and the Poles finding common cause in suppressing the Orthodox Christian faith.

The development of radical thought, particularly with regards to communism did not make headway in fragmented nineteenth-century Poland. Each uprising or revolt, whether in Prussian, Russian or Austrian-held territory, suppressed the Poles ability to speak freely. This resulted in a large number of Polish *émigrés*. It was during the period of 1832–92 that the beginnings of Polish socialism began. *Émigrés* living outside Poland established intellectual groups, such as the Democratic Society founded in 1832, whose ethos, while not directly socialist, concentrated on the rights of workers (Dziewanowski, 1959: 3). As time went on Polish *émigrés* became more involved with socialist movements. For instance, Rosa Luxembourg (1871–1919) was Polish born, and worked extensively in the creation of the German Communist Party as well as being an important contributor to communist ideology through her writings. Similarly, men like Jachim Lelewel and Adam Mickiewicz concentrated on legitimizing agrarian communism. Lelewel in particular remained in close contact with the Communist League – the organization for whom Marx and Engels had written their Manifesto (Dziewanowski, 1959: 4).

The nineteenth-century socialist movements by Poles (mostly *émigrés*) remained largely agrarian in nature. Poland had no great mass of industrialized workers like that found in Britain. Poland had gone from a feudal system to being an agricultural producing area for the three empires within which it had found itself incorporated. This legacy meant Polish socialism was different in character than its other Western European counterparts. Curiously, while most socialist movements tended to be transnational, Polish socialism often emphasized the need to re-establish a free Polish state. The point being that Poland should become a democratic country and take her proper place in Europe. Calls for democracy in the 1980s used similar arguments. Although much of nineteenth-century Polish socialism was vague and contradictory, it did set the ground work for its development in the twentieth century.

Perhaps the most significant aspect of the late eighteenth-century partition of Poland was the economic retardation it caused. Poland had become a peripheral agricultural area to the three empires. The nineteenth century, for Western Europe, brought the development of industrialized capitalism. However, Polish subjugation during this period meant that its development was fragmented and the production of primary commodities continued to play a larger part in its economy than that of many other European countries.

This legacy, unfortunately, has gone a long way to defining Poland's role in the world economy in the twentieth century. If we look at trade figures for the CEECs before the communist collapse of 1989, we will observe that 54 per cent of its exports to the developed OECD economies were made-up of mining, food and fuels (UN, Economic Commission for Europe, 1988: 294). The legacy of peripheralization remained. There continues to be a healthy debate as to when and why Poland became peripheralized. Wallerstein's world system approach puts it back before the sixteenth century, whereas critics of Wallerstein, such as Brenner, put it closer to the late seventeenth or early eighteenth century (Wallerstein, 1974: 125ff, 451 and Brenner, 1977: 25–35). Regardless of which view one may hold it is obvious that by the nineteenth century Poland was well and truly integrated into the world economy and its place was secured albeit as a peripheral economy.

The industrialization that did occur in Poland only further reflected its hinterland status. Out of a total of 15 million Poles, the majority (9 million) lived in Russian-held Poland. There were just 3.5 million in Prussian-held territory and Austrian Poles numbered a mere 2.5 million (Grabiec, 1974: 10–11). Large-scale industrialization occurred in the Russian part of Poland where the workforce was the largest. The conditions of a Russian-Pole industrial worker was far worse than a worker in Austrian or Prussian-held Poland. Even by the early twentieth century, by which time wages and standards had slightly improved, a Russian-Pole working in industry would earn 25 per cent less than a Silesian miner (Germany's poorest paid worker) (ibid.: 157–8). It was the appalling working conditions for the majority of Russian-Poles that spawned twentieth-century Polish socialism. By 1893 the Polish Socialist party was formed which aimed to fuse the philosophy of Marx with Poland's goal of national liberation (Dziewanowski, 1959: 21).

By the early part of the twentieth century Europe began to experience political turbulence. The great empires of Austro-Hungary and Russia were showing signs of instability caused by widespread national movements and imperial conflict. The international system was revealing the tension between capitalism, aristocracy, nationalism and the frustration of the disenfranchised. The two defining events were, of course, the First World War and the Russian Revolution. Once war had broke out between the great powers Polish nationalism resurfaced. It was the first time since 1772 that Polish re-unification had appeared to be a real possibility. This is not to say that there were no differences between Austrian,

Prussian or Russian Poles. Throughout the First World War, the three groups of Poles supported different sides. However, by the end of the war most Poles in all three areas had come to the conclusion that Poland should be reinstated as a totally independent sovereign state. There had been some talk in the latter part of the war about the Kingdom of Poland falling under the Russian Empire, but this was rejected. The Russian empire was in any case made defunct after the October 1917 Bolshevik revolution.

With the defeat of the Austro-Hungarian empire in 1918 the CEECs stood ready for a total redefinition. The collapse of the German, Austrian and Russian empires created the opportunity for the rebirth of the Polish nation. this rebirth was not, however, without its difficulties. Although Poland was recognized by 1918, following the Treaty of Versailles, it received no direct war reparation through the Treaty, and the boundary agreements reached put her in conflict with her neighbours (Epstein, 1973). During the immediate post-war period Poland found herself in a series of border wars. The Polish–Soviet war was fought in 1920 over the eastern border Poland shared with Soviet Union (Gerner, 1985: 43). It also found itself in conflict with Lithuania during 1920, when Polish General Lucjan Zeligowski headed a campaign to seize the Vilnius region. Lithuania never forgave Poland for this act and diplomatic ties between the two countries were not re-established until 1938 (Burant, 1993: 397).

Polish foreign policy during the inter-war years was fraught with difficulty. Tension over borders combined with large ethnic minorities made policy-making a hard task. Nevertheless, Poland did manage to enter into a Pact with Germany in 1934 and the Soviet Union in 1932 (renewed in 1934), an accomplishment only marred by the brevity of the agreements (Kinder and Hilgemann, 1978: 155). Poland was also having its problems domestically. Between 1919 and 1937 it had to grapple with the nationalist tendencies of its own ethnic minorities, agrarian land reform, government instabilities, failure of their republic and finally a military *coup d'état*. In 1935 a new authoritarian constitution following the military coup was enacted which was billed as 'guided democracy', but essentially ended parliamentary democracy (ibid.: 155). The Poland that was invaded by Germany, was not a particularly democratic one. Having said this, Poles living under the authority of Polish Generals were better treated than Poles who fell under the control of the Nazi Generals.

After 21 years of precarious independence, Poland again ceased to exist as a country in September–October 1939. It began with the German invasion of western Poland during September 1939, which was quickly followed by the Russian invasion of eastern Poland in late September/ early October of the same year (Macartney and Palmer, 1972: 411). Germany made few apologies for the military action in Poland. The Russians, however, felt they needed a political excuse for their invasion. As the Soviet armies started to advance on Poland, Moscow announced that 'as the Polish state had ceased to exist, Russia's obligations towards it had become null and void, and it was her duty to intervene and protect her Ukrainian and White Russian brethren' (ibid.: 411). Regardless of the political rationale, by the end of 1939 Poland had been carved-up between Germany and the Soviet Union. Stalin, in particular, did not want the Polish state to remain in any form and incorporated the country into the Ukrainian and White Russian republics. Some Poles, including the entire government, escaped to Romania.

At the close of the war the allies had to make a decision regarding the future of Poland. In February 1945 at the Yalta conference, Churchill, Roosevelt and Stalin, in addition to sorting out the shape of the post-war world, decided upon the fate of Poland. Poland was to be liberated. Its western border was to be decided by treaty and its eastern border was to be at the old Curzon Line[2] (Kinder, 1978: 209). In reality, however, Poland became a satellite state to the Soviet Union and found itself behind the iron curtain during the post-war years.

The events of 1989 were largely driven by Poland's dissatisfaction with the Soviet Union and its own Communist Party during the post-war era. The incorporation of Poland into the Soviet sphere of influence meant the severing of many contacts with Western Europe (Gerner, 1985: 47). There was two sides to this severing. Many of the Polish exiles in Great Britain chose to stay rather than return to a Soviet controlled Poland. Western culture, something that formally Poland had identified with, was actively discouraged. Those with post-war influence in Poland, were to be those Poles who had spent the war in Russia or on the Russian front. Russian Poles, a number from wealthy families such as General Jaruselski, were sent to Soviet labour camps. Both men and women were later conscripted into the Polish contingent of the Russian army and given a strong induction into Soviet communism. They were then put in Polish fighting units and sent to the front. These units had been taught that they were to liberate Poland so that she could take her place in the Soviet Union.

At the end of the war it was the 'Soviet-Poles' that were given positions of power in Poland. There were few Polish Jews left. They had been largely exterminated by Hitler. The Germans had been removed and parts of Byelorussia and Ukraine had been retaken by the USSR. Poland's brave new world after the war, therefore, was to be largely constructed by 'Soviet-Poles'. First, because it served Stalin's political purpose, but, secondly, because of the high attrition rate among the young during the war. Six million people were killed in Poland during the war – which was more than one-fifth of the pre-war population – the majority of those lost were the young (Rosenberg, 1995: 145).

There may have been a 'third way' for Poland had the West been more flexible towards countries with communist parties. Poland's isolation did not happen overnight but grew during the post-war decades. Ultimately, Cold War tensions soured Poland's relationship with the IMF, the WB, and the West in general.

Directly after the War in 1946, Poland requested US$600 million in a reconstruction loan from the WB. Negotiations were slow and when a package was approved the amount of the loan was reduced to just US$45 million (Bjork, 1995: 90). This money was only to be used for very specific development assistance. By the 1950s Poland became wary of both the WB and the IMF. The WB's strict conditionality, and American 'MacCarthyist' attitudes to communist countries, prompted Poland to withdraw its membership from both organizations.

Although Poland belonged to the Communist bloc and held membership in Comecon (the Soviet trading bloc) and the Warsaw Pact (the Soviet military alliance), its communist experience was less severe then in other communist bloc countries. Unlike many Soviet and East European countries, Polish agriculture was never successfully collectivized and much of the agricultural production remained in private hands. In 1956, a common Soviet-Polish declaration was signed which effectively de-Stalinized Poland signalling a change in Soviet government attitudes. The declaration mentioned that: 'the union and the fraternal bonds should become broadened and confirmed and be developed on the basis of complete equality . . . sovereignty and non-interference in internal affairs' (Gerner, 1985: 47). After 1956 Poland remained connected to the Soviet Union through the Communist Party, but the declaration had given it greater freedom to construct its own government and institutions, in its own way. Nevertheless, compared to Western freedoms, political life in Poland for the majority of the population would have been restrictive. Multi-party elections and freedom of the press were not permitted. Despite these obvious restrictions in the years after 1956 successive governments would attempt to attain some form of popular support in an effort to create legitimacy.

4.2 Events leading up to 1989

The lack of a proper system of representative government resulted in an increasingly unenthusiastic citizenry. In recognition of the political danger that this situation posed the Gomulka regime (1956–70) undertook to increase the level of political legitimacy. However, this was not to mean democratic reform. Under the government in which Wladyslaw Gomulka (1905–82), was First Secretary, Poland reversed the agricultural collectivism that existed, allowed greater freedom for the Roman Catholic Church, increased cultural freedoms to a certain degree and permitted workers' councils in factories and mines (Gerner, 1985: 48). These small freedoms were soon whittled down as the government feared loss of control. However, Polish communism ceased to be as authoritarian as other varieties, resulting in a Polish civil society that survived in a fairly robust form, particularly in the workers councils.

Inevitably, increased freedom lead to increased expectation and desire. During the 1960s and 1970s a variety of political demonstrations took place. In 1968, students took to the streets to protest the censoring of a nineteenth-century classic Polish play whose topic was on the Russian oppression of Poland in the early nineteenth century (Gerner, 1985: 48). Workers in the Baltic ports demonstrated in December 1970 over the issue of large government food price rises. The political situation was very tense and the government ordered troops to shoot a number of the workers to put down the movement (see The Kubiak Report, 1982: 3). In many ways the riots of 1970 were the beginning of the end for Polish communism even if it would take another 19 years for a full collapse. The riots had seriously damaged the legitimacy of the Gomulka government and as a result he resigned as leader. He was replaced by Edward Gierek, whose first task was to regain some of the political legitimacy lost during the Gomulka years. The healing process was initiated by increasing state payments to farmers who produced meat and grains; quotas were removed and many farmers were given formal property rights to their farms. This went a long way to solving the common problem of food crises through the 20 per cent increase of the production of both grain and meat during the 1970–73 period (Gerner, 1985: 49).

The Gierek regime endeavoured to usher in a new era for Poland by creating a new economic development strategy. The strategy rested on the need to increase Polish exports, and to import Western technology to retool/modernize Polish industry. This marked departure from former policy was to be financed by borrowing from the West and repaying with hard currency accrued through increased exports to the West.

Although theoretically plausible, Gierek's plan did not, in practice, give the results expected.

Gierek's strategy – which primarily consisted of borrowing from the West in the hopes of boosting international exports – is striking in its dependancy on Western approaches to capitalist development. It was a curious mix of trying to acquire western standards of living while maintaining state control of the economy. Democratization was not considered an option. This strategy was bold, as the investment was all front loaded with moneys initially going into modernization of factories. Importing Western technology and retooling factories was not itself a guarantee of Western export markets.

Gierek's economic strategy marked the re-entry of the Polish economy into the international capitalist system. The year 1989 despite Fukuyama's 'end of history' argument, was not as solid a break as many portrayed. What 1989 did mark was renewed interest by the West of the CEECs after the dissolution of the USSR. Despite Western political attitudes during the Cold War, many of these countries, Poland in particular, had been integrating into the world economy from the 1970s onwards. Western popular perception saw countries behind the iron curtain as being completely cut off from the West. However, it seems reasonable to assume that if Poland were borrowing Western capital, it was exposing itself to Western capitalism. Import/export regulations, Western loan conditionality and business/government contacts with the West would all have had an impact on the Polish economy.

In the early 1970s Gierek's economic reforms seemed to be working. Between 1971 and 1975 total investments in Polish economy increased 18.4 per cent annually and industrial investments grew by 21.9 per cent. With increases in investment and production came the rise of living standards. In 1974 alone, personal income grew by 17 per cent (Gerner, 1985: 49). The growth of the Polish economy far outstripped expectations. Estimates for its growth between 1971 and 1975 were approximately 42 per cent but in reality the figure was closer to 90 per cent. The same holds true for the expected increases in real wages. The assumption was that they would grow by 39 per cent but in 1975 the growth was closer to 70 per cent (Fallenbuchl, 1982; Gerner, 1985: 49).

Indeed, in the early 1970s Poland seemed to offer the possibility of enjoying the best of both worlds, namely eastern bloc security with Western growth. By 1975, however, cracks in the system were starting to appear. Many of the problems which confronted Poland at this time were not of its own making. Crop failures, due to precarious climatic conditions caused a renewed domestic food shortage. Internationally,

Nixon had taken the US off the Gold Standard in August 1971 (see Section 1.3 of this books), which effectively ended the Bretton Woods system of fixed exchange rates. The Arab–Israeli war of October 1973 sparked off the first round of Organization of Petroleum Exporting Countries (OPEC) oil shocks (December 1973). These two major international economic development brought about economic recession in the developed world. Poland, following its recent entry into the world of export-led trade growth, found itself hit quite hard.

Poland cannot be held accountable for the nature of the international economic system during the mid-1970s nor was it responsible for the poor weather conditions during the early-1970s. However, it can be taken to task for a number of policy decisions which exacerbated a difficult situation. The major weakness in the Polish economic strategy was that it did not have sufficient mechanisms to ensure that incoming investment was funnelled to companies or sectors which exhibited the greatest potential for export growth. The bureaucratic structure in Poland was heavy and cumbersome. Investment and high-priced imports were often spread out across-the-board, instead of concentrating resources in growth areas. Even worse, some costly imports were procured for projects not originally in the strategic plan. Too often, once imports had been acquired, the government did not have financial or other resources needed to complete the project. Some of the imports were, therefore, wasted. Moreover, much of the economic growth in Poland was domestic not export driven. Internal wealth based upon the zloty did not result in the acquistion of hard currency necessary for foreign loan repayment. In the mid to late 1970s the Polish economy started to flounder. Unlike the early 1970s when reality outperformed expectations, actual export figures were well below estimated targets (Fallenbuchl, 1980).

By 1976, the food crisis had become serious and the Polish trade balance revealed increased imports and decreased exports. The government tried to stop the flow of imports, but this only halted the modernization of many sectors and ceased projects to which millions of zloty had already been allocated. Food price rises of basic commodities only produced wildcat strikes and street demonstrations. Gierek's hope that a modernised Poland would see its exports outstrip its imports would remain unfulfilled. Moreover, Poland's economic failure spawned unrest which engendered new political restrictions on pre-1970 freedoms (Gerner, 1985: 51). Poland's poor economic condition only worsened during the late 1970s, and by 1980 Poland's debt was a staggering US$24 billion (Prust, 1988: 3–12). This figure looks even worse when one realizes that as much as 96 per cent of Poland's total export earnings would have been allocated to servicing its debt (WB, 1987: 17). The failure of Poland's economic strategy left the country in a vulnerable position.

Between 1980 and 1982 Polish society was involved in a series of confrontations with the communist regime (Sanford, 95: 106). This marked the beginning of societal movements which would ultimately bring down Poland's single party government. Two important players were the Workers' Defence Committee (KOR) and the Foundation Committee for Free Trade Unions (WZ-WZZ). These organizations provided the initial intellectual and worker opposition to the communist state (ibid.: 107). KOR was a crucial precursor to free trade unions. WZ-WZZ performed a largely educational function, but did train individuals such as Lech Walsea who would later help in the creation of the political movement Solidarity.

The catalyst for the emergence of Solidarity occurred in 1980. The government was in crisis over continued foreign borrowing to subsidize the Polish economy. The subsidization of food prices was a major cost to the government and in 1980 it decided to raise food prices. The societal reaction was similar to that of the 1970 Christmas-time food price hike. Strikes broke out throughout the country, but the greatest concentration was in the Lenin Shipyards in Gdansk. Lech Walesa, then a shipyard electrician, became the leader of the Strike Committee. The unrest moved to include over two hundred enterprises organized under the name of the Interfactory Strike Committee (MKS), of which Walesa also became leader.

The most significant outcome of these strikes was a compromise by the Soviet and Polish government to allow free trade unions not attached to the Communist Party or its government ministries (Mason, 1993: 37). This compromise saw the creation of the 'Solidarity' trade union. Within sixteen months of the union's creation it had twelve million members or over two-thirds of Poland's total workforce (of 16 million) (Mason, 1993: 39). Solidarity was more than a trade union, it also functioned as a social–political organization which went some way to meeting the Polish peoples' need to articulate their dissatisfaction with the political system.

Solidarity's massive popular support revealed it as a real threat to the Polish Communist Party. Soviet pressure forced the Polish government to replace the Polish, Party leader, Stanislaw Kania with General Wojciech Jaruzelski, who was already Defence Minister and Prime Minister. In the autumn of 1981, the Soviet Army undertook threatening military manoeuvres along the Polish border. Jaruzelski, a strong supporter of Soviet communism, wrote in his memoirs that he feared a Soviet crackdown in Poland as had occurred in Hungary in 1956, Czechoslovakia in 1968 and Afghanistan in 1979 (Rosenberg, 1995: 128). Whether through fear of the Soviets or a bid to preserve his own government, Jaruzelski decided in December 1981 to declare martial law, arrest the leaders of Solidarity and forbid its existence (Mason, 1993: 40). The economy had stagnated and martial law remained in force until 1983. Momentum for change had been retarded. Even after 1983, it took until the late 1980s before dissension once again manifested as public demonstration.

Martial Law and the general political clampdown in Poland also effected its relationship with the broader world economy. The import–export drive in Poland during the early to mid-1970s had brought it to the attention of West. This was reawakened in the early 1980s with Solidarity's movements against Soviet-style communism. This coincided with the era of the Reagan Presidency (1981–89) in the US and Thatcher's premiership (1979–90) in Britain. The strong anti-communism of these two administrations meant that they were willing to encourage policies in the Eastern bloc that would embarrass the Soviets. As a result of this mildly sympathetic political climate, Poland during its 1980–81 economic crisis, looked to the West for assistance. One possibility was reapplication to the IMF, but conditionality was to prove a problem. However, the Polish government throughout the time of martial law maintained full contact with the IMF. In 1982 a number of economic measures were introduced with regards to price deregulation, wage controls, decentralized control over enterprises and the devaluation of the zloty (Bjork, 1995: 92). These measures were unsuccessful, according to the IMF, as they did not aid the emergence of a market-driven economy.

Poland had difficulties in implementing economic reforms. However, the IMF felt that the Polish government needed encouragement in its exploration of pro-liberal ideas. The US and the IMF appeared more interested in introducing Poland to capitalism than to democracy. Nevertheless, the Polish government was aware of Western expectations and in 1986 General Jaruzelski allowed an amnesty of political prisoners (most of whom were Solidarity members) in the hope of softening international opinion. The US administration, although wary, did agree to drop its opposition to Poland's reapplication to the IMF and the WB. It regained both its memberships in 1986, a full three years before the collapse of communism. Poland's introduction to liberal democracy began with liberal capitalism, but its introduction to democracy had to wait.

Despite Polish government intentions at reform, and prodding by the IMF and WB, it found it difficult to sustain change. On the one hand, the price increases and wage constraints of liberal reforms were unpopular, on the other the Polish government needed to maintain good relations with the IMF from whom they would have to borrow to service their cumbersome debt. It was an all too familiar narrative in the international political economy of the late twentieth century.

In many ways, the talk of Poland's transition to a market economy after 1989 is somewhat misleading. Their economy was certainly heavily state controlled before 1989. Nevertheless, despite the nature of its domestic economy, Poland's international economic relations during the 1980s did not differ greatly different from many developing countries whose economies were considered capitalist. With Poland's reintroduction to the IMF and WB in 1986 came renewed rounds of debt renegotiation. IFIs wanted to remain tough on Poland, but the IMF saw an opportunity to push Poland for a 'second stage' of reform (Bjork, 1995: 93). The pressure resulted in the Polish government's attempt to implement a price and income operation. It was again an attempt to raise prices and cap wages and again it was met with unrest and demonstrations. Between 1986 and 1988 the government relented and even allowed large wage increases.

The Polish government's position became increasingly difficult. It was pressurized by the IMF to do something about its policy shortcomings, and pressurized by the public to leave things as they were. The continuing government compromises turned the Polish economy into a destabilized merry-go-round – although it kept going this was only because it was rolling down hill. In 1988, Polish debt had grown to US$40 billion, nearly double the 1980 figure of US$24 (Mason, 1993: 41; Bjork, 1995: 91). Workers continued demands for wage increases and price capping led to rampant inflation which reached 60 per cent in 1988. In response to these economic problems, General Jaruzelski's government attempted a further price liberalization in 1988. It was met with stiff opposition. This time the political mood of the people had changed.

4.3 Collapse of communism

The events of 1988–89 in Poland are much studied, but contesting views of events are put forward. Stephen White *et al.*'s (1993) work, *Developments in East European Politics* sees the Solidarity movement as largely responsible for the end of communist rule. However, Tadeusz

Kowalik, a contributor to Marguerite Mendell's and Klaus Nielson's (1995) volume, *Europe: Central and East* claims that Solidarity had lost its grass roots base and was not particularly a guiding light in the transition from communism (Kowalik, 1995: 93). Others have pointed to Gorbachev's *glasnost* policy and suggested that Jaruzelski could no longer expect military support from Soviet Russia for the maintenance of his authoritarian regime.

Another argument regarding the cause of change in Poland, rests upon the need for systemic economic reform. Considering the harshness of these measures it could only be undertaken by a government that had the support of its people. The WB's departmental director, Eugene Lari, recognized as early as 1987 that, 'Any viable attempt at structural change in the Polish context had to enlist . . . the country's life force . . . managers, workers, peasants, and society as a whole' (Bjork, 1995: 94). It is one of the great ironies that IFI pressured reforms helped bring about the downfall of the communist government, but then the subsequent 'free' Poland had to adopt far harsher economic policies if it were to gain access to international credit. Economic conditions for the majority of Poles during 1990 to 1993 were drastically below 1988 living standards, but the Polish people accepted from capitalism what they rejected from communism.

Many members of Solidarity who had worked diligently for democracy in the 1980s had a highly romantic view of what liberal capitalist democracy actually was. First, there was an intellectual muddling between capitalism and democracy. Although they can go together, they do not have to, and what is more, some argue that capitalism works better in authoritarian regimes. An ironic Polish saying of this period goes as follows: 'Poles want a German-style economy, a Swedish-style social democracy, combined with American-style consumerism, while keeping communist-style job and state security.' It was in short, an impossible dream.

The end of the communist regime began in the Spring of 1988 when increased food prices brought on strikes and demonstrations, not unlike those of 1980–81 which had caused martial law. During the spring strikes, workers were largely sticking to economic demands, but the nature of the world had changed and Polish strikes no longer brought Soviet tanks to their borders. Solidarity supporters became more brave and by August 1988 the demands were not only economic but political as well.

One of Solidarity's demands related to state legislation which had made membership to Solidarity illegal. The Polish government was concerned and wanted the strikes to stop. The Polish Interior Minister, Czeslaw Kiszczak, went to meet Lech Walesa to say that if he could get the strikers to go back to work, the government would discuss legislation pertaining to Solidarity (Mason, 1993: 41). Getting the strikers to stop would prove difficult. Although Walesa was the nominal head of the old Interfactory Strike Committee, many factory leaders were afraid of 'selling-out' to the authorities. However, Walesa was able to negotiate with worker representatives to end the strikes. This resulted in three important developments. First, it confirmed Walesa's position as leader of Solidarity. Secondly, it changed the way the public had hitherto dealt with the government. Finally it allowed for the establishment of the Round Table Negotiations among the government, the Roman Catholic Church and Solidarity (Mason, 1993: 41).

These negotiations were the first of their kind and sent a signal across the CEECs that serious change was in the offing. In April 1989, a number of agreements were reached. Some of the more important developments included the reinstatement of Solidarity, which would henceforth be allowed to compete democratically for 35 per cent of the parliamentary seats in the *Sejm* (Poland's restructured lower house); the calling of parliamentary elections and giving Solidarity the right to air time on television and radio, in addition to producing their own newspapers.

The Polish senate was also reformed to allow for free elections to that body. This signalled the end of Poland's authoritarian single-Party system. The agreement stated that non-Party politicians would be allowed to contest 161 of the 460 seats in the *Sejm* and all seats in the Senate. Elections were held in June 1989 two months after the agreements were signed. Although Solidarity was under-prepared and under-resourced it won all the available seats in the *Sejm* and all but one in the Senate. Timothy Garton Ash, who was in Poland during the election, said he was struck by how Solidarity supporters were unaware of their level of support. The government, which controlled the printing of ballots, had created an awkward system of colour-coded sheets for different political bodies in which, instead of ticking the box of the chosen candidate, a voter would have to go through hundreds of names and cross out all unwanted candidates. The majority of Poles took the time to cross out the names of those people who had held power in a system without elections (Garton Ash, 1990: 27).

Moscow's reaction to this was very low key, even approving. Soviet bureaucrats had started to refer to their governments' policy as the 'Sinatra Doctrine' as opposed to the Brezhnev Doctrine. This being a reference to Sinatra's hit of the early 1980s, 'My Way', alluding to the letting go of the CEECs. It was a signal to the entire area that they could experiment with change without Soviet interference. It was telling that the humorous title of Moscow's new policy referred to an American song.

4.4 The new regime: privatization, investment and government policy

In Poland during September 1989 Tadeusz Mazowiecki became Prime Minister. His Deputy Prime Minister and Minister of Finance was Leszek Balcerowicz.[3] The Deputy Prime Minister drafted a plan in 1990 which would bear his name. The Balcerowicz Plan was an attempt to 'leap' to the market. This policy had popular support as Poles in general were tired of the type of piecemeal approaches which in the past had not solved Poland's economic problems. With this kind of support Balcerowicz lifted price controls; turned the zloty into a convertible currency (9,500 zlotys = US$1); removed trade barriers to imports and eliminated most government subsidies to state-controlled enterprises (Mason, 1993: 45). The original intention of these measures was the same as those of the defunct Jaruzelski government, namely to reduce government deficits in order to stem the tide of growing debt. The system of government might have changed but the problem remained the same.

Balcerowicz's plan of economic transition appeared neat and well organized. The actual process, however, would present serious challenges. The plan introduced the conversion to private ownership of government assets, as well as placing restriction on wages. The result of government restrictions on wages resulted in a restriction of the domestic money supply which, in turn, reduced the ability of Polish citizens to purchase goods and services. Lack of domestic investment capital resulted in the Polish government's growing need for foreign investors. This created the climate for a series of what some academics called 'spontaneous' or '*nomenklatura*'[4] privatizations. Persons who still held government positions got involved in privatising nominally bankrupt state companies with an eye to turning them into viable commercial companies. This in itself would not have been a problem, but many of these *nomenklatura* allocated shares to themselves or company 'insiders' at very low prices (Meany, 1995: 280). Another suspect method of privatization would see those with political power strike private agreements with foreign buyers. These unofficial agreements often siphoned off state resources by renting state equipment at low prices or exporting items at subsidized prices (Staniskis, 1991; Frydman *et al.*, 1993: 183). The exact number of such deals remains open to dispute with some claiming that as many as 40,000 *nomenklatura* firms were privatized, while others hold that a mere 100 enterprises were effected, mostly in the industrial sector.

Privatization was only one of Poland's problems during those early months of 1990. The task of changing the entire economy from a command-structured socialist model to one driven by market forces (except for wages which remained controlled), posed a serious challenge. No person or group could be sure that their actions were appropriate in the sense that the situation was without historical precedent. It seems ironic that Solidarity's first government (made up of former radicalized workers) should promote a plan that included wage caps. Indeed, many Solidarity members felt betrayed by the policy and a noticeable split began to occur between party members (Kowalik, 1995). Nevertheless, the Solidarity government implemented the Balcerowicz Plan in full. The influence of the IMF, which had suggested that there may be a possibility of international assistance from their organization, as well as a stabilization fund for the zloty, and most importantly generous debt relief, was easily detectable (Stanislaw, 1992). If the Solidarity government had not instituted the Balcerowicz Plan they could have caused Poland to lose its access to credit through the IFIs.

The Balcerowicz Plan's programme of 'jumping' directly into the open market was, however, a complicated affair. There remained, for example, the workers' councils which had been given an enhanced role in 1981 and given further legislative sanction in March 1990. These councils had the right to dismiss managers without having to gain permission from the Ministry of Industry. This resulted in 307 out of 1,700 state managers being laid-off, during 1990–91 (90 per cent on the advice of these councils) (Meany, 1995: 281). The councils justified their existence by acting as independent ombudsmen which diligently observed the deals between *nomenklatura* and private business. Many economists, however, said they were a force which could block the privatization-induced layoffs resulting from privatization (Engelberg, 1990: 10). Given the government's commitment, however, the move towards privatization was continued.

A stumbling block remained as to what would be the best mechanism to use for privatization. The Solidarity Government introduced a number of measures intended to speed the move to the market. During 1990 bans on private ownership were lifted paving the way for legitimizing small firms especially in the food and retail part of the service sector. In 1990 more than 500,000 small private business appeared. This development, coupled with a few large scale privatizations increased private industrial output by 8.5 per cent during the 1990–1991 fiscal year (Mason, 1993: 46).

Legitimizing small firms proved easier than privatizing large state enterprises. Domestically Poland had people who could manage small-scale retail shops and food service. However, because personal accumulation of wealth was not permitted under the old system there were no wealthy industrialists to buy up large state enterprises and turn them into private companies. It became increasingly clear that the big state firms would need to be dealt with differently from those small enterprises slated for privatization. In short, the creation of a free market was going to take careful government planning.

In September 1990, the Privatization Law created the Ministry of Ownership Transformation, more commonly known as the Ministry of Privatisation or MOP. This ministry was created to oversee privatization of large state firms. Previously privatization had been dealt with by Poland's Ministry of Finance (MOF) in the office of the Government Plenipotentiary for Ownership Transformation. This office had been trying to halt the 'spontaneous' privatizations and drafted the legislation for the 1990 privatization law (Meaney, 1995: 282).

The MOP was created to take over all aspects of privatization, but particularly large state enterprises. In addition to this it provided an information point for individuals and enterprises who needed to know how to embark on appropriate privatization strategies. The MOP also had the daunting task of coming up with new privatization programmes, and providing training to professionals involved in corporate governance and the securities market (Frydman *et al.*, 1993: 178). In large part the MOP was created to provide an intermediary body between those firms slated for privatization and those actually doing the privatizing.

The MOP was specifically designed to do an end run around the MOI, which was the government body in charge of state-owned companies. This ministry was looked upon with some scepticism. Some considered it too full of past bureaucrats, although how this could be totally avoided is unclear. The MOI did not enhance its image when it made it clear from the outset that it did not favour rapid privatization. The Solidarity Government thought that the task would be better trusted to an autonomous ministry whose existence would end with the end of the privatization process.

The task would prove immense. There were approximately 7,000–8,000 state-owned enterprises, 3,000 of which were under direct control of the central government (Meaney, 1995: 282). Poland's privatization law and the creation of the MOP coincided with the suspension of the September instalment of IMF's stand-by loan. This was despite the IMF's strong approval for the Balcerowicz Plan. They were satisfied with Poland's reduction of its national deficit and the convertibility and stabilization of the zloty. They were disappointed, however, with Poland's continuing problem with inflation. Although the Balcerowicz Plan had reduced inflation from the high of 2000 per cent in 1989, in 1991 it was still running at an annualized rating of 70 per cent (Mason, 1993: 46). The IMF was in a quandary. It did not wish to relax its conditionality with regards to lending money, but it also wanted to point to some form of success in the CEECs. The hardships produced by neo-liberal reforms were not encouraging other countries in the region to continue their 'jump' to the market. The compromise decided upon by the IFIs was to involve Poland in a 36-month funds agreement, in the hopes that this financial 'carrot' would keep Poland on the path of transformation to a market-driven economy.

The process of privatization was heavily dominated by foreigners through their involvement in the MOP. About half of the personnel were Polish and half foreigners. Non-Poles were concentrated mostly in the mass privatization programme. The privatization programme was the brain child of Jan Lewandowski, who was to become Minister of Privatization under two different governments. Basically the scheme decided upon was to give all adults (i.e. 18 and above) voucher/coupons which could be exchanged for shares. These shares would make up 'National Investment Funds' (NIF). This mass privatization plan aimed to transfer approximately 60 per cent of ownership of newly commercialized enterprises to NIFs. These national funds would be made up of foreign/domestic investment banking, and accountancy/consultancy firms, whose task it would be to keep tabs on the performance of enterprises which fell under the jurisdiction of the fund. Certain individuals from the banking and consultancy world would be invited to join the board of directors of the newly privatized enterprises in the expectation that they would get involved in enterprise management and restructuring (Meaney, 1995: 284).

At the beginning of the MOP's mandate it hoped to get 400 enterprises to take part in the privatization scheme on a voluntary basis. However, after a screening process, in which profiles of companies were translated into English, a shortlist 204 enterprises was compiled (Meaney, 1995). The main component of the plan revolved around distributing the shares of the NIFs to the adult population as a whole. The shares were not to be distributed right away and there was also to be a cost involved. The NIFs were to operate for at least 18 months before shares would be sold. Although every adult citizen was permitted to take part in the scheme, two costs would be incurred; (1) the programme fee of US$20 (which allowed participation); and (2) the cost of the share itself (although each citizen would be given initial certificates or shares for free which they could choose to keep or sell). The prices were intended to float on the market after the parliament had established an initial base price through the stock exchange or street brokers. These prices would be listed in newspapers and other media (Frydman *et al.*, 1993: 195).

When the mass privatization plan was first conceived it was thought that 30 per cent of the shares would be retained by the state and 10 per cent would be given to the workers. To spread the shares out still further it planned that each individual enterprise's shares would not be held by one NIF. Instead, it was hoped that one-third of an enterprise's shares would go to a lead NIF, with another third being shared out to the remaining NIFs of which there were to be approximately 10.

The NIFs were to be structured in much the same way as the private enterprises where tender selection committees would be made up of Polish and foreign investment bankers. The NIFs would be managed by a supervisory board, mostly Polish but not exclusively, and management boards to be controlled by foreign investment banking firms, etc. Foreigners were given a high profile in the process. Members of management board were to be promised a small fee after 5 years and a big fee after 10, the increase was to be based on portfolio growth and value (Meaney, 1995: 285).

Poland certainly had the will to privatize but it suffered throughout from the problem of underfunding. Compared to the East German Treuhand which had 2,000 employees, the 300-strong Polish MOP was tiny. As a result Poland was constrained to make extensive use of foreign consultants. They figured prominently in deciding which companies would be privatized. Their involvement was not limited to mass privatization, they were also deeply influential in the sectoral privatization's which emerged around mid-1991. The term 'privatization' in the context of post-1989 Polish development is, however, a bit of a misnomer. Banking, accounting, and consulting firms would get together to study companies contained in specific sectors (clothing, tobacco, etc.) and consider their suitability for privatization. The practical effect was, however, to slow down the process of privatization. There were rumours that many companies felt mass privatization was a bad idea.

For example, the controversial area of tobacco was put under sectoral privatization. It took until November 1995 before the Polish tobacco industry was privatized. When it was, 65 per cent in the Augustow-based plant (one of the five major enterprises) was bought by the UK-owned branch of British American Tabacco for US$88 million (EIU country Report, *Poland* (1995): 23). In fact, many companies initially studied under the Polish sectoral privatization plan still await their full privatization.

There was also concern about the extent of foreign influence. The MOP had the right to give foreign managers a proxy to run firms under their jurisdiction: managerial power meant the ability to keep or let go whom they pleased from the existing enterprise structure. There was a popular fear that Poland was leaving itself open to foreign asset-stripping. However, using Foreign Direct Investment as a basis for the transition process inevitably meant an increase of foreign influence.

FDI was an intregal part of Jeffrey Sachs' plan for Poland. Sachs worked with the MOP to create its privatization package. He referred to the place of FDI in the transition phase to capitalism as his 'conceptual breakthrough'. FDI was supposed to take the place of any kind of Marshall Plan for the East. Instead of giving the area funding to modernize (which would have left domestic assets under Polish control), FDI alone was supposed to fulfil that role. Unfortunately many Polish policy-makers assumed that if they made their currency fully convertible, and liberalized prices, capped wages and privatized government companies, FDI would automatically result. Indeed many Westerners seemed to confirm this assumption. The IMF, WB and the OECD at separate times highlighted the need for the CEECs to arrange their institutions and economies in such a way as to be attractive to foreign capital. In its 1994 report, the OECD emphasized its view that 'the privatisation process must extensively rely on FDI' (p. 3). The influence exercised by Western policy experts in Poland at this time explains the rush to privatization. There were those in Poland who would have preferred to restructure state enterprises first, hoping thereby to make them worth more on the open market. This was not permitted by the MOP. Unfortunately, this meant that firms were sold without an attempt being made to improve them first and as a result often fetched ludicrously low prices.

However, Poland's attempted adherence to IMF loan conditionality and its policy initiatives based on the advice of Westerns did not go unrewarded. The Polish government under the Balcerowicz Plan felt it deserved more than piecemeal debt relief. They had IMF approval and democratic legitimacy following the June 1989 elections which the Polish government felt should count for something. To this end they proposed the creation of a US$1 billion stabilization fund. The money was to be pledged from the UN, US, Japan, and the EU, and was to be administered by the Federal Reserve Bank of New York. The governments involved agreed to the establishment of the fund which was created in 1990, but the fund was linked to Poland's continued policy of transformation along neo-classical economic lines (Bjork, 1995: 100).

Poland's willingness to conform to IMF conditionality and its governments' move to the market during 1990 did not solve its problems. Even if it had attracted substantial FDI, the problem of debt remained. Over two-thirds of Poland's debt was not with the IMF but with the Paris Club. The Paris Club differs from the better known London Club of IFIs as it is not controlled by commercial banks, but is under the direct control of national governments. What Poland wanted was debt reduction (or more precisely, debt forgiveness). In international lending circles 'debt forgiveness' is usually considered a non-negotiable issue. The February 1990 Paris Club meeting refused to even entertain the notion. Instead the Poles had to work for a rescheduling agreement which they were fortunate to get. With US$10 billion in principal payment falling due in 1991, Poland was granted an eight-year moratorium on repayments. Unlike many CEECs, Poland was able to secure some much needed debt relief.

Were Poland's policies borne out of a belief in the neo-classical economic agenda or out of a desire to integrate with Western Europe? Two years after the inception of the Balcerowicz Plan one of its co-architects confirmed that he felt 'shock therapy': 'was the only possibility which would allow Poland the chance to attain a place in the European economic order...without...serious sacrifice we did not have a chance' (Kowalik, 1995: 101). Polish policy-makers had been convinced that they had to move to a market-driven economy. They were also convinced that there was only one right way to do it. Therefore, the neo-liberal agenda was continued. The Polish people, however, were not as committed to the neo-liberal agenda as the government was, particularly when economic 'shock therapy' started to have negative results on the domestic economy. The press, in particular, was scathing. Confidence in the government began to be undermined. During 1991 and 1992 privatization received a particular bad press when it was discovered that KPMG–Peat Marwick was brought in to be consulted on the privatization of insurance companies in Poland. The advice given by KPMG was to break up the Polish PZU company, which until then had handled all foreign coverage. This move was interpreted as a method to weaken the Polish insurance industry and make it easier for foreign operators to enter the Polish market after its full liberalization in January 1993 (Meaney, 1995: 286).

There were other examples which led to a general souring of Polish popular attitudes towards transformation. Soon Solidarity's economic policies began to sour relationships within Solidarity itself. Zbigniew Bujak[5] a senior member of Solidarity and directly involved in the initial success of Mazowiecki's government, began as an enthusiast about Poland's economic reform. He was quoted in the summer of 1990 as saying:

> I consider it feasible . . . that we promote a program to march towards Europe . . . either the working class will make a great leap, and become a highly qualified middle class and remain in the vanguard of society or it will refuse to undergo this transformation, and it will change into a force which will block any progress. Either it will bring us to Europe or it will shut the door to it before our noses.
>
> Kowalik, 1995: 94

However, by the end of 1991 he had revised his former support, thus further tarnishing Solidarity's image. In the months following the implementation of the Balcerowicz Plan, Bujak was disappointed with the results of 'shock therapy' and eventually renounced it altogether. By 1991 he was saying:

> I apologise for the fact that the ideals of Solidarity have not been realised or have been realised in a perverse manner. I apologise for the indifferent and ineffective economic reform, for the many bankruptcies, for the number of people without work . . . many friends of mine from our previous underground activity now complain to me: we did not struggle for such a Poland. This was not our vision during those years.
>
> Kowalik, 1995: 95

After this Bujak was himself evicted from the Solidarity Party, and the Solidarity Party was partially rejected by the voting public at the 1990 presidential polls. At the end of 1990, Mazowiecki made a very poor showing in the presidential elections. The subsequent Bielecki government also went down to defeat during the October 1991 parliamentary elections. The political situation was tense. The fact remained that it did not matter which party was in control – all of them would be faced with financial constraints and pressure from the IMF, WB, IFIs, etc. After the October 1991 election there were as many as 18 parties in the *Sejm*, but none of them had more than 12 per cent of the vote (Mason, 1993: 47). It took the grudging co-operation of a number of parties just to come up with a ruling coalition. The process of reaching an agreement on establishing a ruling coalition took 6 weeks and the government disintegrated after 6 months. After another series of coalition attempts, a seven-party coalition was established under Prime Minister Hanna Suchocka. By this stage Lech Walesa had been elevated to President.

The political situation went from bad to worse as many factories continued to close or be privatized increasing unemployment at a time when inflation remained around 30 per cent (Mason, 1993: 48). By the middle of 1992 there were close to 6,000 strikes taking place throughout Poland. The population wanted the issue of unemployment to be properly addressed. Little did they realize that unemployment was an accepted component of the neo-classical model of capitalism. Ironically, the Polish population started to desire a more authoritarian style of government. Opinion polls revealed that most people in Poland wanted governance 'with a strong hand', particularly with regard to giving the government special powers to rule. The same polls also illustrated a disturbing Polish trend toward anti-Semitism in which 40 per cent of those taking part in the poll said that Jews[6] 'played too big a role in the country's public life' (Mason, 1993: 49). These polls revealed a reversion to 1930s-style xenophobia. Many had already forgotten that the authoritarian government of Jaruselski had not solved their economic ills, nor had Hitler's extermination of the Polish Jews brought any tangible benefits. Ultimately, these opinion polls reveal the desperate way in which the Polish people had begun to cast about for an answer to their problems. Nationalist and populist parties began to spring up and gain popularity. It was a politically dangerous situation without an obvious solution. In the November 1995 elections Lech Walesa was unseated as president of Poland by the former Communist Party activist Aleksander Kwasniewski. It was perhaps a sad commentary on a man who had during the 1980s personified Poland's struggle against authoritarian government. Walesa had, however, become a controversial character in part because of the inherent problems of moving from electrician/ labour activist to Head of State. Despite Walesa's fight for democracy he did not reconcile himself to the lack of authoritarian control it involved or the rising popular criticism it entailed. As a result he was continually trying to gain greater executive control over the running of the country. Always a pugnacious fighter, a *sine qua non* of success in any struggle with a powerful elite, once Walesa became President, this aggressiveness began to be interpreted as arrogance or rudeness by the population. Even so, he still maintained a strong following and the 1995 presidential vote was close even after the second vote, but in the end he was voted out of office in favour of a former communist.

Many of the voters felt confused, they did not want to vote for a former communist, but many had become disillusioned with Solidarity. There was also an element of nostalgia for the past as most people were actually better off under the communists. Kwasniewski, however, was not a Jaruselski-type communist. His policy platforms were somewhat similar in fact to those of centre-right European social democrats. In his speech after the election Kwasniewski promised to continue along the road to liberal-economic reform as well as pursuing Poland's candidacy for membership in the North Atlantic Treaty Organization (NATO) and the European Union.

The move back to the communists was basically a way for the population to register disappointment with current government policy. Liberal capitalism had not given the majority of the Polish people what they had hoped for. The move to a market economy entailed far higher human costs than any had expected (see further details below). It was the results of these policies – the attempt to make the move to the free market – which ultimately brought down Walesa and created the turbulent situation in domestic politics which brought the communists back to power. For many in Poland the transition to the free-market became synonymous with their experience of increased poverty.

4.5 The results thus far

The last section was an overview of privatization and the transition to a market economy. It examined the process and the policy prescriptions. This section, however, does not look at how privatization or 'shock therapy' was conceived but at the outcome of translating neo-liberal ideas into a commercial and state system. It begins by pointing out the influence of neo-liberal economic approaches, particularly the model of 'shock therapy'. This model was intended by its champions to solve the problem of converting an entire area to a capitalist market-driven system. Sachs in his 1994 article 'Understanding Shock Therapy' actually said that his ideas, translated into policy would lead to 'a recovery of human freedom and a democratically based rise in living standards' (Sachs, 1994: 25). Sadly, Sachs was confusing the ideal of social emancipation and democracy with the ideal of market capitalism.

The conflict between ideals and policy outcomes was serious in Central Europe. It was definitely a case of Western experts, or Western-trained intellectuals, trying to put into place a pure form of capitalism. Actual Western European levels of state ownership were not considered, nor its history of economic development which often diverged from pure capitalism. Standard neo-classical economic theory assumes that capitalism would have to have open trade, full currency convertibility, and the establishment of the private sector as the engine of growth (Sachs, 1995). If this definition of capitalism is accepted, then most of the OECD countries have, at different times, not been fully capitalist. Any scholar of the GATT will be able to illustrate that the wealthiest countries also have the most intricate of trade barriers making the criteria of an 'open' economy somewhat dubious. During the Marshall Plan (1948–58), for example, the US actually tolerated European trade barriers to allow their economies to re-establish themselves. These lessons were not applied to the CEECs after 1989 (Keegan, 1993: 17). Moreover, as we have seen post-war Western Europe did not have fully convertible currencies until 1958, which coincidentally was a period of rapid growth, making the argument for a convertible currency also suspect. In fact, in 1947 the US Congress had initially made a US$4.4 billion loan to the UK contingent on London allowing the full convertibilty of sterling, but this proved to be a calamity[7] and was suspended within a month (Keegan, 1993: 18). The last criteria, that of the private sector as the engine of growth, reveals a limited understanding of the role of government in the establishment of a research and development capability, especially in Europe and East Asia. Even in the United States, the development of the internet was first pioneered by the American military. The neo-classical agenda, therefore, goes against past practice. The neglect of history and the outcomes of the transition might have been unintentional, but the concept of quickly converting the CEECs to liberal capitalism was definitely a marriage of neo-liberal ideology and the interests of Western private capital.

The first step of breaking up Comecon was to prove disastrous for many of the inhabitants of the Central European countries. According to a 1994 OECD report, the fragmentation of Comecon alone accounted for one-third of Poland's decline in industrial output in the post-1989 period. In Table 4.1 we see that Poland's industrial output dropped by 17 per cent which also explains the 22 per cent drop in real earnings. A portion of blame can be ascribed to the insistence of the IMF inspired neo-liberal Balcerowicz Plan that Poland establish a convertible currency. When the zloty became a hard currency, East European

Table 4.1 Poland: Changes in Level of Economic Development, 1989–94 (% Change from 1989)

	Poland	**Hungary**	**Czech Republic**	**Slovakia**	**Slovenia**
GDP	–9.1	–18.5	–20.0	–23.0	–16.0
Industrial output	–17.2	–21.7	–36.3	–41.0	–30.6
Real earnings	–22.0	–15.5	–18.4	–23.6	–22.9
Investment	–5.8	–14.3	–19.2	–25.9	–21.8
Exports	16.6	3.2	27.8	5.5	18.0
Imports	66.2	62.6	29.1	16.3	27.1
Inflation	30.0	3.1	2.5	2.5	177.0

Source: World Economy Research Institute, *Poland, International Economic Report 1994/1995*, Warsaw, Warsaw School of Economics, 1995: 32.

and Soviet firms found it difficult to buy Polish goods because they did not have enough foreign exchange. In 1991 alone Poland's exports to the former Soviet Union dropped by 90 per cent (Mason, 1993: 47). The break up of Comecon was hastened by these ill-conceived developments.

Separating Central Europe from Russia was bound to create problems. The whole thrust of Central Europe's economy during the Cold War had been to service both its own and the Soviet Union's vast internal market. By encouraging these fledgling market economies to go for an export market-driven economy meant that their products had to compete abroad with sophisticated products from Western Europe and America. Conversely, both Central Europe and the former Soviet Union's domestic markets also became flooded with Western products. As a result, all Central European countries now suffer from a negative trade balance. This position is particularly difficult when the countries in question carry a heavy debt burden.

To illustrate the magnitude of the change in trading patterns, Polish trade flows in the late 1980s are compared with that of the mid-1990s. This was after all, a relatively short space of time. In 1986, the Soviet Union took about 69 per cent of Polish exports, in short, the majority of their goods serviced the Soviet (mostly Russian) market (Lewis, 1993: 271). Trade figures in Table 4.2 show that by 1994 over half of Poland's exports went to Western Europe. The translates into a 63.6 per cent drop in Central European trade with Russia.

The figures in Table 4.2 represent the extent to which the Balcerowicz Plan of the leap to the market was successful. It was all part of the wider plan to guide Poland towards Europe. Indeed, in 1991 Poland did become an associate member of the EC with full membership expected

Table 4.2 Poland's Biggest Trading Partners in 1994

	% Of imports	% Of exports
Germany	35.7	27.5
Netherlands	5.9	4.6
Russia	5.4	6.8
Italy	4.9	8.4
UK	4.6	5.3
France	4.0	4.5
USA	3.4	3.9

Note: Poland ran a trade deficit in these years, but these figures do not show this as all countries are not included.
Source: World Economy Research Institute, *Poland, International Economic Report 1994/1995*, Warsaw, Warsaw School of Economics, 1995: 122.

soon after the year 2000. The Association Agreements between the Central European countries and EC, only further severed Central Europe from its traditional market in Russia. This process was intensified through the application of rules-of-origin regulations. Europe would only accept produce that had a certain percentage made in either Poland, (pre-1993) Czechoslovakia or Hungary. This effectively destroyed an economy of scale that could have been achieved by keeping Central Europe linked, in terms of industrial production, with the former Soviet Union. The shock and slump this caused was substantial as the figures in Table 4.3 reveal. During 1990, Poland's industrial output dropped by almost one-quarter. Although the situation improved in 1991, industrial production continued to show a 11.9 per cent decline in these years.

Today, supporters of the 'Shock Therapy' model of market capitalism point to Poland's success between 1993 and 1995. It is true that in 1995 Poland was one of the fastest growing European economies. However, growth figures can be very deceptive. While it is true that Poland's 1995 GDP growth rate increased by approximately[8] 5 per cent this would have had to be sustained for at least 20 years to make up for the losses experienced during the early years of economic transition when levels

Table 4.3 Poland's Industrial Production (%)

	1989	1990	1991	1992	1993
Poland	–0.5	–24.2	–11.9	3.9	5.6

Sources: H. Schmieding, 1993: 216; EBRD, 1994.

of production were dropping by as much as 24 per cent a year. More worrying still is the fact that, although FDI was expected to overhaul and modernize the Polish economy, most of Poland's growth in recent years has been based on selling traditional products to Germany at cut-rate prices. The structure of the Polish economy has not changed radically with the arrival of capitalism.

It was a boon for Poland to receive as much US$7 billion in 1995 from crossborder trade with Germany, but there is a limit to the profits which can be expected from this trade. The demand for raw materials and semi-processed goods was strong in 1994/95, but these are not the sectors on which to concentrate if Poland wishes to achieve long-term success as an international exporter. This puts Poland in a somewhat vulnerable position in the sense that its growth has been based on exports to Germany and other EU countries. If Western European countries experience any kind of economic recession, then Poland will feel the effects particularly sharply. Over half its exports go to the EU with Germany taking up 35.7 per cent of that total (EIU Country Report, *Poland*, 1995: 3) If Poland is to be successful it will need to do some careful government planning with regards to economic restructuring in order to encourage growth and development in those sectors producing more highly processed goods. Unfortunately, the neo-liberal agenda in Poland has resulted in a heavy concentration on *laissez-faire* economics, which has prioritized short-term profits over long-term restructuring.

To date, Sachs has refused to concede that Poland's economic crisis during the 1990s was caused by 'Shock Therapy'. In 1993, he claimed that Poland's problem had nothing to do with its economic reforms but rather the collapse of trade with the former Soviet Union. This is not without its irony considering that Sachs himself was the designer of the European hub-and-spoke[9] trade regime (Gowan, 1995: 17). Later, Sachs was to point to communism as the underlying cause of the problems experienced by Poland even though the wages of the average citizen and industrial production were actually higher during Jaruzelski's time. The London-based *The Economist*, a publication which had supported Sachs' initial neo-liberal suggestions, claimed that while 'all the post-communist economies suffered deep recessions . . . much of this hardship was, however, the legacy of communism's failure, not the product of capitalism's arrival' (*The Economist*, 1994: 24). Gowan points out that none of the neo-liberals considered that the slump was caused by 'capitalism's arrival'. Some strong supporters of neo-classical/neo-liberal economics even refused to believe the evidence of the impending

Central European economic crisis during the early 1990s by calling into question the accuracy of the figures. Nevertheless, Stanislaw Gomulka, a pro-IMF conservative academic, calculated the average fall in GDP during the transition phase was over 40 per cent and even an OECD study admitted that ultimately the policy of 'Shock Therapy' turned a difficult situation into a catastrophe (Stanislaw, 1994: 23; Gowan, 1995: 18).

Economic policy has remained fairly tight, considering the debt load that Poland is carrying. The country is basically forced into reducing its deficit if it wishes to maintain its access to the European Union. Under the existing European Agreements Poland has to hold its deficit below the 3 per cent rate laid down in the 1992 Maastricht Treaty. Considering that Poland is now heavily trade dependent on Europe, it has little choice but to comply if it wishes to keep its European market share. Linked with this development is the requirement to reduce the general import tax, which stood 5 per cent in 1995, before being reduced to 3 per cent in 1996 and abolished completely in 1997 (EIU Country Report, 1995: 12). Therefore, while Poland is desperately trying to save its market access gains to Europe, European and other foreign products have had open access to the Polish market since 1997. This is an arduous way of introducing a fledgling economy to global capitalism. It is hard to see how it will avoid a further trade deficit with Western Europe in coming years.

Foreign influence was not only found in the import trade sector: it also became evident in structures of ownership. In Poland there was at first, an expectation that the national investment funds would be short-listed in a tender by the relevant MOP Committee, made up of Polish and foreign investment banking, accounting, and consultancy firms (Meaney, 1995: 284). However, all the leading bidders eventually turned out to be foreign firms. Even the success of small-scale privatization was marred by the fact that although 500,000 new small businesses were created in 1990, 150,000 of these failed or were liquidated by 1992 (Mason, 1993: 46). The painful process of transformation was made more difficult by the tendency of transnational capital and banks to try to derive short-term profits from the CEECs. Morawetz suggests that privatization and the final collapse of state socialism brought about a new qualitative stage for the chances of western business in the CEECs. Direct control of the production process by Western foreign direct investment was now possible (Morawetz, 1991).

During 1995, there was a slowing of the transition process as the government had to deal with the social problems created by the transition. This deliberate slowdown of the transition process rather than decreasing FDI actually increased the inflow of moneys to Poland. In part this can be explained by the opportunities for foreign companies to purchase almost entire sectors of the Polish economy at far below the going market rate.

The 1995 figures reveal that private sector investment growth made up a total of 38 per cent of all investment, compared to 33 per cent in 1994 (EIU Country Report, 1995: 6). Overall growth for investment in Poland was between 10–15 per cent. On one level this was good news for Poland because it represented a much needed inflow of money into the area. But the question of control of capital still remains. Large parts of the Polish economy have now ceased to be Polish. As mentioned earlier, the speed of privatization resulted in low prices for old state enterprises allowing Western multinationals to buy entire strategic sectors. Most do not have any desire to import large amounts of new investment, rather they have purchased these sectors simply to increase their global market niche. The most sought after companies have been in such sectors as cement, pharmaceuticals, chemicals and telecommunications.

It took the much troubled mass privatization programme the best part of 5 years (1990–95) to get its programmes up and running. Citizens 18 years and over were permitted to purchase share certificates for 20 zloty (or about US$8). The initial plan hoped that as many as 20 million adults out of the 28 million eligible would take part in the scheme. The MOP will keep these certificates available for at least a year and have been promoting them heavily. After a period of 2 years these certificates will be exchangeable for freely traded shares within the NIFs. These shares have performed in unexpected ways. On the secondary money market there was a huge amount of speculation. By the week starting 26 February 1996, the 20 zloty shares had jumped in value to 90 zlotys. However, at the end of trading Friday 8 March 1996 the price had gone up to 110 zlotys (Central Europe Today, 1996). As the price rose so did the concentration of those shares in the hands of those people who had money. It will be interesting to see whether this concentration of wealth will intensify in the future.

This does not mean that privatization is by any means complete. Part of the problem is that most of the viable companies have already been sold, and the state sector is left with the true dinosaurs that many Westerner investors would not even want for free, such as the old technology industrial steel plants. The state sector in December 1994, was left with 3,610 such firms. Critics of the government are concerned that the money making firms have been sold and the remaining firms will deplete scarce government funds. Such a situation will only further confirm neo-liberal views that governments are incompetent at managing businesses. Being left with the poor performers, however, is not a fair test.

In Poland and Hungary, 55,000 enterprises were bought by Western multinationals by 1993 alone (Gowan, 1995: 41). The crux here remains one of price. Although many enterprises were sold this did not translate into a huge amount of foreign capital. If we look at UNCTAD's (1994) *World Investment Report*, we see that, while developed countries can expect an average of US$18 million in invested foreign equity capital and most developing countries pull in about US$4 million, the average in each of the CEECs has been US$260,000 (per buy-out). Very few foreign buyouts are above the price of $1 million. Added to this is the privatization process which declared enterprises technically bankrupt, yet prohibited government from restructuring these enterprises before they were sold. Moreover, there was a lack of available credit and a collapse of domestic markets. With these kinds of policies, foreign multinationals were able to buy many of Central Europe's strategic sectors with a minimum of capital. This outcome can be ascribed to the 'Shock Therapy' model of development, a model which caused one of the most serious recessions in the CEECs since the post-war era.

The commercial banking sector has also been attempting to privatize itself, but during the last 5 years only three out of the nine major bank privatizations have been completed. The sluggishness of this reform will create some difficulties for Poland. As mentioned earlier a $1 billion stabilization fund was set up for Poland in 1990. Originally this money was designed to be part of the policy of 'Shock Therapy', but this money was never used for that purpose, in part because of the reluctance to invest this money in social spending to alleviate the problems of the poor. Again, the split between the project of democratization and human emancipation as opposed to the project of capitalism, is evident. Even though this money was available generally it was considered good practice to use it for the purpose of bank reconstruction, provided that all the major banks were privatized by 1996. However, obstacles remain and it is difficult for the Polish banking structure to transform itself. This is because banks under the old socialist system did not need to offer the range of services that will be expected from Western investors. It is in the area of commercial banking that lack of infrastructure or practice is the most noticeable.

The effect of 'Shock Therapy' did more than create commercial problems in Poland, it also intensified the disparities between its regions. Investment, both national and foreign, tends to be concentrated in economically developed areas. This, in turn, excludes the hinterland

and increases the disparities between rich and poor. In Poland, workers are four times more likely to be unemployed if they are living in a rural *voivodship*[10] than if they are urban dwellers. Moreover, their children are almost twice as likely to suffer from infant mortality. Foreign capital and foreign aid is concentrated in the country's richest regions, such as Warsaw, Gdansk and Katowice, while some of the poorest regions have yet to receive any substantial Western investment. The statistical data provided by the Polish Central Statistical Office gives solid evidence that these rising disequilibria in terms of the distribution of wealth and development is creating a situation of relative deprivation. Data about the shares of the different groups over time in net household income illustrates, that in comparison with 1985, the richest 30 per cent have gained, while the less fortunate 70 per cent of the population have lost.[11] Considering these figures, the government's response, introducing an even more distressing form of economic liberalization is remarkable. The town of Mielec, in Rezeszow is the site of a government 'special economic zone'. The government is trying to attract investment into this poor area by offering companies even better terms and give-aways, while ensuring that worker benefits and social services are kept to a minimum. Benefits include a 10 year tax holiday combined with 50 per cent tax relief in the 10 years thereafter. However, zones of this kind do not tend to bring long-term prosperity and attract multinationals who locate in these areas to specifically avoid social costs. Unfortunately, development in many peripheral regions in Poland is inadequate, therefore towns are willing to do much to attract foreign investment.

The most immediate legacy of 'Shock Therapy', a legacy even more serious than the creation regional disparities, has been the increase in unemployment. In 1989, unemployment was approximately 7,000. Within 2 years this figure had skyrocketed to 2 million, representing some 12 per cent of the total workforce (Mason, 1993: 46). The policy-makers which created the neo-liberal transition policies expected unemployment as a by-product of the introduction of capitalism. *The Economist* in 1989 had already informed readers that the implementation of 'shock therapy' was thought by the Polish government to have already cost 400,000 jobs (Gowan, 1995: 17). Many Western economists, however, were unofficially expecting up to 3 million, which is close to present levels (ibid.). In the first quarter of 1990, unemployment was at 1.5 per cent but by the final quarter of 1994 the unemployment rate had risen to 16 per cent which translates into 2,838,000 people out of work (out of total workforce of about 16 million) (Bossak, 1995: 72–3).

Of all the aspects of shock therapy's rapid decollectivization, the most disturbing were its social ramifications. Basically only a third of the population can today afford a comfortable lifestyle. Another third survives by hard work. While the remaining one-third has been experiencing different levels of poverty as defined by the UN. Distressingly, the poor were financially better off during Stalin's time. The WB, during a study of Russia defined the poverty line as the money needed to buy enough food to maintain normal body weight. This seems a somewhat draconian definition. Under the United Nation's International Children's Emergency Fund's (UNICEF) definition, those who fall below 2,300 calories a day are suffering from malnutrition. In 1989, the Polish population was well fed and malnutrition (i.e. 2,300 calories and below) was negligible, however, 3 years later in 1992, almost 18 per cent of Poles were suffering from malnutrition (UNICEF, 1994). Despite these statistics Poland was actually one of the bright spots during the transition process. In Russia 37 per cent of the Russian population fell below the WB definition of poverty in 1992, with the figure for children climbing as high as 46–7 per cent. The average Russian pension is not sufficient to buy enough food to maintain normal body weight (Gowan, 1995: 22). No matter which criteria is applied poverty increased in Poland and in the region as a whole.

The general state of health of those living in transitional economies dropped. Many of the health problems are stress related. A UNICEF Report cited stress induced stroke and heart disease as accounting for 32–80 per cent of the increase in deaths. Added to this, of course, is the problem of poorer diet, psychological stress and depression which seems to have translated into a dramatic rise in murders and suicide. In Poland, the increase in the suicide rate between the period of 1989 to 1993 was 133 per cent (UNICEF, 1994). The lower levels of health have also given renewed impetus to epidemic-type diseases. Typhoid, diphtheria and tuberculosis are on the increase after a long period when they were rare. In the former Soviet Union alone diphtheria increased 109 per cent in 1992, and had risen to by 290 per cent in 1993 (Gowan, 1995: 23).

These figures are never truly addressed by neo-liberal policy-makers, who accept human discomfort as a by-product of the transition from a command to a market-driven economy. Research has tended to concentrate on Poland's industrial output and export figures. Many have pointed to the up-turn in Poland's export economy since 1993 for which liberal policy-makers in both the Polish government and the IFIs have been willing to take credit. A similar level of responsibility has not been accepted for the social problems created by the transition.

The situation has changed since Poland's acceptance as a candidate country for membership in the EU (see Chapter 7). It will likely continue to improve economically, but income inequality may continue to be a problem. The current government is suggesting reform of the tax system in which there will be no grading according to income. The suggestion is to eliminate the three rates of 19 per cent, 30 per cent and 40 per cent in favour of a flat personal income tax rate of between 17–19 per cent. (EIU Country Report, *Poland,* 1998: 15). This is thought to increase income disparity. However, despite problems of social inequality, the worst of the transition process is over. Nevertheless, it is unfortunate that the adoption of Western norms and values, particularly economic practices, should have had to come at the price of the 1990–93 recession. This economic collapse could perhaps have been avoided if a more flexible developmental approach had been employed at the start of the transition.

Poland's connection with the EU and its relationship with Germany in particular has ensured that its economic development will be henceforth tied to Western Europe. During the last 4 years Poland's economic performance has dramatically improved. As can be seen in Table 4.4, its GDP has shown marked growth since the 1993 recession.

Poland's recovery has been highly dependent on its trading relationship with the EU. A full 32 per cent of its exports are being sent to Germany (EIU Country Report, *Poland,* 1998: 5). There is no denying that from the point of view of economic development, Poland's

Table 4.4 Polish Economic Indicators

Economic indicators	**1993**	**1994**	**1995**	**1996**	**1997**
GDP at current prices (zloty bn)	155.8	210.4	286.0	362.8	445.1
Real GDP growth (%)	3.8	33.3	26.8	20.1	15.9
Consumer price inflation (%)	36.9	33.3	26.8	20.1	15.9
Industrial output growth (%)	6.4	12.1	9.7	8.7	10.8
Exports ($bn)	13.6	17.0	22.9	24.4	27.2
Imports ($bn)	15.9	17.8	24.7	32.6	38.5
Current-account balance ($bn)	–2.3	–0.9	5.5	–1.4	–4.3
Reserves excluding gold ($bn)	4.1	5.8	14.0	17.8	20.4
Gross external hard-currency debt ($bn)	45.2	42.6	42.3	40.9	39.3

Source: EIU Country Report, 1998: 13.

relationship with the EU has been beneficial. The fact that it is now an EU candidate country has enhanced its economic stability. Moreover, all these factors have helped Poland maintain its democratic reforms. The last parliamentary elections were held in September 1997. A coalition government took control on 20 October 1997. The parties of the coalition are Solidarity Electoral Action (AWS) and the Freedom Union (UW). These parties are in turn coalitions of other smaller groupings of political parties. Nevertheless, these parties have been successful in maintaining a functioning government with the legitimacy of a popular mandate.

Poland's success has actually encouraged the belief that 'shock therapy' was not only justified, but necessary. This belief has been manifested in the return to politics of Leszek Balcerowicz. As we have seen, he was the author of the 1990 Balcerowicz Plan which was a major component to the 'shock therapy' model of development. Balcerowicz, was appointed as finance minister and the chair of the cabinet economic committee after the 1997 elections. His anti-inflationary stance and belief in the free market has been thought to have boosted the confidence of foreign direct investors. However, it could be argued that the role played by the government's free marketeers in Poland's economic success has been over-estimated, just as the important economic role played by Poland's relationship with the EU has tended to be under-estimated.

It is now obvious that Poland's transition is nearing completion. In the OECD's 1998 *Economic Survey of Poland* it applauded the country's overall economic performance, as well as its foreign direct investment levels, which in 1997 reached US$6.6 billion. (EIU Country Report, *Poland*, 1998: 13) It has largely met Western targets regarding fiscal standards. Poland has also been successful in re-focusing its trade towards the West. Within the space of eight years it has gone from being a country strongly tied to the former Soviet Union, to one embedded in the Western global political economy. However, this new found status has not come without a price. Although Poland's growth and development have been good since 1996, it has become more vulnerable to the unpredictability of global financial markets. Growth forecasts for 1999 are not hopeful as the instability in global financial markets are expected to effected EU growth in general, on which Poland is now particularly reliant. If Poland's economy suffers in the following year, it should perhaps be remembered that the solution does not rely upon applying the same types of policies that caused the 1990–93 recession.

4.6 Summary comments

What general trends can be seen in Poland's transition process? First, the entire project was, from its very conception, based upon the presumption that the transition would return Poland to its place among the capitalist countries. The process had two main components. The first was political and was concerned with the introduction of democracy. Poland's democratization project was, however, heavily influenced by the economic transition. The liberal economic 'shock therapy' policies that the first Solidarity government introduced created a backlash against the government. The voting public blamed the government for the economic hardships they experienced during the 1990–93 recession. Confusion set in between capitalism and democracy. The negative effects of capitalism, such as job losses, were often attributed to the process of democratization. The re-election of communist politicians after the 1990–93 recession would increase the tension between the political and the economic process. The increase in income and regional disparities as well as high levels of unemployment added to the political pressures faced by Poland's fledgling democracy.

The second component of the transition was economic. The transition, through privatization of state-owned firms, liberalization of trade, and the creation of a convertible currency, did create a functioning market economy. However, the process of privatization would increase the presence of Western influence. Foreign ownership and foreign investment played a large role in Poland's reintegration into Western capitalism. The investment and policy advice given to Poland was not value free and supported a specific neo-classical view of capitalism. These views in turn led to outcomes favourable to the capitalist hegemony, such as increased Western ownership of Polish assests. Ultimately, the policies prescribed to Poland would result in the country's dependence on Western markets generally, and EU markets in particular.

5
Czech Republic

The Czech Republic, like Poland and Hungary, has experienced the transition from a communist command economy to a market economy. However, unlike the other two, the Czech Republic experienced a break-up with its former co-republic, Slovakia. The end of Czechoslovakia, marked an end of an era, but it was not accomplished through violence. All three of the countries examined in this study are contrived state constructs brought into existence after the First World War and the collapse of the Austro-Hungarian Empire. This is particularly true of Czechoslovakia which was an attempt to create one state out of the traditional kingdoms of Bohemia and Moravia and the Slovak provinces of Hungary. Considering that its creation was heavily influenced by the West it is not surprising that its re-introduction into the world economy would also be Western dominated. In this chapter we supply a case study of the history and current changes to what was Czechoslovakia and concentrate predominately on the Czech Republic after its 1993 split with Slovakia.

5.1 Brief history of the Czechs

It is difficult to examine Czech history in isolation. Its background is intertwined with its neighbouring republics and former kingdoms. Its inclusion with Slovakia dates only from 28 October 1918 making Czechoslovakia a state with a fairly brief life span (Wightman, 1994: 255). However, the areas containing ethnic Czechs and Slovaks have existed since before the Middle Ages. Unfortunately, these groups' awareness of each other has often translated into Czechs feeling strongly that they are different from Slovaks and vice versa even though their languages are mutually intelligible.

Back in the ninth century both areas were under the Great Moravian Empire, but after this time they were to go their separate ways. The Slovak peoples came under control of the Magyars (ethnic Hungarians) while the Czechs were to create a kingdom of their own which was to have a significant impact on Medieval Europe. The Holy Roman Emperor, Charles IV, set up the first university, the Charles University, in Central Europe in Prague in 1348. By the early fifteenth century the Czechs were at the forefront of a Protestant movement begun by Jan Hus, the Rector of Charles University. Jan Hus who was burned at the stake in 1415, and his Hussites were to be responsible for the establishment of the Czech Kingdom as a largely Protestant power. It was not until two hundred years later, after their defeat by Austria at the battle of the White Mountain in 1620, that the Czech kingdom was forced to convert back to Catholicism by being incorporated into the Catholic Habsburg Empire. Religion was to become one of the defining features of the difference between the Slovak's and the Czechs, the former remaining more rural and loyal to the Roman Catholic Church, the latter were to associate Catholicism with their take-over by the Habsburg Empire. Greater urbanization and industrialization, Hussite Protestantism and a sense of an independent history was to spawn the Czech nationalism of the nineteenth century. Despite differences, the Slovaks and Czechs continued to affect each others' history. The nineteenth-century Czech nationalist movement was influenced by Slovaks as well as Czechs. Intellectuals such as the Slovak poet Jan Kollar or the archaeologist Pavel Josef Safarik helped to revive Czech as a literary language in the nineteenth century (Wightman, 1994: 255).

A political domestic irritant of what became Czechoslovakia was not the relationship between its two main ethnic groups, but dissatisfaction voiced by the German minority living in their territory. During the 1920s and early 1930s this dissatisfaction was dealt with by various political processes, such as allowing German minority parties to participate in the state government. This changed, however, with the rise of Nazism. As Hitler's popularity increased in Germany, the Sudeten Germans in Czechoslovakia became more vocal and extreme in their nationalist demands. The German Sudeten party in 1935 was to win 67 per cent of the Sudeten German vote. The Sudeten Germans were to receive the backing and encouragement of Hitler and in 1938 the leader of the Sudeten German Party, Konrad Henlein, announced the 'Carlsbad programme', which called for reparations to be given to the Sudeten Germans for the discrimination they had suffered after 1918. The relationship between the Sudeten Germans and Nazi Germany was to culminate in the 1938 Munich Agreement. At the Munich conference, the United Kingdom and France (in the presence of Mussolini), following the policy of appeasement towards Hitler, signed an agreement with Germany allowing the cessation of the Sudetenland from Czechoslovakia to Germany (Kinder and Hilgemann, 1979: 157).

This appeasement policy sealed Czechoslovakia's fate. The country's President, Benes, was to resign in frustration at what he and many in his government felt was a betrayal by the Western liberal democracies. By 15 March Hitler's troops had begun their invasion of Czechoslovakia. Benes went into exile for the duration of the war. Slovakia was to be set up as a puppet state under the pro-fascist leadership of Josef Tiso, whereas the Czech lands of Bohemia and Moravia were to be put under the direct control of Nazi Germany as a protectorate.

During the war Benes campaigned for the restoration of the Czechoslovak state. He felt that it was important that the country be re-established complete with its pre-1938 borders. The victory of the Allies in May 1945, made this possible. Benes returned to Prague in 1945, after the territory, minus Ruthenia, had been liberated. He again took-up the position of President, although the situation was now very different from that of pre-1939. In the first instance, the Sudeten Germans were forced out from the Czech lands by a state sponsored deportation. As many as 3 million Sudeten Germans were expelled in this manner, justified according to a principle of 'collective guilt'. This post-war act remained a bone of contention between modern-day Germany and the Czech Republic. In October 1996 the German and Czech governments negotiated the wording of a joint declaration that they hoped would resolve outstanding historical grievances.

While the Sudeten Germans had been forcibly removed, the Slovak peoples remained, and after the war there was a move toward granting Slovakia greater autonomy. As a result the Slovak National Council was established in Bratislava. Although Benes was interested in the emancipation of the Czech and Slovak peoples, he remained Czech-centric. Moreover, he seemed caught between wanting democracy, but not wanting the political criticism that often accompanies it. He tried to reduce the number of official parties permitted to run for office. His fear of instability caused him to prohibit any parties that had had dealings with the Nazis (in fact the majority of established parites at that time). The anti-Nazi sentiment would translate into pro-Soviet sentiments. This in turn would result in the growing popularity of the communist party.

Before the Second World War the communists had not done well in Czechoslovakia. A change in attitude occurred because it was mostly the Soviets that had liberated the Czech and Slovak lands at the end of the war. The German occupation, particularly of Czech lands, had been oppressive and frequently brutal. There was also an underlying distrust of Western Europe. Many had not forgotten the 1938 Munich Agreement and the West's abandonment of Czechoslovakia. Not unlike Western European fondness for the allied countries that had liberated them, both Czechs and Slovaks formed a special bond with the Soviet Union. The ture condition of those living under Stalin was not yet known. Indeed at the July 1945 Potsdam conference he was often referred to as 'Uncle Joe' by the Western press. A romanticized view of the Soviet Union and the post-war liberation enabled the communists gain 38 per cent of the vote in the May 1946 election in Czechoslovakia. They were to become the single largest party in the country, with the Czech population providing the majority of their support.

The Soviet Union, although a palpable influence, allowed Czechoslovakia to maintain its democratic and parliamentary traditions. Unfortunately, this state of affairs was only to last two years. In February 1948, the all-party coalition that had managed to run the country since the war started to disintegrate. A dozen ministers resigned, none of whom belonged to the communist party. The Soviets sponsored a move to increase the presence of communist party members. President Benes was forced to head a new government that was mostly made-up of communists. This was to prove the beginning of the end for Czechoslovak democracy. Over the coming months the government was to bring in a new constitution that made it virtually impossible to establish a non-communist opposition party. Benes refused to ratify the new constitution and subsequently resigned from office. Over the course of the next two decades Czechoslovakia was to become one of the worst Central European countries in terms of the denial of freedom of speech and expression. The show trials in Czechoslovakia, during the 1950s were as bad, if not worse, then those constructed in the Soviet Union.

Czechoslovakia was accused of being more Stalinist than Stalin's Russia. Perscution was not limited to political opponents of communism, members of the ruling party were also targeted. There were repeated 'purges' from the party, with members being accused of having, bourgeois nationalist, Zionist, cosmopolitanist, Titoist, sympathies. The reform of Stalinist-style government did not come from within Czechoslovakia, but was largely due to the softening of methods within the USSR itself after the death of Stalin. However, chage was not instantaneous. Stalin died in March 1953, but the Czechoslovak government continued to promote 'hardline' policies for several years. In June 1953, it conducted the brutal suppression of peaceful workers' demonstrations in Plzen and other Czech settlements. Show trials were still prevalent in Czechoslovakia during the mid-1950s despite Khrushchev's denunciation of Stalin at the Soviet Communist Party 20th Congress in 1956. It was not until Khrushchev's renewed campaign to de-Stalinize the Soviet bloc in 1961 that the Czechoslovak government began to discontinue its more oppressive political practices (Brown and Wightman 1977: 188).

Over the course of the next decade the political situation in Czechoslovakia began to slowly improve. There was a connection between the gradual lessening of political repression and the realization that the economy was stagnating. The Stalinist model of economic development had proved successful in transforming the economy to heavy industrial production but by the early 1960s the model was beginning to show signs of failure. In 1963, for the first time since the Second World War, national incomes began to decline. During the 1950s political repression had stifled any meaningful discourse regarding solutions to Czechoslovakia's economic and political problems. The loosening of political control meant that academics, intellectuals and professionals were now freer to discus their country's problems. Czech civil society, which had been kept down since the 1938 Munich Agreement became evident again as economists, sociologists and political analysts began debating economic and political reform programmes for Czechoslovakia.

This period, leading up to the 1968 Soviet invasion of Czechoslovakia, became known as the 'Prague Spring'. This period saw a partial rehabilitation of political opponents executed during the Stalinist era. Censorship was also greatly reduced. In January 1968, the First Secretary of the Party, Antonin Novotny, was replaced by Alexander Dubcek. Dubcek had been the leader of the Slovak Communist Party and was chosen to respond to demands for greater political reforms. The Communist Government in Czechoslovakia had controlled the delivery of all economic and political goods. When the system began to fail the population viewed this as a failure of everything to do with the Communist Government. Dubcek set about creating an agenda of radical political and economic change. His slogan was 'socialism with a human face'. This policy, however, worried many of the old-guard communists, since it suggested that existing socialism was inhumane.

The reforms were not a break with the Soviet Union. It was, in fact, more of a case of trying to increase the level of democratisation within the Czechoslovak Communist Party. Added to this was the move to give greater autonomy to certain state businesses as well as allowing greater freedom in workers' councils. Moreover, Slovakia was to gain its long awaited status as a separate republic within a properly federated Czechoslovakia. With the benefit of hindsight, the suggested changes seem tame, but however modest they stimulated an increased desire for change. Dubcek's reforms gave liberation of all kinds their own momentum. Art, philosophy and science began to flourish as never before under Communism. The freedoms, however, did beg the question as to why reforms should be limited to 'democratization' of the party rather than the introduction of full-scale democracy.

The Czechoslovak government tried to assure the Soviet Union that they would remain loyal members of theWarsaw Pact and that membership of CMEA (Comecon) would not be affected. Nevetheles, the changes in Czechoslovakia let to the creation of a 'social market economy' which presupposed trade with the West. At the same time, although the government continued to pay lip-service to Marxist–Leninism, school and university curricula in the social sciences began dropping the study of strict communist dogmas. It was an indication that the influence of the Soviet Union was on the wane.

Not unlike the Velvet Revolution of the late 1980s, many of the communist-bloc Central European countries were quietly trying to introduce reform. Dubcek and those in his government lobbied their neighbouring countries for support in an attempt to get a broader reform front going among the Eastern bloc countries. Unfortunately, as we have seen in Chapter 4 on Poland, The Polish leader, Wladyslaw Gomulka was not interested in substantial change. His colleague, Janos Kadar of Hungary was interested in reform but was gun-shy of the Soviets, an understandable attitude given the recent memory of the 1956 Soviet invasion of Hungary. Czechoslovakia had to face the Soviet Union alone.

The Soviet government was always particularly concerned with any changes within Czechoslovakia because of its long border with Germany, which made the country one of the most important front-line border states separating the Soviet Union from the West. So strong was the abhorrence of German influence that the Soviet Communist Party would often accuse dissidents of collaborating with Germans when trying to publicly discredit them. The Soviet paper *Pravda* would often publish fabricated news items on German aggression to justify Soviet manoeuvres close to the borders of the Central European countries. These tactics were also used to show Soviet displeasure with Dubcek's policies.

Despite Soviet posturing, Dubcek and his government continued on their path of modest reform. There were demands for the rehabilitation of all victims of the terror under Stalin. In addition, a movement was afoot to investigate the whole 'terror' phenomenon which would have basically meant an investigation of the Communist Party itself. This, in turn, might have led to scrutiny of the behaviour of the Soviet Communist Party and, ultimately, an end to the legitimacy of Soviet rule.

Repression of Czechoslovakia remained difficult. Part of the problem for the Soviets was that there was no open violence against communism. Neither were there any mass popular movements which might have given the Soviet army an excuse to come in and re-establish the former order. Instead, a quiet liberation of the press and personal freedoms was underway. Seeing this Soviet Union instead tried diplomatic means to talk or cajole Dubcek out of his continued reform programme. These tactics were bolstered during the early summer of 1968 by repeated Soviet military manoeuvres on the Czechoslovak border.

The issue came to a head in August 1968. Not only had Dubcek not backed down from his reforms, but he had called for an extraordinary Party Congress with a view to gaining support for even more far-reaching reforms. Determined to avoid these developments the Soviet Union invaded Czechoslovakia on 21 August 1968. The invading army was made up mostly of Soviet troops, but included token contributions from Bulgaria, Hungary, Poland and East Germany. By taking Prague the Soviet-led force had placed the invaders in an invidious situation. They did not want to dismantle all Czech political institutions because they had originally been the work of the Soviet-inspired Communist Party. However, there was only one way to ensure that these institutions did not organically reform through political change, and that was through occupation. As a result, Soviet armies remained stationed in Czechoslovakia until after the collapse of the Soviet Union in 1989.

After the 1968 invasion a period of 'normalisation' ensued. Over a period of time all the liberalizations that had been allowed were slowly withdrawn. Only the creation of a federal system of the separate Slovak and Czech republics remained. Dubcek was dismissed in April 1969 and replaced with the hard-line communist, Gustav Husak. The renewed clamp down destroyed any remaining romanticism left towards the Soviets and the Communist Party. The pretence of pro-Soviet and pro-Marxist propaganda was missing. There was to be no more cajoling, the post-Prague Spring policies of the new Czech government was simply one of control. Between 1969 and 1971, the Czechoslovak Communist Party lost 25 per cent of its members as it expelled suspected reformers and pressurized others to leave (Wightman, 1994: 257). Although there was to be no return to Stalinist-style executions, the political mood was bleak. The more control needed, the greater the system's lack of popular political legitimacy.

Underlying these political problems was the economy which continued to ossify. Before the Second World War, a democratic Czechoslovakia had enjoyed a Gross National Product (GNP) per capita (US$380) close to that of Austria (US$400) (Gelb, 1991). Indeed, during the inter-war years Czechoslovakia was one of the most industrialized countries in the region. The Czech lands in particular produced world-class products. The stifling of creativity which followed the imposition of the post-war communist regime was to destroy much of their indigenous capacity to produce competitive products. The direction of trade was reoriented from western Europe towards the Soviet Union. Despite the Czech lands' well-established market share in certain light industrial goods, they were encouraged to invest predominantly in heavy industry. Even though Czechoslovakia remained one of the wealthiest of the Central European countries, by 1990 its per capita GNP was only 25 per cent that of Austria (Dyba and Svejnar, 1994: 94).

Despite impressive growth, particularly during the 1949–53 five-year plan, when net production increased by 10 per cent per year, economic stagnation set in during the 1960s (Dyba and Svejnar, 1994: 97). Dubcek's reform's had led to renewed economic growth in the 1965–68 period, but the clamp-down after 1968 led to further economic contraction. The end of Dubcek's reforms coincided with a worldwide recession precipitated by the OPEC oil shocks of the early 1970s. The poor weather that had brought hardship to those in Polish agriculture had a similar effect in Czechoslovakia. Bad weather, poor terms of trade and continued repression of political freedoms stifled Czechoslovak economic performance during the 1975–80 period when growth rates dropped to about 3.6 per cent per year. Although the Soviet Union had committed itself to maintaining military control of Czechoslovakia, its tactics of repression were ineffectual in dealing with economic decline. Moreover, as Zdenek Suda said in 1980, the Czechoslovak Communist Party faced 'not only a hostile majority of the non-organised population but also considerable opposition among the rank and file party membership, who questioned the legitimacy of the prevailing order' (Suda, 1980: 378). The political mood generally was uninspiring which made for poor performance in most aspects of Czechoslovak life.

The early 1980s witnessed no economic or political upturn. The OPEC oil cartel had raised the prices of most of the world's commodities making imports more expensive. At the same time, the continued lack of product development and economic flexibility meant that Czechoslovak products were not doing as well as they should have done abroad. This was combined with a general recession and rigid government practices. The result was a drop in growth to 1.8 per cent during the first half of the 1980s (Dyba and Svejnar, 1994: 97). The growth rate simply stagnated over the later part of the decade. By the end of the decade Czechoslovakia was in trade deficit with both the Soviet Union and Poland. It also had to use Comecon export credits to finance its exports to Third World countries. Ultimately, the government turned to Western financial institutions for loans.

5.2 Events leading up to 1989

The economic deterioration of the 1980s stimulated renewed political protest, albeit in a less open and organized way. During the late-1970s certain dissident groups began to emerge. The most prominent being Charter 77. This group campaigned for civil rights and liberties that, in theory, should have been allowed under the 1975 Helsinki Agreements and by the Czechoslovak constitution. One of the group's most prominent members was Vaclav Havel. Although destined to become the Czech President after the fall of communism, at the time Havel was a playwright whose work had been banned since 1969. Charter 77 was not heavily supported during the late 1970s, with original signatories totalling only 242. By the end of the 1980s, however, the number had grown to almost 2,000. As a potential pressure group, Charter 77 was not particularly successful in gaining civil rights during the communist era, but it did perform a valuable function in terms of disseminating information about human rights abuses. It also acted as a focal point for those dissatisfied with the government.

By the mid-1980s, Gorbachev's *glasnost* in the Soviet Union led to a relaxing of political and economic controls. The rest of Central Europe took this as a sign that they, too, would be permitted a certain amount of latitude for political and economic reform. The Czechoslovak government, however, resisted change. Despite internal pressures from groups like Charter 77 to compromise, they still refused to condemn the acts of repression undertaken during and after the Prague Spring. The changes that did take place where mild and did not signify any fundamental change in the way the Czechoslovak government operated. In December 1987, Husak, the General Secretary of the CPZz, resigned. However, Husak's resignation did not signal any radical policy shift. His replacement, Milos Jakes, was known to be responsible for the purges after the Prague Spring. Moreover, he was openly hostile to any suggestion of the rehabilitation of those involved in the 1968 reforms. If anything, Jakes was to prove more repressive than his predecessor. Public protests were dispersed with unnecessary force. In March 1988, the police brutally broke up a quiet candle-lit vigil in Bratislava by Roman Catholics demanding greater religious freedoms and support for the recognition of human rights. This proved to be a political turning point.

The repression was unsuccessful in deterring protesters. In August 1988 demonstrations were held by thousands of dissidents in Prague's historic Wenceslas Square, to press for basic political reforms. This was followed in October by another huge public demonstration on the 70th anniversary of the creation of Czechoslovakia, reaffirming the protesters commitment to reform. Demonstrations and protests continued. In January 1989, citizens gathered to commemorate the suicide of Jan Palach. Palach had set fire to himself in 1969 to protest Dubcek's capitulation to the USSR's demands to rescind the 1968 reforms. Despite months of protests and demonstrations the government refused to relax its attitude towards dissidents. Police continued to break up demonstrations harshly. Vaclav Havel, himself, was arrested and given a jail sentence of 9 months.

In an attempt to suppress on all types of public assembly, the government introduced new legislation in an attempt to prevent further demonstrations. The population, however, was strongly motivated by the idea of greater democracy and freedom. Now clamp-downs only seemed to spur them to further public actions. Moreover, support for the government was fading even within the state authority. The federal Prime Minister, Ladislav Adamec, wrote a formal complaint regarding police brutality, and Cardinal Frantisek Tomasek, the Archbishop of Prague, publicly observed that 'brutal violence cannot suppress our citizens' desire to enjoy the measure of freedom which has become an accepted feature of 20th century life' (Wightman, 1994: 258).

The cycle of demonstrations and repression continued until November 1989. During that month Students had gained permission to stage a demonstration commemorating the death of those students killed by the Nazis in 1939. After the police had dispersed the crowd, an unsubstantiated rumour regarding a student being killed during the demonstration spread through the city. Soon the entire country was in revolt at this news (later this rumour was found to be untrue). Demonstrations began to occur throughout the country, with an enormous gathering taking place in Prague on 24 November 1989. Reports suggested that half-a-million people had gathered to demonstrate. It was at this moment that the 60-year old Alexander Dubcek re-emerged. Havel joined with other dissident groups to create a Civic Forum representing a kaleidoscope of reform-orientated groups. A two-hour general strike was held on 27 November 1989 after which the authorities capitulated and agreed to negotiate with the dissidents. This day marked the beginning of the end of communist rule in Czechoslovakia.

5.3 Collapse of communism

After the continued resistance of the government to change, many were surprised with its reaction to the November demonstrations. It was the beginning of what was to become known as the 'velvet revolution'. The majority of the Communist Party leadership, including the General Secretary, suddenly announced their resignations. By the 10 December, Husak, who had stayed on as President, stepped down after swearing in a new Government of National Understanding. A junior minister was left to head up the outgoing administration in which only 10 of the 21 cabinet seats were held by communists (Wightman, 1993: 53). This unprecedented move was followed, in late December 1989 by Dubcek becoming the chairman of the Federal Assembly and Vaclav Havel being installed as President. What had been unthinkable a few short months previous, had come to pass. The communists had resigned and a new caretaker government had been established to oversee the holding of free democratic elections.

The date of 8–9 June 1990 was chosen for the election to Federal Assembly and the Czech and Slovak National Councils. A system of proportional representation, last used in the 1946 elections, the last free elections of the pre-war era, were brought back with some modifications. A threshold was put in place requiring a party to gain 5 per cent (Czech) or 3 per cent (Slovak) in the National Councils to qualify for seats. Also voters could only put down a preference for up to four candidates.

In the run-up to the June 1990 elections there was a general mood of optimism and consensus building. Tensions between the Czech and Slovak political movements were not overt. The remaining communists in the regime continued to resign as it became clear that the old system had disappeared. The elections themselves witnessed an unprecedented 96 per cent turn-out of the eligible electorate, with Civic Forum winning 51 per cent of the Czech Votes. Similarly, its sister party in Slovakia, Public against Violence, won 34.9 per cent of the vote. Along with the small Christian Democratic Party, these two groups formed a new coalition to make up the federal government. The constitutional structure of the political system included a federal assembly and two national parliaments. This constitutional structure would have awkward political repercussions. The problem revolved around a requirement that all major federal legislation had to have the approval of at least three-fifths of the deputies in the House of the People (Federal Assembly), and also three-fifths support in each of the separate Czech and Slovak parliaments, under the House of Nations, the federal upper house. This arrangement was to prove a thorn in the side of a new government that would need to make many ground breaking changes. It also had the unfortunate consequence of heightening the tensions between the Czechs and Slovaks, most particularly among the politicians themselves. Petr Pithart, a jurist, author and former dissident, was appointed to lead the Czech cabinet. The Slovakian cabinet, on the other hand was led by, Vladimir Meciar, an amateur boxer who had worked as a provincial company lawyer and was said to have had suspect dealings with the communist secret police. This chalk and cheese element ran through much of Czech and Slovak relations at this time. The liberation of 1989 meant democracy and economic liberalization to the Czechs, but, to the Slovaks it was seen as an opportunity to exercise their long-repressed national aspirations. Many in the Slovakian government were not truly committed to economic restructuring and their political aims were often based on a desire for statehood. The Slovakian situation was different to that of the Czechs in that the changes to a market economy would lead to an unequal burden falling on the Slovaks. The Czech Republic managed to control unemployment which rarely rose above 3 per cent in the post-1990 period. In Slovakia the rate was closer to 12 per cent. Moreover the Slovakian economy had concentrated on armaments manufacturing, which left it in a particularly vulnerable position after the end of the Cold War which led to a collapse in the global armaments market. Slovak politicians and pundits exacerbated this problem by being outraged at the move to change the Slovak economy away from producing lethal weapons. There remained a strong attachment to ideas of socialism and a paternalistic role for the state. Unfortunately this was also combined with elements of strong anti-Semitism and a chauvinism towards all things non-Slovak. Its not surprising that the ruling elite would soon be at loggerheads with the Czechs (Ulc, 1996: 338).

The Slovak attitude toward the Czechoslovak federation was soured by the Czech assumption that they held the torch of enlightenment and that the Slovaks where needlessly dissatisfied with their level of sovereignty. The level of intransigence on both sides became apparent when the entire political process became bogged down in what was known as the 'battle over the hyphen'. While there was general agreement that the term socialist should be dropped from the official name of the republic, the Slovaks strongly objected to the name remaining the Ceskoslovenska Republika. It was felt that the name demonstrated the subordinate way in which the Czechs viewed the Slovaks. Eventually the name Ceska-a-slovenska Federalni Republika (CSFR) was decided upon. But the political rows over this issue had resulted in no one being satisfied with the outcome. Not surprisingly, post-communist Czechoslovakia, only lasted three years. Although constant and repeated negotiations took place to try to come to a mutually acceptable solution, Slovakia remained committed to its aspiration for separate statehood. In some cases factions in Slovakia went from the sublime to the ridiculous in trying to glorify their national aspirations. Otto Ulc recounts how the extreme nationalists, mostly supporters of the Slovak National party, performed a rite of bizarre historical revisionism when they decided to commemorate the foundation of the Hitler-sponsored Slovak fascist state in 1939. Moreover, they wanted its president, Josef Tiso, who was executed as a war criminal for sending tens of thousands of Jews to the gas chambers, to be exonerated. Unbelievably, a plaque honouring this president was unveiled in October 1990. This coincided with the exact day of an official visit of the Israeli president, Chaim Herzog (Ulc, 1996: 340). This insensitivity and lack of concern for outside opinion was fairly typical of nationalist sentiments in Slovakia at that time.

By 1992, the Czechoslovak state had reached an impasse and had ceased to be able to function as one country. The situation was brought to a head in the 1992 elections when the electorate voted along nationalists lines. In Slovakia, not a single pro-federation party made it over the 5 per cent threshold for representation in parliament. In fact 70 per cent of the Slovakian electorate voted for parties whose platform was the secession from Czechoslovakia. In the Czech Republic, like so many other Central European countries, the dissidents who were responsible for the fall of communism, were denied a second term in office in their try for a second term. The Civic Forum had collapsed in 1991 and in 1992 its successor the Civic Movement did not even attain the 5 per cent needed to remain an official party. It was the new Civic Democratic Party (CDP) that took the lion share of the votes. The CDP leader, Vaclav Klaus, became the new premier. He formed a coalition government comprised of a right-of-centre party as well as four centrist parties. Klaus, unlike the former premier Petr Pithart, had no dissident credentials and was not committed to holding onto Slovakia 'at all costs'. After a series of short, acrimonious and unsuccessful negotiations, Klaus handed the Slovakian leadership an ultimatum. They had to choose between taking part in a meaningful federation or accepting the dissolution of Czechoslovakia, which would also mean an end to Czech subsidies to Slovakia. The Slovak Premier, Meciar, accepted the offer of independence as this was what he had long advocated. The final day of the 72-year-old state of Czechoslovakia was 31 December 1992. Although this dramatic turn of events still mystifies many Czechs, Slovakia had basically won its freedom to be a poorer, yet sovereign, country.

5.4 The new regime: privatization, investment and government policy

With a few exceptions (e.g. Interior Minister Jan Ruml), the government which controlled the newly created Czech Republic on 1 January 1993 was devoid of most of the people involved in the collapse of communism in November 1989. Klaus and his CDP felt themselves to be modernizers, and the bulk of their political platform concentrated on portraying themselves as a stable party which could push through a coherent reform programme. However, their job had been made easier by reforms already put in place at the beginning of the transition process. During the summer of 1990 the Federal Parliament had put forward a comprehensive programme designed to restructure the economy. Alena Nesporova in her 1995 work on Czechoslovak industrial restructuring, points out that there were three main pillars to this economic plan:

> (a) quick privatisation of state assets; (b) liberalisation of prices, and (c) liberalisation of foreign trade. The two last elements were based on the internal convertibility of the national currency (convertibility on the current account). The main priority for macroeconomic policy was to maintain the internal and external stability of the economy by means of tight monetary and fiscal policies.
>
> Nesporova, 1995: 183

This was not to be an easy task for those in government. Like many of the CEECs, the legacy of Soviet influence, combined with national communism, had encouraged the ideal of the 'industrial worker' especially the worker in heavy industry. The emphasis placed on heavy industry was out of keeping with what was actually needed or appropriate. In the case of Czechoslovakia and the post-January 1993 Czech republic, the economy needed not only to be privatized, but also to be completely restructured. The service sector was small, and research and development into new product technologies had not been strongly pursued. As a result pre-1989 Czechoslovakia's per capita steel production was 50 per cent higher than that of Austria or Germany, and three times as much as that of France (Handl *et al.*, 1995: 56). Similar statistics also exist for heavy industrial goods such as cement. In addition to this challenge Czechoslovakia had a much smaller private sector than its other transforming neighbours. In 1985, the private sector made up only 0.3 per cent of the workforce and this had only grown to 1.2 per cent by 1989. (Handl, 1995: 59) The big challenge for the newly independent Czechoslovakia was, therefore, to privatize without creating the massive levels of unemployment experienced elsewhere in Central Europe during the 1990–93 period.

Despite its structural problems, Czechoslovakia did have some advantages over other countries in transition. The most striking was Czechoslovakia's lack of debt compared to its neighbours. While Czechoslovakia's gross foreign debts were US$7.9 billion (or US$510 per capita), Poland's was double this and Hungary's was four times this amount. Czechoslovakia went into its transition phase with a debt service ratio of 19 per cent of GDP which was unique in the former Eastern bloc and acceptable to the World Bank (Nesporova, 1995: 181). In addition to this, those living in Czechoslovakia were used to a government that practised fiscal austerity. Moreover, the trade union movement was comparatively weak in Czechoslovakia compared to other Central European countries (Campbell, 1996: 69). This created a political culture better able to accept the harsh realities that the transition process placed upon it.

Towards the end of 1990, the Czechoslovak government had set a policy which aimed for zero growth in money supply, and a budget surplus of 1–1.5 per cent. These measures were obviously designed to tackle inflation. However, by 1992 inflation had reached 52 per cent. The government responded by bringing in even tougher restrictions on the money supply and attempting to realize a 2–2.5 per cent budget surplus. These measures were in the context of making the koruna fully convertible, a move which involved triple devaluation of the currency against the US dollar. Reducing inflation caused difficulties for the population at large, especially the new class of entrepreneurs. But it was brought under control and the rate dropped to 17–18 per cent by 1993 (Dyba and Svejnar, 1994: 99; Shirong: 1994: 18).

The policies above were all part of the larger programme of creating a market economy in Czechoslovakia. From the beginning of January 1991 prices began to be liberalized. Approximately 85 per cent of consumer and producer prices were freed, a move which coincided with a capping of wages and the imposition of a 20 per cent import duty (Dyba and Svejnar, 1994: 99). Similarly government subsidies were cut to industry and agriculture. As a percentage of GDP, Czechoslovakia's government was spending approximately 16 per cent on government subsidies in 1989. By the end of 1990 this figure had dropped to 3.5 per cent. This represented a massive reduction in subsidization, and a good portion of these cuts being accomplished by slashing subsidies on food products (Handl *et al.*, 1995: 58).

These policies were implemented at a time when momentous changes were also occuring in the structure of Czechoslovakia's international trade. The collapse of trade with the former Soviet Union was to be as dramatic in Czechoslovakia as elsewhere in Central and Eastern Europe. Exports to the Soviet Union in 1990 represented over 54,000 million koruna. By 1994 this number had dropped to 15,655 million koruna.[1] Only its trade with developing countries remained unchanged (Nesporova, 1995: 185). The West and the EU in particular, now became Czechoslovakia's main trading partners. Moreover, trade with Germany mushroomed in the years of 1990–94. If we look at Table 5.1 we see that exports to Germany in 1990 amounted to 27,639 million koruna, but by 1994 this had quadrupled to 120,570 million koruna. By 1995, over 55.1 per cent of exports and 56.4 per cent of imports were with the EU (EIU Country Report, *Czech Republic and Slovakia 1996–97*, 1996: 24). These figures are all the more impressive when one realises that the trade statistics after 1993 refer to the Czech Republic alone, minus Slovakia (see Table 5.1).

These trade figures are, in large part, a testament to the speed of the privatization process. Even before the 1993 split of the Czech and Slovak Republics, the private sector made up more than 50 per cent of the Czech Republic's GDP (Mladek, 1995: 125). This figure is striking, particularly if we consider that during the same period over 85 per cent of the industrial output was still controlled by state-owned firms (Rutland, 1994: 268).

Kristian Palda, an academic at Queen's University in Canada, who worked with the Czech Ministry of the Economy as a consultant in 1995, points out that there was no coherent division between the types

Table 5.1 Czechoslovak/Czech Merchandise Trade with Main Trading Partners (in korona mns, exchange rate 1990–94 approximately US$1 = 30 koruna)

Formerly planned economies		**Czechoslovakia**			**Czech Republic**		
		1990	**1991**	**1992**	**1992**	**1993**	**1994**
Slovakia	exports	–	–	–	–	82,628	66,979
	imports	–	–	–	–	65,564	60,201
Soviet Union	exports	54,159	65,298	39,963	22,142	17,269	15,877
	imports	51,410	96,572	90,580	52,661	36,910	35,864
Poland	exports	13,394	24,351	16,232	11,918	10,477	15,655
	imports	20,370	15,106	13,458	10,005	9,406	12,103
Hungary	exports	8,841	14,397	15,080	7,789	8,635	10,788
	imports	8,147	6,233	6,137	3,334	5,096	4,832
Developed countries							
Germany	exports	27,639	83,972	107,510	81,544	100,128	120,570
	imports	31,734	69,350	101,524	78,724	95,314	107,511
Austria	exports	12,717	19,489	25,776	17,927	23,147	29,805
	imports	23,124	27,281	37,688	26,636	29,175	34,291
Italy	exports	6,630	14,989	21,250	15,445	19,113	20,199
	imports	5,436	11,062	20,297	14,115	17,648	22,289
France	exports	5,662	8,093	10,380	6,318	7,372	10,383
	imports	4,203	7,986	18,724	18,389	11,491	15,468
USA	exports	1,639	3,328	5,700	4,321	6,901	8,820
	imports	1,368	6,277	16,645	14,856	11,254	14,267
UK	exports	5,521	6,265	7,715	5,700	11,418	11,349
	imports	6,862	6,511	9,498	7,789	10,131	12,785
Switzerland	exports	4,790	3,672	4,699	3,269	4,473	5,607
	imports	10,048	8,193	8,556	6,443	8,405	9,419
Japan	exports	1,592	2,129	2,772	2,499	1,914	2,569
	imports	1,144	3,803	7,641	6,572	6,542	8,466
EU	exports	67,016	135,898	176,025	130,950	162,898	189,003
	imports	76,561	111,894	176,125	140,057	160,035	191,055

Source: Statistics reproduced from EIU Country Profile, *Czech Republic and Slovakia 1996–97* (1996): 26.

of privatizations that took place in Czechoslovakia and the post-1993 Czech Republic. However, he does suggest that there were four main categories in which most of the privatizations would fall: (1) restitution; (2) small privatization; (3) municipalities and land; and (4) big privatization (Palda, 1997: 85–7). It was restitution which, from the first helped to increase the percentage of the workforce involved in the private sector. Initially, the Czechoslovak government was apprehensive about entertaining the notion of property restitution. It feared that many foreign exiles or their descendants might come and make claim to property which had been re-allocated by the Communist government after the war. As a compromise the government decided in 1990, to consider restitution with regards to property nationalized at or after February 1948. The choice of 1948 as the cut-off date proved crucial, for during the war all companies which employed more than 500 workers were taken over by the state, along with property owned by Sudenten Germans. This basically meant that only those who were Czechoslovak citizens and residents on or after 1948 could make a legitimate claim to restitution. This does not mean that the issue of restitution was easily solved. There remains controversy and conflict over a number of restitution cases. Having said this, however, the process of restitution had been crucial in creating a private sector and a bourgeoisie in present-day Czech Republic.

The largest impact of restitution was in the commercial, real estate, restaurant and retail sectors, as well as in agriculture. Palda's research suggests that by the end of 1994 property to the value of between 70 and 120 billion koruna (or US$2.5–4.3 billion) had been returned to post-1948 owners. The lack of property evaluation hampers estimates of the value of the returned property, it is usually assumed that this type of privatization represents 10 to 25 per cent of what the Czechoslovak government owned in apartments and retail holdings post-1948 (Palda, 1997: 85).

Restitution did not cover all small privatizations. Small privatizations occurred in tandem with that of major government-owned property restitution, but dealt with uncontested properties. The method of privatization employed was that of public auction. For the most part the state identified smaller self-contained businesses and auctioned them. The small firms in question ranged from small to medium-size industries, accommodation and retail. Only those people resident in Czechoslovakia were eligible to take part in the bidding for property. It is estimated that more than 22,000 small business were reprivatized in this fashion. For businesses independent of property, the government auctioned off a series of 2–5-year leases. The breakdown was approximately 23 per cent small business, 21 per cent local production and services and 10 per cent restaurants (Handl *et al.*, 1995: 59). This type of privatization was completed toward the end of 1992 and greatly facilitated the resuscitation of a property-owning middle class in Czechoslovakia.

The third type of privatization – municipalities and land – had more to do with public administration than returning property to private individuals. Under communism Czechoslovakia was a very centralized system and local government had been all but eliminated. Under the transformation legislation of 1991, it was decided that local municipalities would be reconstituted and given authority for local government. As part of this programme, unclaimed apartment buildings, urban land within municipal boundaries and former state property holdings were returned to over 6200 municipalities. Alongside this form of administrative restitution was the privatization of agricultural land. The main aim here was to privatize the nationalized co-operatives (Kolchozes) as quickly as possible. In Czechoslovakia there were over 1,200 co-operatives, most of them agricultural. These were sold off and became either companies or private co-operatives. Some of these businesses were then leased again by the private owners to individual leases. Despite widespread bankruptcy of these types of privatized companies/co-ops, they currently number approximately 1,300 and represent a value of about US$7.7 billion (Palda, 1997: 86).

Restitution and small business and municipal/land privatization represented the areas which would provide the largest private-sector activity in Czechoslovakia. However, it was only a small portion of what the state owned. For the government, the most serious challenge remained that of 'big' firm privatization. These firms represented wide cross-section of the economy from banking, steel, public utilities and energy to chemical manufacturing. The only thing these firms had in common was their government ownership. Following the transformation legislation of October 1991, which was based on the 'big-privatization' legal framework of April 1991, it was decided to attempt to turn these large state concerns into some form of joint-stock enterprise. The solution was a form of voucher privatization whereby the ownership of these companies were transferred to the population as a whole through the issuance of share vouchers to workers in respective industries. The first part of the process was to be directed by the then acting Minister of Privatization, Tomas Jezek. Basically the existing management of the state firms was told to come up with a viable privatization plan for their respective firms. These plans were to present not only accounting data but also a credible strategic plan for the enterprises' future. Managers were aware that outside groups whether domestic or foreign, also had the right to submit a strategic plan for their enterprise. This forced the existing management to take the process seriously, for if a rival interest were to come up with a plan that the Ministry of Privatization found more appealing, existing managers might find themselves under threat from alternative privatization plans (Mladek, 1995: 125).

Preparing the state-owned companies was only part of the project. The other task was laying the groundwork for those who would purchase shares. The intention was that Czechoslovak citizens would purchase these shares, although foreign buyers were not completely excluded. During the first wave of privatization some 3 per cent were sold to foreign firms (Nesporova, 1995: 185). In certain sectors deemed 'strategic' such as banking and the financial services, the government reserved the right to maintain a controlling number of enterprise shares. These strategic firms only numbered around 50 and were completely dwarfed by the 4,500 firms which were adopted under existing privatization plans. The number of adopted plans was large but represents only a small proportion 23,000 privatization projects submitted to the MOP for possible adoption. Voucher privatization employed a system whereby voucher books were sold for 1,000 Koruna. These booklets contained 1,000 investment points and cost about 20 per cent of the average monthly wage (Palda, 1997: 86–7). An individual could hold on to the voucher points or give them to an investment privatization fund (IPF) which would diversify the holdings of the small investor. These investment funds also tried to encourage the small investor to sell his/her vouchers. Many offered to pay 10 times the original price for the vouchers within a year of the small investor joining the fund. Before the first wave of privatizations in January 1992, 80 per cent of the population had bought vouchers and 72 per cent of these people entrusted their money with to some 220 private investment funds (Rutland, 1994: 267). This process did not create any extra investment capital in the Czechoslovak economy, but it did rally the population behind the transition project giving the transformation an added legitimacy and degree of popular participation.

After the split between the Czech and Slovak republics in January 1993, the Czech government decided to continue with the privatization as planned and there have been a number of waves of 'big' firm privatization. The first began in May 1992 and the second finished at the end of 1994 (Slovakia only participated in the first wave). A quarter of the industries in the Czech Republic were involved in the first privatization. Around 1,320 firms were privatized at this time and 65 per cent of the assets were purchased through the voucher method. This wave of privatization may have been as dramatic as the figures might suggest. Many firms are nominally private, but 27 per cent of shares are held by the state-controlled Fund of National Property (FNP) for sale at a later date (Rutland, 1994: 267).

The second wave of privatization involved 861 companies, of which approximately 15 per cent had not found a purchaser in the first wave. The take-up in this second round was very good, with 96.3 per cent of tendered companies being sold. During these two waves of privatization some 480 billion koruna worth of property was transferred from government to the private sector. Of this, some 350 billion koruna can be accounted for by voucher privatization (Palda, 1997: 87). After the second privatization in 1994, the majority of the 'big'[2] state-owned enterprises were floated on the private stock market. What remained in government hands was either considered 'strategic' or were least attractive to private buyers. Nevertheless, the government can be credited with some success in privatizing state-owned industries. The Czechoslovak and later the Czech authorities had attempted to restructure their economy away from a dependence on heavy industry. It also liberalized prices, capped wages, cut government subsidies, re-oriented trade from the former Soviet Union to Western Europe and completed a significant amount of its privatization programme by the end of 1994. These efforts placed the Czech Republic in a stable economic situation.

5.5 The results thus far

There is no doubt that until 1998 the Czech Republic was considered one of the most successful examples of a transition from a command to a market economy. Its government has often cited its ability to maintain low levels of unemployment as evidence of its success. Nevertheless, Czechoslovakia, and later the Czech Republic experienced economic problems not dissimilar to its Central European neighbours.

As mentioned earlier, fiscal restraint had long been a feature of government policy. Moreover, the general conservatism of its political culture meant that the population as a whole did not have as high an expectation of the results of the transformation. Not that the population did not experience economic hardship. From 1990 through to the end of 1993 Czechoslovakia saw its real GDP decline by 1.2 per cent in 1990, 14.2 per cent in 1991, and 7.1 per cent in 1992 (Sojka, 1994: 40). This drop in GDP could be linked to an overall drop in industrial output which fell by a third between 1990 and 1992. The decline in industry meant pressure was put on employment, productivity and real wages. There was also a serious problem with the state healthcare system where many sections have still to be privatized, at a time of declining real wages. Added to this is the lack of affordable housing for workers. The construction of flats decreased from 55,000 units in 1989, to 18,000 in 1994. Despite a considerable increase in recent construction there remains an unfulfilled demand for over 400,000 flats (Handl *et al.*, 1995: 65). The combination of a decline in real wages, undermined government healthcare, and lack of affordable housing led to general dissatisfaction among workers. However, unlike the Polish trade unions, the Czech trade unions were weak and not as accustomed to political strike action. As a result, they accepted a 23 per cent drop in real wages in 1991. There was very little strike activity between 1989 and 1994 and in most cases conflictual issues were solved wage bargaining. However, on March 1994 there was a strike consisting of approximately 40,000 trade union members. It prompted by the government's attempt to amend the Labour Code to allow short-term contracts, release restrictions on pregnant woman working night shifts, and raise the legal retirement age. The changes to the Labour Code worried trade unions and more than 600,000 members signed a petition to signal their concerns about the suggested amendments. There were also other issues such as a ban on unions in the civil service and the undercutting of old age pensions. The government, however, went through with the amendment which was passed in the lower house with a large majority (102 for, 16 against) (Brokl and Mansfeldova, 1995: 305).

Despite an even larger strike demonstration in December 1994 involving 500,000 people who stopped work for 15 minutes, the government largely stuck to its policy of tough economic reform. Considering the drop in wages, industrial decline, and high inflation (20 per cent in 1993), the Czech workforce has been fairly controlled with regard to strike action (EIU Country Report, 1996: 5). This is not as strange as it might seem if we realize that 6 years after the reform began the Czech unemployment rate was only 2.8 per cent (Steiger, 1996: 204). During 1994 to 1996, the unemployment rate floated from 2.5 to 3.5 per cent (WIIW, 1996: 382). At face value the statistics appear impressive.

There are, however, those who criticize the various post-January 1993 Czech governments for not being tough enough during the transformation process. They cite the low level of unemployment as evidence for this. The argument against government policy suggests that the low unemployment rate is symptomatic of under-employment. Many feel that there are people working for the remaining state-owned companies that, if proper restructuring had occurred, would now be jobless. Economic research at the Union Bank of Switzerland claims that often low unemployment is a sign that a country has not yet undergone real structural change and suggests that the Czech Republic's true unemployment rate would likely be around 8 per cent (Steiger, 1996: 204). However, the government, itself, explains the low jobless rate as being the cause of the policy effecting the unemployed. An unemployed worker receives 60 per cent of the average wage for the first 3 months with 50 per cent during the following 3 months. After 6 months workers can apply for welfare benefits, but, can only receive them if they continue to actively look for employment (Steiger, 1996: 204). This type of employment policy does seem to encourage workers back into the work force, but, can only be a partial explanation for the low unemployment rate. There must also be job vacancies to which workers can apply. The steady growth of the Czech economy has meant that there were double the job vacancies in 1995 that there were in 1994. Undoubtedly this contributed to the low jobless rate.

What is often missed by those studying the low employment rate in the Czech Republic, is the probable connection between its stable economic performance and its rejection of the high unemployment model of 'shock-therapy' during its economic transition. Undoubtedly, there are employees who are being subsidized in many of the remaining government run enterprises. However, by allowing them to remain there in the short-term, the state helps to maintain a stable political situation within which to bring about its wider economic restructuring programme. Moreover, by privatizing small industries first and allowing property restitution, these industries are now employing many workers previously employed in state-enterprises. Realistically, however, the unemployment rate will likely rise in the future as the final stages of privatization takes place. Slowly the excess labour in state enterprises will be shed, leaving the workers to find their own way in the privatised economy. If we look at Table 5.2 we get a sense of the performance of the Czech Republic during the transformation phase.

These statistics show the dichotomies which exist in the Czech Republic. The real growth rate in 1995 was up to 4.8 per cent and the level of investment had increased to 411.1 billion koruna. In addition, the CDP's government had been mostly successful at balancing its budget and even running a surplus. On the other hand, the problems of fiscal restraint have caused a slow down in housing projects and an increase in the level of domestic debt. This has been coupled with a growing trade deficit in which imports, particularly from Europe, have been more successful than Czech exports.

During 1997 the Czech Republic current account deficit developed into a currency crisis. The seriousness of the situation prompted the government to spend US$3 billion on supporting the Czech koruna (Czech Republic, *Factbook*, 1999: 10). The attempt was unsuccessful and the Czech central bank ultimately had to let the koruna float. This only further exacerbated the current account problem as imports continued to outstrip exports. Deficit financing led to the creation of an external

Table 5.2 Czech Republic: Selected Economic Indicators, 1990–95

Indicator	1990	1992	1993	1994	1995
Population per 1000	10,362.7	10,317.8	10,330.6	10,336.2	10,330.8
Real growth rate (%)	–1.2	–6.4	–0.9	2.6	4.8
Gross investment (koruna bn)	146.6	200.9	256.1	332.6	411.1
Housing construction (1000 units)	44.6	36.4	31.5	18.2	12.7
Unemployment rate	0.8	2.6	3.5	3.2	2.9
Housing construction: Growth rate (%)	–19.0	–12.8	–13.4	–42.4	–30.3
Govt budget (koruna bn): deficit (–) surplus (+)	–1.0	–1.7	+1.1	+10.4	+7.2
Gross debt (US$ m)		7,082	8,496	10,694	16,549
Exports total (US$ m)			13,204.6	14,254.7	17,085.5
Imports total (US$ m)			12,858.5	14,970.6	20,885.9

Source: Figures reproduced from WIIW, 1996: 76.

debt problem in the excess of US$20 billion (Czech Republic, *Factbook*, 1999: 10). The Czech Republic's poor economic performance forced its government to implement to two austerity packages during 1997.

The effects of fiscal restraint were to damage the popularity of the Civic Democratic Party under Vaclav Klaus. Klaus's party was also implicated in a scandal with regards to senior members of the government being involved in the misuse of investment funds and insider-trading on the Czech Stock Exchange. Despite this, CDP remained in control of the government until the general elections of 19–20 June 1998. However, Klaus had resigned as Czech Prime Minister the previous December because of the political scandal. Although the CDP had lost some of its popularity domestically, international financial organizations have been on the whole approving of the economic policies implemented by the Klaus government. The international financial community was, however, dismayed with the June 1998 elections which gave the left-wing Czech Social Democratic Party (CSSD) 32 per cent of the vote (Rose, 1998).

The June 1998 elections returned no party with a clear majority. As a result the CSSD, with the largest percentage of the vote, began to look for coalition partners. In an unusual move, it entered into negotiations with the former ruling CDP which had managed to acquire 27.7 per cent of the vote (Rose, 1998). The negotiations would result in the Civic Democrats signing an coalition agreement which allowed the CSSD to form a government. The Czech parliament is, therefore, made up of a left-right coalition.

The composition of the new government has had two major effects. First, the CSSD promised during its election campaign to weed out corruption in the government. The concentration on investigating the wrongdoing of members of the past government has diverted time and resources away from the Czech government's responsibilities *vis-à-vis* EU accession agreements. During an October 1998 visit the European Commissioner responsible for EU enlargement, Hans van den Broek, stated that the new government had lost valuable time since the June election and that it was now trailing behind the other five countries which are in line to begin substantive negotiations towards EU membership in November (Friedrich, 1998). Secondly, the CSSD had also promised to increase social spending even if this were to result in deficit spending on the part of the government. However, it is difficult to see how this would work in a coalition which includes the fiscally conservative CDP. Moreover, the upper house, the Chamber of Deputies, remains dominated by representatives sympathetic to the right-wing conservatism of the former government. It is likely that the nature of the coalition will force the CSSD to rein in its desire to increase public spending considerably on pensions and child benefit. It is likely the IMF and other Western lenders will also encourage the Czech government to stay the course of reform already embarked on by the Klaus government.

5.6 Summary comments

How is the Czech Republic's transition similar to the that of the other two Central European case-studies and how is it different? The similarities between the examples are based upon the general process of democratization and economic restructuring. As Poland and Hungary, the Czech Republic was faced with the daunting task of creating a democratic state while developing a market economy. It faced the same challenges in terms of privatisation and currency convertibility. There were, however, some important differences. The Czech Republic, unlike the other two examples in this study, experienced a split with its former federated partner, Slovakia. The break up of Czechoslovakia was an added complication to the transition process. Despite the problems caused by Slovakia's desire for nationhood, the post-1993 Czech Republic seemed poised to have the best economy in Central Europe. It had a low debt ratio, and its democratic leadership was made up of technocrats willing to adopt economic policies that would integrate it into the West. Moreover, the Czech population seemed less inclined to react negatively to fiscal conservatism.

What happened between 1994 and 1998 to change the Czech Republic from a frontrunner for EU membership to a country experiencing a serious financial crisis? The answer lies in the West's attitude towards financial deregulation. As explained earlier in this study (see Section 1.3), there is an erroneous assumption that the creation of a deregulated financial sector is similar to creating a free market in tradable goods. While the Czech Republic had success freeing up trade in goods, the fledgling Prague stock market and the new financial investment funds suffered from instability and corruption. Western advice followed a familiar pattern and suggested that the solution to financial instability was the introduction of even more severe neo-classical economic solutions in the form of austerity programmes. The outcome of this process has been not only to facilitate the spread of Western practices in the Czech Republic but also Western ownership of assets.

The political ramifications of the way in which the Czech government has adopted Western advice has seen a growing tension between the democratic process and the economic transition process. The 1998 election results show a clear increase in support for left-wing political parties. The current government is being encouraged by Western organizations to continue on the path of economic reform. The electorate, however, has been calling for policies that concentrate more on the project of fairness and social responsibility. The tension between the introduction of capitalism and the maintenance of the initial objective of creating a democratic emancipated society will continue to be evident in the Czech Republic in years to come.

6
Hungary

This chapter deals first with the history of Hungary before moving on to more recent events. It looks at the collapse of communism and the attempt to move Hungary towards a market-driven economy. Hungary differs from a number of CEECs in the sense that it has been very suspicious of 'shock therapy' and austerity measures. The story of Hungary's conversion to capitalism is one of a struggle between liberal hard-right influence, and those in Hungary who wish to model themselves on more social democratic models similar to Austria or Germany.

6.1 Brief history of Hungary

Medieval Hungary was a monarchy ruling a territory three times as large as the present day republic. Its history shared the turbulent nature of the other Central European countries. In the early part of the sixteenth century the Ottoman Empire attempted to take over the Kingdom of Hungary. At the Battle of Mohacs the Turks killed King Louis II of Hungary (1516–26) and the Kingdom was divided among the Hapsburgs, the Ottoman Empire and the principality of Transylvania. Hungary was not reunited until the end of the seventeenth century when the Hapsburg Emperor, Leopold I (1657–1705), managed to push the Turks out of Hungary and the occupied areas of Transylvania. This turn of events made Hungary an important part of the territory held by the Hapsburg monarchy (Macartney and Palmer, 1972: 3, 12, 21, 42). Although owing allegiance to the imperial court in Vienna, Hungary had managed to acquire political autonomy. This political independence was enshrined in the Ausgleich compromise of 1867, which established a dual monarchy in which Austria and Hungary owed allegiance to the Habsburgs, but had completely independent legislatures, constitutions and political administrations. There were joint agreements on trade, taxation and transport which were covered by renewable 10-year agreements. Any expenditures that fell under joint jurisdiction was paid for through customs duties and separate national contributions. The Austro-Hungarian Empire was held together through the institutions of the Habsburg monarchy and the imperial army. However, the day-to-day running of Austria and Hungary was completely separate and the governance of each part of the empire thus significantly different. Male suffrage, for instance, was introduced in Austria before the First World War, whereas Hungary continued to maintain a more archaic political structure until the break up of the Habsburg empire in 1918.

The break-up of the Austro-Hungarian Empire was a direct result of their being on the losing side of the First World War. Vienna was forced to agree to the same armistice terms as Germany. Under these terms the defeated Central European powers were forced to give up considerable territory. Similarly, the Wilsonian principles of self-determination would encourage ethnic minorities within the former Austro-Hungarian empire to lobby for independence at the Versailles Conference. As a result Hungary lost two-thirds of its territory leaving many ethnic Hungarians (Magyars) living under the jurisdiction of other states. The problem of large ethnic groups outside its borders plagues Hungary to the present day.

After 1918, the Hungarian government declared Hungary a republic in protest over its treatment under the armistice. By 1919, it had a socialist government under the leadership of Bela Kun. This development was inspired by the Bolshevik Revolution. The Soviets, however, saw this development as a threat. Lenin in particular, was quick to criticize Hungary's attempt to establish a 'dictatorship of the proletariat'. The experiment lasted only 133 days and its collapse was attributed to a number of inter-linked causes, such as the lack of successful land reform, the large reduction in Hungarian territory and an ineffective Communist Party (Molnar, 1978: 20).

The collapse of Kun's government stimulated a political move towards conservative values. In the inter-war period Hungary reverted to a right-wing authoritarian style of government, and the pre-1918 royalist constitution was reinstated. The throne remained vacant and the head of state was given the title of regent. In 1920 Admiral Miklos Horthy de Nagybana was appointed as regent and held that position until 1944. Horthy's government was stable but conservative with all major posts being held by noblemen. Horthy's government last 22 years and was replaced by force when Germany put pressure on Hungary to establish a fascist government.

After the war, communist rule returned to Hungary, but unlike the short-lived Bela Kun government it was not a domestic grass-roots movement. Communism was imposed through the presence of the Soviet Army which occupied Hungary during 1945. However initially, the domination of the Communist Party was not complete: during the post-war years Hungarian governments were made up of a number of popular coalitions. Nevertheless, even though parties such as the Small Landholders Party had more seats than the Hungarian Communist Party (HCP), the HCP had the backing of the Soviet Union. Leaders of other parties were often intimidated into resigning. This, combined with pro-Soviet propaganda, proved successful and by 1948 the majority of the other democratic parties had become subsumed into the ruling party which took on the new name of, the Hungarian Workers' Party (HWP).

Over the course of the next 10 years, Hungary would be governed harshly by the Communist leader, Matyas Rakosi, who transformed Hungary into a highly industrialized state, but the human cost was high. Land was forcibly collectivized and hundreds of thousands of the regime's opponents were sent to labour camps. The AVO, Hungary's Department for Defence of the State, was in charge of internal state security. This department was a Hungarian version of the Soviet KGB and would not allow any opposition, peaceful or otherwise, to the Rakosi government.

The years of oppressive government in Hungary spawned a powerful groundswell of opposition. After Stalin's death in 1953 a branch of the HWP were eager to bring about reform. There were those in the Soviet politburo who were not unsympathetic to the notion of reform. It was Imre Nagy, a former Hungarian Minister of Agriculture, who was the catalyst behind the reform movement. Reform would prove difficult because the Soviets began sending mixed signals regarding what constituted acceptable policy. During the Khrushchev era internal power-plays within the Kremlin would result in erratic Soviet foreign policy. Hungarian politicians were allowed to begin reform but then would be reined in sharply as Soviet policy shifted.

In 1953 the Hungarian Premier Rakosi, was forced to stepdown. Over the course of the next two years Nagy was put in charge of the administration. His work was an attempt to de-Sovietize Hungary. In particular, Nagy tried to encourage political pluralism and a radical reorientation of foreign policy. These moves were watched nervously in Moscow and in March 1955 the Kremlin had Nagy forcibly removed. Two Kremlin-approved successors came and went quickly. Eventually, in July 1956 a pro-Stalinist, Erno Gero, became leader of the Hungarian Party, replacing Rokosi, who had held the post after stepping down as Premier.

The Soviets reactionary behaviour stimulated calls for a popular uprising. The stage was set for mass demonstrations. Beginning in Budapest in October 1956, crowds as large as 200,000 strong gathered in front of the Parliament building. What started as an anti-Soviet demonstration soon grew to a movement that demanded Nagy's return and the continuation of parliamentary reforms. Nagy was not himself a particularly radical person. He remained a communist and was from a poor rural background. The plight of the less well-off continued to be his concern, but unlike many Hungarian dissidents he continued to believe that the solution would be found in communism. However, his vision of communism did not include violence, repression and incarceration. It was his move away from the Soviet Union, especially his declaration of Hungary's independence from the Warsaw Pact, that was to bring down the weight of the Soviet military.

Soviet troops invaded Hungary occuping Budapest on 4 November 1956. The troops took over the government and arrested Nagy. Both he and the other members of the government were taken back to Russia and were coerced into signing a confession of treason. They were then hung in June 1958. Two thousand others would be killed and an additional 20,000 incarcerated as the Soviet Union attempted to stamp out any remaining resistance to their rule. A taboo on even mentioning Nagy's name remained until the 1980s. No one, without fear of reprisal, could admit that Nagy had stood for a political reform movement that championed greater democracy and accountability. The Soviet version had branded Nagy as a counter-revolutionary and a usurper.

The 1956 invasion and its political repercussions were to have an enormous impact on Hungary's political culture. It was the single most important event for Hungarians in the post-war era. As a result, one of the first orders of business after the collapse of the Soviet Union was the rehabilitation of Imre Nagy on 16 June 1989.

6.2 Events leading up to 1989

Immediately following the 1956 uprising, the political climate grew more oppressive. However, many hoped that some sort of eventual reform would come about. It was not just Hungarians who fought against the 1956 Soviet invasion. In fact, over a thousand Russian soldiers deserted the Soviet army and fought with the Hungarian revolutionaries (Wollner,

1995). Lack of benefits and accountability had already begun to take its toll on the entire Soviet system.

Janos Kadar[1] took over the Hungarian government after Nagy's removal. He became the Secretary of the renamed Hungarian Socialist Workers' Party. Under his leadership, a highly repressive clean-up operation was carried out which led to the execution or imprisonment of the majority of those responsible for the 1956 revolution. Following this political clampdown, He decided that some form of conciliation was needed. Kadar was not interested in undermining his own position nor did he want to attract the attention once again of the Soviet Union. Political reform was, therefore, out of the question. However, some scope did remain for a form of cultural and economic reform. Furthermore, the Communist Party itself needed to increase its legitimacy if it was to survive. When the party was restructured in December 1956 it retained only 12 per cent of the former party members. (Toma and Volgyes, 1977: 31)

In 1961, Kadar and his party began to introduce a slightly more relaxed regime. Police intrusion lessened and as did the strict regulations on changing professions. Kadar's policy was designed to encourage apathy. His famous quote 'he who is not against us, is with us' suggests that he was satisfied to relax restrictions provided that the population did not come out against his government (Swain, 1993: 67). During the early 1960s, Kadar's government created a 'social compact' and came to an arrangement with the Soviet Union. Basically Kadar was able to trade loyalty to the Soviet Union abroad with greater freedom to experiment at home. Unfortunately, this meant that Hungary did send troops to join the Soviet Army when it invaded Czechoslovakia in 1968.

Part of this new internal freedom was the New Economic Mechanism (NEM), which came into force in January 1968. This had grown out of the deliberation that began in the 1964 Plenum of the Central Committee of the Party. Basically this committee was looking at ways of introducing comprehensive reform. In order to avoid political conflict those working on reform treated economic development as a technical problem and avoided discussing the ideological implications of the changes they were suggesting (Richet, 1981: 26). The result was a move away from the previous strict governmental control of the economy. Sector decisions were taken out of the hands of ministries and devolved down to the level of manager. In addition, state farms were given greater individual freedom to become autonomous co-operatives rather than being directly controlled by the government. The manufacturing economy was also given some freedom to produce goods other than those from heavy manufacturing. The Soviet Union had pushed Hungary into developing a heavy industrial sector even though she had few natural resources for this type of industry and subsequently had to import the majority of the necessary raw materials from Russia and the other Soviet Republics.

With the arrival of the NEM the idea of market-driven prices became accepted. Indeed, the freeing of the economy soon began to show dividends. As in Poland the idea of the dual compromise, which traded lack of political representation for greater economic prosperity, seemed to be working. For the next 5 years growth in the national income would rise by almost 7 per cent a year (Gerner, 1985: 97–8). Had Hungary continued along this path of slow economic reform it might have found itself in a rather strong economic situation in 1989. Unfortunately hard-liners in the Party disapproved of the new 'liberties'. During 1972–73 they exerted pressure to have the reforms rescinded. Their timing could not have been worse in the sense that their desire to impede the development of Hungary's burgeoning private sector coincided with the oil price shocks of December 1973. There followed a re-introduction of direct government controls over state-owned enterprises and an increase in government subsidies as well as tariff protection. However, Hungary remained dependent on the international market for oil. Notwithstanding Russia's plentiful oil supply it insisted on selling it to Comecon members at current international market prices. Moreover, it would only accept a portion of the oil payment in the 'soft' Comecon currencies, the rest having to be paid for in US dollars. In 1974, the man largely responsible for the design of the NEM, Rezso Nyers, was dismissed. The financial prognosis for Hungary was not good. The dearth of forward-looking strategy in Hungarian economic policy led to a large increase in the country's trade deficit, which in turn forced the government to borrow money in order to be able to subsidize state companies. This caused a serious deterioration in Hungary's terms of trade, which saw the balance-of-payments level drop by 20 per cent between 1973 and 1980 (Gerner, 1985: 99). It was a downward spiral that would leave Hungary with a gross external debt of over US$11 billion by the early 1980s (EIU Country Profile, *Hungary*, 1996: 3). Lack of confidence in the government became increasingly obvious. In 1976, a survey was carried out which revealed that if there had been free elections in Hungary the results would have given the Social Democrats 42 per cent, Christian-Democrats 27 per cent, a peasant party 17 per cent,

Conservatives 6 per cent, and the Communists 5 per cent (Kovrig, 1979: 430). At the grassroots level there was clearly very little support for the government in power.

The struggle between the devolution of economic control and its subsequent recentralization characterized much of the 1980s in Hungary. Starting in 1978 an austerity programme was launched which attempted to cut down the need for foreign borrowing. However, the second oil shock of 1979 increased pressure on Hungary and a series of austerity programmes came and went between 1980 and 1988. After 1980 industrial wholesale prices were based on the import cost, and the subsidization of domestic foodstuffs decreased. State-owned restaurants were leased to private individuals and private shops were permitted. In 1982 Hungary became a member of the IMF, the WB and the EBRD. Coincidentally, the current Vice-President of the EBRD is Miklos Nemeth, the Hungarian Prime Minister from 1988 to 1990 who was instrumental in opening Hungary's borders with the West. He left his party after losing the 1990 elections, and took the EBRD vice-president's post (Bozoki and Lomax, 1996: 191).

Hungary's move away from communism occurred earlier than Poland and the Czech Republic's. By 1985, Hungary had developed a private sector and although the government remained socialist its philosophy was closer to Western European socialism, than to Soviet communism. It was a far cry from many centrally controlled economies in the CEECs. In 1980–81 legislation was passed reducing the number of ministries. During this period small-scale semi-private businesses were actually encouraged. By 1982, even the government itself was making self-criticism. Hungary's Foreign Minister at the time, Frigyes Puja, stated that economic relations with the West should not only be improved, but that foreign participation should be encouraged (Puja, 1983: 9). The head of the Institute for World Economy of the Hungarian Academy of Science, Jozsef Bognar, went even further pointing out that Hungary's acclimatization to the non-socialist world went beyond the purely economic, since it involved a growing change to Hungary's cultural and social structure (Bognar, 1982: 34). Increased political awareness continued to stimulate political debate. In 1986 a meeting was held in Lakitelek, which was attended by populist writers, economists and historians. A number of reform-minded members of the party also attended this meeting. Kadar's consensus-building was beginning to dissolve. Many institutions were beginning to demonstrate their independence and even members of the party seemed uninterested in preserving party unity.

6.3 Collapse of communism

By 1987 discontent had started to become organized. A reform wing of the Party and other social groups banded together to form the Patriotic Peoples' Front (PPF). This group was an umbrella organization for groups and individuals who wanted reform. Debt continued to be a problem, doubling between 1977 and 1979, and doubling again between 1985 and 1987. This gave Hungary the dubious honour of having the highest per capita debt in the whole Central European region (Swain, 1993: 68). Strain was showing at all levels of economic activity. Research and development (R&D) suffered as lack of revenue caused across the board cuts in research. Product development was cut by the same amount without reference to any type of selection process. By the late 1980s calls for a more focused policy toward R&D investment was made, but by that time it was already too late (Balazs, 1994: 283).

The situation seemed to call for a new direction. The PPF sponsored their Secretary-General, Imre Pazsgay, to write a discussion paper. The paper was entitled 'Turn and Reform' (1987) and suggested a complete refurbishment of the Hungarian economy. More importantly, the paper made a direct link between economic reform and the need to move towards economic pluralism. A second meeting of the populists was held at Lakitelek in September 1987 and there the Hungarian Democratic Front (HDF) was formed.

The government did make attempts at this time to introduce incremental economic reform. The banking system was reformed in 1987 to allow for competitive banking rather than having one state-run bank. By 1988 personal income tax and value-added taxes were adopted. The difficulty remained, however, that the only part of the economy which seemed to be flourishing was the liberalized small-scale industrial sector. Hungary was seen as one of the most progressive of the communist countries during the 1980s, but this could not be attributed to its government. In fact, the sectors that were successful were in areas where government had relinquished a portion, or all, of management control.

Many Hungarians had to work for a private firm or in the black market, in addition to their state job, in order to make ends meet. Some took on two jobs, but numerous people had three. Despite this, real wages continued to decline and dropped 10 per cent between 1979 and 1984. This situation was the breeding-ground for dissatisfaction and despondency. Hungarian social scientists during this period became aware of a noticeable drop in the belief of solidarity. Hungarians began to speak more in terms of the individual than the group. After 1986 it seems the population began to lose faith in the government's ability to achieve socialist targets or even deal successfully with economic problems (Swain, 1992: 7–32).

The time seemed ripe for reform. Janos Kadar, celebrated his 75th birthday in 1987 and it became obvious that he could not remain much longer as the leader of the Hungarian Socialist Workers' Party for much longer. Young members of the party had grown up under the more liberal regime of the later Kadar and did not carry the same fear as those that had lived through the 1956 uprising and the purges that followed. They were to become a strong force for change. Over the course of the first few months of 1988, these changes began to be apparent. Karoly Grosz, who had become the Chairman of the Council of Ministers in 1987, was nominally in control of the party. However, the moves towards reform had placed him in an awkward situation between the reformers of the party, on the one hand, and the Hungarian politburo, which was still headed by Kadar, on the other. He began to lose control as demonstrations became frequent. On 15 March 1988 over 10,000 people marched through Budapest to celebrate the 140th anniversary of the 1848 uprising against Austrian rule, and used the opportunity to demand the initiation of real reform. The underground free press started to openly distribute their publications. A radical youth party was established in April 1988 called the Federation of Young Democrats (FYD) (Rady, 1994: 327–8).

The FYD, together with other groups trying to effect democratic change, banded together into a confederation named the Network of Free Initiatives. This coalition was quickly renamed the Alliance of Free Democrats, and they soon began to demand democratic reform. The party conservatives were still not ready to relinquish their control of power. Kadar during a March 1988 meeting of the Central Committee managed to get the Committee to agree to slow down the pace of reform. This had the effect of splitting the Party even further causing the expulsion of four Party members who would not agree to the retrenchment. Even at this stage, despite his age, Kadar thought he could control the Hungarian executive and remove the impetus for change by supplying a few concessions to the reformers. However, the days were gone when Kadar could regain popularity by easing the rationing of salami (1979) or allowing the sale of perfumed soap in Hungarian shops (1980). Opposition became even more noticeable when members of the Communist Party refused to renew their membership cards when they came up for renewal. By the early months of 1988, 45,000 party members had not renewed their memberships representing a full 6 per cent of the total (Rady, 1994: 328). The party conference of May 1988, forced Kadar out of the executive and kicked him upstairs with the honorary post of Chairman of the Party. Even this token was taken from him in 1989. He died 3 months later.

The new power-brokers were lead by a team of four: (1) Rezso Nyers, the architect of the scuttled NEM; (2) Imre Pozsgay, the former secretary-general of the PPF; (3) Miklos Nemeth, the liberal secretary of the party's central committee (1987–88); and Gyula Horn, who would soon become Prime Minister. All these men had been involved with the past regime in one way or another. The reason Hungary's transition to democracy and a free-market was so peaceful was because the reformers had been part of the old political machine and were themselves destined to be part of the new regime. They were a group of technocratic modernizers, cut from a very different cloth than the former communist ideological revolutionaries. While Polish reformers were ideologically committed to the ideal of liberal capitalist democracy, the same could not be said of Hungarian reformers. The arguments used by the reformers centred on the 'inefficiency' of the Hungarian political system in the modern world, rather than the need to introduce liberal values. Democracy was only accepted as necessary in so far as Hungary was expected to be able to compete in the global market place (Bozoki and Lomax, 1996: 190). The technocratic attitude towards the transition seemed to diminish the anti-socialist backlash experience by most other countries in the region. The credibility of ideas such as 'socialism' were never to disappear from the Hungarian political scene and in the 1994 election parties professing socialist or social democratic values were to get over a third of the popular vote.

6.4 The new regime: privatization, investment and government policy

Similar to many countries in transition, the majority of those involved in stimulating change in 1989 were to find themselves defeated by the very system they created. Change in Hungary did not occur in a vacuum. The changes in Poland in particular gave Hungarian policy makers the confidence to exert their own independence from the Soviet Union. The situation in Hungary in 1989 was substantially different from that of 1956. The Soviet Union was not only allowing change but also in some cases actually encouraging it. Gorbachev, in particular, was very supportive of the reformers in the Hungarian communist party. Imre

Pozsgay, in a bold political move, announced in January 1989 that what had happened in 1956 was not a 'counter-revolution' but a 'popular uprising'. His announcement broke a political taboo that Hungarians had to live with for a generation. Moreover there were no reprisals from the Soviet Union. In negotiations between the reformist communists and the opposition, a consensus was soon reached. On 11 February 1989, the central committee of the Party announced that Hungary would henceforth be a multi-party democracy. By March of the same year they were preparing to participate in a coalition government (Swain, 1993: 71). An Opposition Round Table was created by a body which referred to itself as the Forum of Independent Lawyers, who banded together with eight opposition organisations. On 13 June 1989 the party leadership agreed to negotiate with the Opposition Round Table and three days later the bones of Imre Nagy were disinterred from the common graveyard they have been flung 31 years earlier, and given a hero's burial. Although there would be months of heated negotiation and free elections would not be held until March 1990, for many Hungarians it was the rehabilitation of Imre Nagy and his public funeral that marked the true beginning of political freedom in their country.

During the summer of 1989, the communist party thought that it would still be able to maintain the benefits that it had gained during its long reign simply by setting up a coalition government. However, the Free Democrats and the Young Democrats refused to sign the final political agreement until a referendum had been held as to whether the communist party should be allowed to keep its properties, workplace branches and militia. There were also disagreements over how the president should be chosen. The Free Democrats and the Young Democrats were successful in their bid for a referendum which was held just after the fall of the Berlin Wall in November 1989. The results were very clear cut, with over 95 per cent of the population in favour of disbanding the Party's properties. This event put an end to the reformist communists and the hopes of Imre Pozsgay. The Hungarian Socialist Workers' Party attempted to burnish its image by changing its name to the HSP and handing over its property and militia to the state. Pozsgay remained a strong force in the party but the actual leader was Rezso Nyers. Despite its skilful handling of the negotiations with the Soviet Union for the removal of troops, the HSP was not destined to be the successful party in the 1990 elections, which was won by an alliance of the Hungarian Democratic Forum, Alliance of Free Democrats, Independent Smallholders' Party, Christian Democratic People's Party and the Federation of Young Democrats. The HSP only managed to obtain 8.5 per cent of the popular vote. Many thought that this would mean the death of the party. In 1994, however, they staged a remarkable comeback when they won 54 per cent of the vote and retook office. This result was to a large extent due to popular worries created by the economic transition.

For the new government the economy was one of the most pressing problems it faced. Given its economy policy advantages, Hungary should have advanced ahead of many of the other countries during the transition period. Hungary had been trading internationally for decades, and since 1968 a certain level of privatization had been allowed to exist. The autonomy of many state managers had also created home-grown Hungarian entrepreneurs. A good example here was the creation of Fotex. Originally created in 1985 to process film, it soon became a large public firm with a chain of film developing stores, optical outlets, crystal stores and a crystal factory. By 1994 it was one of the most prominent Hungarian firms and its stock was regularly traded on the Budapest Stock Exchange (Lane, 1995: 183). Although Hungary was exposed to capitalism earlier than some of its Central and Eastern neighbours, it was not to produce the results one might have expected. Despite Hungary's ranking as one of three likeliest contenders for EU membership, alongside Poland and the Czech Republic, it does not outperform its neighbours.

In part, Hungary's economic malaise in the early 1990s was somewhat similar to that of Poland and the Czech Republic in the sense that it suffered from debt, restructuring and a loss of trade with its former patron, the Soviet Union. This does not, however, explain everything. The answer may lie in the increased sophistication and independence of both its political groups and private entrepreneurs. Where Poland had been quite 'led' by the policies of Jeffrey Sachs and were keen to please the IMF, Hungary was more independent and its policy makers had their own vision of how the transition should be conducted. Hungary is one of the few countries in the former eastern bloc that did not go for a 'shock therapy' model of mass privatization. Neo-liberalism was not as accepted in Hungary as it has elsewhere in the region. It is likely that Hungary's independent policy-making and continued commitment to social values affected the IMF's decision to give Poland debt relief but not Hungary.

The Hungarian elections of 25 March 1990 were to produce a government headed by Josef Antall. The new government was a coalition of a centre-right persuasion who were committed to converting Hungary into a market economy. The term Antall actually used was 'social market economy'. His vision was of private ownership and enterprise coupled with the continuation of decent social benefits. His method was in the early stages not dissimilar to the Czech and Polish experiences. He created a separate bureaucracy, the State Property Agency (SPA), to deal with the privatization process. The task for Hungary was particularly daunting. Despite Hungary's track record of allowing private companies to operate, the state-maintained control of up to 85 per cent of GDP. In comparison, the average for OECD countries would be approximately 15 per cent. The establishment of the SPA in March 1990 was also done to alleviate public fears over the practice of spontaneous privatizations, where former party functionaries would cede ownership of state property to themselves or in combination with a foreign buyer. An especially glaring example would be the Hungar Hotels deal in 1989–90 where the properties were sold into foreign hands at below market value prices (Meaney, 1995: 299).

Curiously, the impetus for privatization in Hungary did not come from government as much as from the managers of state enterprises. The method of privatization resembled much more the British style of case-by-case privatization. This is a much slower process than mass or voucher privatization which was popular in other CEECs such as Poland and the Czech Republic. Those privatization's that were manager-led often resulted in an enterprise not being wholly privatized. Quite often foreign partners would be brought in to purchase a share of the company while the government might retain majority ownership.

The SPA has a managing director and an 11-member board of directors appointed to 5-year terms by the prime minister. It has been given approval for all enterprises with more than 1,000 employees. The SPA is headed up by a minister without portfolio and is not officially considered a ministry. An annual report must by submitted by the SPA to the parliament who in turn establishes the guidelines and policies of the SPA (Frydman *et al.*, 1993: 128).

Out of all the Central European privatization organizations, Hungary's was the least dominated by foreign nationals. Whereas Poland's MOP had foreigners as 50 per cent of its staff, Hungary's SPA had very few. There were no 'young Americans' or returned US-educated Poles dominating policy prescriptions with regards to privatization. The Harvard-style teams invited into many of the other transition countries were not so invited by Hungary. There was a foreign presence in Hungary, but its influence was much more muted than in Poland. Deloitte Touche, the international accounting firm did help in the conception of the SPA and they also provided some training courses funded through USAID. Nevertheless, unlike Poland and the Czech Republic, only one American worked in the SPA during the whole of 1992 (Meaney, 1995: 301).

The SPA agenda does not fit the neo-liberal mould of privatization. It basically had three activities. First, it was to induce a programme of 'active privatization' in which it was supposed to privatize 20 of the most profitable state companies. This unfortunately never occurred in the way planned and by 1992 the majority of these companies had not been privatized. Secondly, the SPA was to act as a watchdog organization, stopping the shady deals that went with 'spontaneous' privatizations. And, thirdly it was to facilitate 'self-privatization' which was basically trying to bring together domestic and foreign companies to encourage joint ventures.

After 1992 there was concern that the privatization process was stagnating. This concern back by a growing concern with regards to FDI. Although the government was not particularly successful in converting public companies into private ones, this did not mean that foreign influence was not occurring in a private capacity. The growth in the Hungarian economy had been stimulated by the small and medium-sized firms which had begun growing in the mid-1980s. There were restrictions on the amount of employees these firms could hire, restrictions which were removed during the transition process. The growth in the number of businesses skyrocketed. But the rise in private property and foreign joint venture companies had little to do with the government-led privatization process. It was the existence of an already partially developed business class that facilitated this indigenous growth, and in turn attracted foreign investment. By 1989 alone, the number of limited liability companies grew by 894.5 per cent and the following year the number of businesses rose by 103.9 per cent (Lane, 1995: 183). Much of this growth was initiated by the setting-up of foreign companies or mergers of already private companies with foreign partners. It is interesting that although Hungary did not adopt the 'shock therapy' prescribed to its neighbours, it received about half of the entire region's FDI (Gowan, 1995: 14). Despite Hungary's lack of commitment to neo-liberal ideas it continued to keep up its payments to creditors and, therefore, continued to be considered by Western lending institutions as a stable country.

The most difficult transition year for Hungary was 1991. The government introduced austerity measures during 1990–91 which occurred at a time of rapidly prices. The result was social and industrial protests. Hungary had to buy its stability by keeping social payments high during this time of transition. The drop in industrial activity of all kinds was taking its toll and the government did not want to reduce subsidies or social welfare payments. These payments were generous compared to Poland, and enhanced Hungary's stability, but they also depleted government revenue at a particularly difficult time. The unemployment rate went from virtually nil to 7 per cent by late 1991 and, even though production everywhere was in decline, the inflation rate jumped 34 per cent. At the same time, the government's deficit rose to 53,100 million forints (in 1994 US$1 = 105 forints) (Rady, 1994: 330). The forint was causing problems because the government had not yet made it fully convertible despite its commitment to reform. Problems with currency convertibility were common throughout the CEECs during the early years of the transition.

Certain members of the government grew frustrated with the slow progress of reform. As with all coalition governments there were strong splits over policy. There were those favouring a quick 'jump' to the market and those who wanted the pace to be incremental. At the end of 1990 one of the top economic advisers of Antall's government, Gyorgy Matolcsy, announced his resignation. He was frustrated that the government did not take his advice and implement a rapid programme of privatization. His criticisms were warranted in the sense that the government had promised privatization, but by June 1992 only 8.3 per cent of state-owned firms had made the transfer from public to private hands. Enterprises that had been sold tended to be purchased by foreign companies through stock issued by the government. The government attempted to handle the criticism of its progress by creating a State Assets Handling Company in 1992. It was hoped that this new entity would deal with state enterprises. The power struggle continued, however, as ministers of finance came and went. In January 1993 Mihaly Kupa took over as Finance Minister and in March announced the introduction of a Czech-like voucher system in an attempt to transfer the stock of state-run industries into private hands (Rady, 1994: 330).

But, the Antall government was in a no-win situation. The demands for change and greater privatization would mean a reduction in subsidies to industry. However, by doing this the government would cause plant closures and unemployment. The fear was that plant closures would be numerous and widespread. In some cases, the bulk of a given industrial sector would disappear. A solution was needed which would offer alternative and private forms of employment. The government tried to facilitate this by establishing a privatization loan scheme in 1992. Loans to the amount of 100,000 forints (US$1,150) were made available to individuals to allow them to purchase shares in outlets that were being privatized (Berry, 1994: 334). Individuals who obtained shares in this way would not be allowed to sell his/her shares until after the loan had been repaid in full. This scheme was done in conjunction with the voucher privatization programme. In addition, the government offered credit at reasonable rates for people interested in taking over state enterprises. In Poland, national policy-makers had been very against any suggestion of employee buy-outs, but this was not the case in Hungary. Alongside the other government schemes, an Employee Stock Ownership Programme was initiated. Unfortunately, new businesses tended to be small and were not capable of absorbing the unemployment caused by the closures of government enterprises.

Regardless of how well each of the schemes was conceived, the problem of a lack of domestic capital remained. Average Hungarian citizens had little money with which to purchase shares and even if they had been given loans many would not, in the short term, have had the funds to repay them. Even though this sector of the Hungarian economy was buoyant, the rate of retail privatization was slow. Many retail shops were run by private individuals who would have a licence from the government permitting their activity. When store managers were given the opportunity to purchase their store, most managers did not have adequate capital to make the purchase. It took an increase in consumer activity to create the funds needed. This explains why the service sector in Hungary did not pick up until 1992. The years 1990–91 had been ones of relative decline as Hungary suffered through the worst part of its transition. However, increased activity in 1992 helped those in the service industry acquire the capital they needed. An unexpected boost came from the increase in foreign tourism. Budapest, in particular, became a much sought-after tourist destination and visitors brought with them what Hungary desperately needed, hard currency. In 1992, tourism was one of the biggest earners of convertible hard currency with over US$1.2 billion coming into country. Tourism, therefore, accounted for 5.6 per cent of Hungary's annual 1992 GDP, which was US$20.9 billion. This was good news for retail and catering units, 9 per cent of which were privatized in 1992, in part because of the availability of extra foreign money (Berry, 1994: 334). The Hungarian economic landscape soon began to change dramatically. In 1993, the private sector was said to have accounted for 50 per cent of the Hungarian GDP. Small and medium firms dominated the private sector as private firms grew from 15,000 to 900,000 by 1993 (Balazs, 1994: 285). In practice this meant that much of the Hungarian economy was being run by novice business people with fledgling management skills and short-term goals.

Although foreign currency acquired through tourism was helpful in contributing to the national current accounts, it did not deal with the still existing problem of restructuring the Hungarian economy. Political tensions mounted over economic performance and would result in the Antall government losing the 1994 election. Social groups were disappointed with the negative aspects of the transition such as crime, unemployment and decreasing standards in health and education. Liberals, however, were disappointed with the lack of progress towards a functioning market economy. When the ballots had been counted in the May 1994 elections, the communist HSP had won 54 per cent of the seats in parliament giving it an absolute majority. The return of the HSP had much to do with the fact that they had no part in the unpopular policies put through by Antall's government. Four years in the wilderness had allowed the HSP not only to criticize government policy but also to give them the opportunity to redefine themselves. Popular Hungarian pessimism towards the privatization process gave the HSP a chance to develop a political platform that would attract votes. Their slogan of 'transition with a human face' was well received by the populace. The hardship caused by the transition process made many Hungarians less concerned with what the HSP had stood for in the past, as long as they stood for a kinder future. Once in office, however, the HSP would find the task of governing difficult. The Hungarian Democratic Forum (HDF) coalition had left behind a legacy of unfinished business. Part of HDF's troubles stemmed from their lack of a clear economic strategy. Moreover, political consensus on the transition process had never been achieved and many social groups simply felt alienated from the whole process, as the popular saying in Budapest went, 'today is worse than yesterday, but better than tomorrow' (Barony, 1995: 68). This summed up how many felt about the economic changes which had taken place between 1990 and 1995.

6.5 The results thus far

Despite Hungary's good record with regards to FDI, it did not survive the transition process unscathed. Throughout the 1980s the Hungarian industrial sector was underfunded and the general structure of the economy, with its dependence on raw materials from outside, was very vulnerable to regional shocks (Balazs, 1994: 285). Industrial production in 1990–93, fell by approximately 30 per cent. Those enterprises with more than 50 employees were particularly hard hit with their production dropping by around 40 per cent. The destruction of state-owned heavy industry was striking. Over a period of three years Hungarian heavy industry was to decrease by 75 per cent. The effect was felt throughout the country as half of the coal mines were closed, the steel industry reduced to a third of its former size and the heavy chemical industry bankrupted (Bossanyi, 1995: 94).

The industrial sector was not the only economic casualty. Agriculture would also be affected by the changes. Hungary's plains are among the most fertile in the world. Agriculture, even after its Soviet-style collectivization remained an important sector and suffered during the transition. Once the Soviet market disappeared post-1989, many Hungarian farms were left with huge surpluses. In livestock alone farms were left in 1991 with 200,000 surplus animals for market (Berry, 1994: 332). Moreover, this sector was not to be helped by the early move towards trade with the EU. Under the European Agreements the one area not covered was agriculture. The EU was trying to deal with its own surplus produce caused by the Common Agricultural Policy (CAP). It was, therefore, reluctant to allow low-priced Hungarian agricultural produce into the already saturated European market.

The collapse of trade with the former Soviet Union was to cause a 40 per cent drop in all exports between 1990 and 1993. Hungary had already made the decision in 1990 that trade with Comecon countries would no longer be done in roubles but in US dollars. This measure was devastating. It soon became obvious that the former Soviet Union did not have access to sufficient amounts of hard currency to pay for its imports. Russia, in particular, could no longer afford to purchase goods from Central Europe if the exchange was to be based on US dollars. This market had traditionally accounted for approximately half of Hungary's exports. The decline spiralled as investment in the national economy decreased by 23 per cent during the period 1989–93. In an attempt to increase trade, the government continued to liberalize border measures. There was an increase in Hungarian exports going to OECD countries with the EU countries showing the largest increase. However, with the increased exports came increased imports. Hungarian's were very interested in acquiring goods from the West. It became fashionable for the *nouveau riche* to drive across to Austria and purchase large quantities of consumer goods to bring back home. Those Hungarians that did not travel were keen to purchase foreign imports at home, and despite food surpluses in Hungary, many preferred to purchase packaged foreign foodstuffs. In 1991 the trade deficit was a serious concern at 91 billion

Table 6.1 Registered Unemployed in Hungary, 1990–94

Hungary	1990	1991	1992	1993	1994
No. of registered unemployed	24,000	158,000	449,000	620,000	580,000

Source: Katalin Bossanyi, 1995: 97.

forints, however, the figure continue to mushroom and by 1993 it grew to 342 billion forints.

The collapse of industrial and other types of production, combined with a serious trade deficit, translated into a large increase in unemployment. Levels of employment declined by 20 per cent during 1990–1991 suggesting a loss of 1.1 million jobs. Privatized companies were growing in number, but still employment lagged behind. During this time 25 per cent of those employed worked in the private sector and by 1995 over half the population was employed in non-public companies. Despite this, employment continued to decline.

The figures in Table 6.1 show the rapid rise in unemployment but this is not the complete picture. Although the official unemployment rate in 1994 was approximately 14 per cent the actual figure is thought to be much higher. This figure only takes into account those who are officially registered, and does not include new graduates who cannot find work but are ineligible for benefit. Also past employees of collapsed industries have little hope of employment. However, they do not remain on the unemployment register. Instead their local authority becomes responsible, and gives them a small living stipend. In addition there are a substantial amount of women who find it difficult to re-enter the workforce after child-rearing, but are not considered unemployed. The actual unemployment figure is thought to be around 1 million people, or put another way, double the official figure.

Many Hungarians, being frustrated with their loss of earning power in the formal sector, have turned to the informal sector (black economy). This hidden economy has become an increasing force in Hungary. Estimates in 1994 suggest that almost a third of the Hungarian GDP could be ascribed to the informal sector. The growth in this sector can be explained by an increase in levels of unemployment and a decrease in the standard of living. Between 1990 and 1993 the real wages in Hungary contracted by 12 per cent. Levels of poverty throughout Hungary increased dramatically during this time. In 1989 only 8 per cent of the population was living below the subsistence level, but this rose to

16 per cent in 1992. Reports in 1993 estimated that 2 million people were living in these conditions. Over 25 per cent of the population were to drop below the subsistence level during 1994. By 1995 one-third of the population was experiencing poverty (Bossanyi, 1995: 94).

The ageing nature of Hungary's population placed an increasing burden on this society in transition. While Hungary's workforce is about 4.2 million (including the unemployed) the number of old age pensioners is 2.9 million. With the drop in wages and the insecurity of the job market it is increasingly difficult for those working to be able to make enough revenue to support their grandparents, or generate enough tax revenue for the government to cover the costs of caring for the elderly. The result has often been poverty for the aged. It is lamentable that senior citizens, who managed to survive Stalinism, the 1956 uprising and communist oppression, must now live out their final years without proper financial security.

Tension continues to grow as problems with the availability of work, the increase in prices and the cost of services cause severe societal stratification. While two-thirds of the population have restrictive means the top third have seen their income rise rapidly. The top 10 per cent in particular have done very well out of the transition. On average the top 10 per cent earn seven times more than the 10 per cent on the bottom (Bossanyi, 1995: 96). The level of corruption is also an issue. Some of the newly rich have not come by their wealth honestly. Organized crime is a problem and a number of individuals from the old regime were able to gain control of state assets and have it transferred, in part, to themselves or other insiders.

The decline in wealth for the bottom two-thirds of society can be partially attributed to the acceleration of inflation. Soaring inflation, especially on foodstuffs, and a decrease in real earnings created a recipe for increasing poverty. The Hungarian inflation rate in 1989 was high at 17 per cent, but this was to almost double and in 1991 the inflation rate was 34.9 per cent. The government was truly concerned about their lack of control over macro-economic indicators. There had been a lenient policy toward the exchange of forints throughout 1990 and 1992. After this the worries, regarding inflation and Hungary's ability to manage its debt with such high inflation, spawned a stronger policy toward control of the money supply. Over the last few years Hungary has undertaken periodic devaluations as well as a sliding devaluation in an attempt to stabilize its currency and control inflation. The forint saw a drop in value of 40 per cent compared to a 'basket' of foreign currencies during spring 1994 and 1995 (Bossanyi, 1995: 97).

Hungary, similar to pre-1993 Poland, found itself in a difficult political and economic situation. Civil unrest was threatening. Strikes and demonstrations were fairly common. Many Hungarians felt that the transition process was leaving them behind. The majority win for the HSP was a testament to this dissatisfaction. Having said this, it was difficult for the former coalition government to maintain debt repayment and finance the transition. It was a situation that the HSP could also not ignore. In 1995, debt servicing accounted for 30 per cent of Hungary's budget expenditure. Since the early 1990s domestic debt, used mostly to finance the budget deficit, has tripled (Bossanyi, 1995: 98).

The HSP having won on a ticket that pledged greater support for those who were disadvantaged by the transition, has had to rescind its election promise. The declining revenues and increase in debt servicing made it unlikely that the government could fulfil its election promises. Since the May 1994 election the living standards of those on fixed incomes have dropped repeatedly. The government in a bid to cut budget expenditures introduced a number of changes to the tax code. State support was cut from programmes that helped young families, large families, and those on long-term assistance. The Prime Minister Gyula Horn, was not eager to put in place reforms that would harm the very group his government had pledged to protect. In March 1995 the liberal economist, Laszlo Bekesi, the finance minister, resigned over his governments unwillingness to deal with the economic crisis. His replacement, Lajos Bokros, was less economically radical than his predecessor. However, over the course of the next year the current account deficit continued to grow and became even more unmanageable. The government brought in a new stabilization programme which further deteriorated tax breaks and subsidies to poor families and university students. The trade union movement, who had supported the HSP during the election, were disappointed at the governments change in policy.

The cost of governing continued to soar and in the first quarter of 1995 the deficit grew to US$1,420 million (Richter, 1996: 60). The trade deficit also grew over this period as imports rose by 18 per cent. Although exports increased by 11 per cent this still left a trade deficit of US$1,545 million (Website: Business Europa Briefing, 8 January 1996). Finance Minister Bokros, tabled a series of austerity measures intended to cut social spending in an attempt to regain control of the budget. However, the Hungarian Constitutional Court ruled the austerity measures as unconstitutional, which further embarrassed the government. In conjunction with these occurrences the IMF discontinued negotiations with Hungary regarding new funding, during September 1996.

The IMF complained that Hungary needed to control its budget deficit and that it would not consider lending more money to Hungary until it had proved capable of controlling its spending.

The government at this stage was in serious need of revenue and began to reform its method and level of taxation. In Hungary, social security contributions are already quite high. Employees contribute 14 per cent of their salary and employers contribute an additional 44 per cent therefore, there was very little room to manoeuvre. The government, instead, chose to look at income tax reform. It is proposed that the zero tax rate for low income families would be abolished and they would have to contribute a portion of their income. Alongside this development is the plan to reduce income tax for those in the highest income tax bracket. Tax reform will also not include the taxation of revenue from interest. The Hungarian government, in its attempt to placate the IMF and international financial institutes has had to put aside its commitment to people in the lowest income bracket.

In March 1995 the Hungarian government put in measures to try to control inflation and debt. There was a 9 per cent devaluation of the forint, and a crawling peg exchange rate management system. An import surcharge of 8 per cent was levied against goods coming into Hungary and businesses were permitted to open foreign exchange accounts in local banks to be used for export receipts (Richter, 1996: 60). This did have the effect of reducing the deficit and by October–November the budget was getting close to being balanced. It was not only the extra revenue from the import surcharges but also the government's tight control on civil service salaries that kept the budget in check. Professionals in higher education also suffered job cuts and salary reductions. In Hungary the civil service and higher education are two of the lowest paid 'white collar' sectors.

Hungary, again like Poland, was rewarded by the international economic community for introducing stricter neo-liberal economic measures. Hungary also attempted to signal its desire for greater foreign investment by agreeing to let foreign companies open their own branches, as opposed to purchasing shares in Hungarian companies, by 1998. In March 1996 the IMF approved a standby loan for Hungary. It was approved for a 2-year period and consisted of US$387 million. The loan was contingent on Hungary keeping its social security spending under control and the national deficit under 4 per cent. In reality, this proved difficult for Hungary. The loan requirements expected that Hungary's monthly crawling peg devaluation would see the forint devalued by 1.2 per cent a month. Similarly there was an expectation under the terms of the agreement that the inflation rate would drop below 20 per cent and that 'real' energy prices would be introduced by 1997 (Website: The Hungary Report, 18 March 1996). Moreover, the money put up by the IMF was never designed to be spent, so it will not be available to Hungary as extra revenue. The purpose of the loan was to demonstrate the IMF's faith in Hungary's current economic policy, thereby, backing Hungary's application to join the OECD. On 23 April 1996 the Hungarian parliament voted 278 to 0 to become the 27th member of the OECD. Many in Gyula Horn's government felt that membership in the OECD would help pave the way for Hungary's eventual membership in the EU.

There is no disputing that the economic measures Hungary took during 1995 and early 1996 made the economy more fiscally sound. Despite restrictive economic policies the economy did not stagnate but continued to grow at a moderate rate. There was a rise in industrial production by 8.5 per cent during the first half of 1995 and export sales grew by 21.3 per cent. There was also a slight decline in unemployment which was about 1 per cent lower during the first three quarters of 1995 than it was during a similar period in 1994. The unemployment rate in January 1995 was 11.4 per cent, but by October it had dropped to 10 per cent (Richter, 1996: 61, 63). As always, there is a need to be cautious about these figures, for they will not capture the long-term unemployed who are no longer eligible for benefit.

Hungary's devaluation of its forint and increased export performance in 1995 helped close the trade gap. Imports decreased by 3 per cent, and exports, in real terms, increased by 4 per cent, bringing Hungary close to a balanced trade budget. For the government, however, the biggest increase in revenue, during 1995, was caused by the acceleration of their privatization scheme. During the first three quarters of 1995 the government seemed to be hesitating on privatization, but this changed rapidly in October and November 1995 when minority shares were sold in all the major Hungarian utilities. Mostly German, French and Italian investors spent US$1.7 billion in order to purchase stakes in six regional electricity distributors, two electric power stations and four regional gas distributors. By the close of 1995 stakes had also been sold in the Hungarian national oil company, and Matav, the Hungarian telecom company. All together, the privatizations in 1995 were to come to approximately 8 per cent of Hungary's GDP and represented around $US3 billion, of which 93 per cent was in hard currencies (Richter, 1996: 64). This revenue began to help Hungary move out of its debt spiral.

When reviewing the macro-economic indicators, the situation in Hungary looked quite optimistic, but for the citizens of Hungary 1995 was a difficult year financially. Attitudes towards government had also shifted as the hope inspired by the HSP dissipated with its subsequent reneging of campaign promises. With strong liberal policies that propose easing tax restrictions on the wealthy, but increasing the tax burden on the poor, cynicism grew. For medium-to-low paid workers the increased tax burden was only one element contributing to their decline in living standards. Food prices rose by 33.5 per cent and the cost of household energy increased by 46 per cent putting serious pressure on low income families. So while export sales increased by 21.3 per cent, sales in the domestic economy came close to stagnating with a growth rate of 0.6 per cent. While there may have been large sums of money coming into Hungary during 1995, it did not reach many Hungarians.

On one hand, Hungary was praised as one of the leading East European countries, and in an IMF study Hungary is complimented on its progress towards a market economy. On the other hand, Hungary's economic policies have led to social trends that may cause some long term problems. Homicides in 1996 had increased by 50 per cent from the previous year and the number of registered drug addicts in 1996 topped 100,000 (Website: Hungary Report, No. 2.2, 1 July 1996). The change in Hungary during this period caused a reduction in the tourist trade, which was down 12 per cent by March 1996. Increased car theft probably had a part to play in deterring tourists during 1996, as this crime grew by 15 per cent during that year accounting for a total of 12,131 cars (Website: Hungary Report, No. 1.50, 20 May 1996). The litany of social impacts runs from increased property crime to a lowering of life expectancy for Hungarian males. Education will continue to be cut as the government tries to reduce expenditure and over 10,000 hospital beds were cut during the mid-1990s.

Hungarian cuts in social spending has been part of the wider project of being accepted into the Western global economy. The West, through financial institutions and foreign direct investment, has encouraged tight fiscal policies based upon neo-classical economics. This has been combined with changes to trade policies which were designed to reorientate Hungary toward the West. This was done with the co-operation of the Hungarian government. The government was keen to cement ties with the West and Western Europe in particular. At the beginning of the transition there was an expectation that the harsh Soviet paternalism would be supplanted by benign Western paternalism. However, meeting Western fiscal standards has inflicted austerity measures upon the general population. During 1995 the coalition government, made-up of the HSP and the Alliance of Free Democrats (AFD), introduced an austerity package in an attempt to reduce the national financial deficit and the already accumulated debt. While the austerity package won praise from international financial institutes, it was unpopular with the average Hungarian citizen. The package caused a 3-year drop in private consumption and an initial drop in wages. However, in terms of macro-economic indicators Hungary's economy has greatly improved in the last year and a half. If we look at Table 6.2 we can see both a drop in external debt and a rise in the GDP.

The figures thus far for 1998, show a continued rise in GDP. Despite the improvement in Hungary's overall economic performance, the general electorate ousted the HSP–AFD coalition government in the Spring of 1998. The Hungarian electoral system is complex and elections are held in two rounds. Voting took place on 10 May 1998 with a second round following on 24 May. The government was to be replaced by a centre-right coalition. The political situation was not without its irony. The Socialist coalition had been responsible for introducing an austerity plan based upon fiscal conservatism. The new-right coalition ran a campaign promising to increase social spending. The new coalition is made-up of the Alliance of Young Democrats (Fidesz-MPP) and the Smallholders' Party (FKgP). The Fidesz-MPP capitalized upon the resentment felt by most Hungarians towards the former government. Although the economy showed strong signs of recovery this did not impact on people's daily lives. The improvement in the economy was led by increased investment and exports, and this did not translate into

Table 6.2 Economic Indicators, Hungary 1993–97

Economic indicators	**1993**	**1994**	**1995**	**1996**	**1997**
GDP at current prices (Ft bn)	3,548	4,365	5,494	6,845	8,341
Real GDP growth (%)	–0.6	2.9	1.5	1.3	4.4
Consumer price inflation (%)	22.5	18.8	28.2	23.6	18.3
Exports ($ bn)	8.1	7.6	12.9	14.2	19.6
Imports ($ bn)	12.1	11.4	15.3	16.8	21.4
Current account ($ bn)	–4.3	–4.1	–2.5	–1.7	–1.0
Total foreign debt ($ bn)	24.2	28.0	31.7	27.7	23.8

Source: EIU Country Report, *Hungary*, 3rd quarter 1998: 5.

Table 6.3 Main Destination of Hungarian Exports, 1997

Destination	% Of total
Germany	37.3
Austria	11.4
Italy	6.1
Russia	5.0

Source: EIU Country Report, *Hungary*, 3rd quarter 1998: 5.

an appreciable increase in the standard of living. Moreover, the distribution of the economic recovery was uneven. Real wages did increase during the 18 months before the election but this was not enough to make up for the short-fall experienced during 1995–96 (EIU Country Report, *Hungary*, 1998: 13).

The current government has made many promises which are based upon industrial protectionism, state intervention and increased government spending. As a result the Fidesz-MPP/FKgP coalition is already coming under attack by the IMF and the OECD. Projections from Western international organizations suggest that the new government will experience fiscal difficulties in 1999, and as a result expand deficit spending and ultimately increase Hungary's external debt. There will be a limit, however, to the extent to which the government will be able to keep its campaign promises. As a candidate country for possible integration into the EU it will have to maintain a certain level of fiscal responsibility. Similar to other Central European countries, Hungary has become seriously dependent upon the EU in terms of export trade.

Another potential problem for the new government is its backing of a strong form of nationalism which is at loggerheads with its economic dependency upon the EU. The electoral swing towards a right-wing form of nationalism is the direct result of resentment of the increased foreign influence in the economy combined with growing wealth disparity. The new government will find it difficult to fulfil all its electoral promises. The Hungarian economy has become increasingly tied to the Western global economy and now needs to be on good terms with its trading partners and international organizations if it is to maintain its success in the current capitalist system. Before the May election the former government signed an agreement with the WB in which Hungary was granted a US$250 million loan to be used in the reform of its pension system. A similar WB loan of £100 million had been granted in

March 1998 to be used for the reform of the higher education system (EIU Country Report, *Hungary*, 1998: 29). These amounts have been allocated in tandem with EU PHARE funding (8 million ecu) and loans for improving Hungarian transport infrastructure (200 million ecu for Budapest underground and 100 million ecu for upgrading of the railway system) (ibid.: 30). For good or ill Hungary is now reliant upon the West and the EU in particular.

The political back-lash against the 1995 austerity measures are understandable, but the national government will find it hard to carve its own way in the face of structural constraints. If the Hungarian government tries to turn back the clock it will probably experience negative repercussions in terms of accessing credit internationally. At this stage in its economic development it can little afford to reject aid and loans from the West. As a member of the IMF, WB, WTO, and the OECD, the Hungarian government will find it hard not to follow the rules of the Western organizations of which it is now a member. When Hungary becomes a full-member of the EU, this trend will only be intensified.

6.6 Summary comments

Hungary's transition, like that of Poland and the Czech Republic's, concentrated heavily on the economic transformation from a command to a capitalist economy. Unlike the other two countries in this study, Hungary's economic system had elements of a market economy before 1989. Since the NEM of 1968, and the subsequent changes allowing a certain level of management autonomy for state industries, Hungary had accepted in principal the existence of market prices.

Did the pre-1989 Hungarian experience of a limited market help it during the post-1989 transition? On one level Hungary's contact with the West and its more export-oriented economy did mean that Hungarian politicians and managers of state-owned industries were more sophisticated in their conception of what a capitalist economy could deliver. Socialism as a concept seemed to be less tainted in Hungary then in the other two examples studied. The term, 'market economy' and 'social market economy' were often used interchangeably during the early years of the transition. Hungarian policy-makers seemed interested in trying to limit foreign influence over the transformation process.

If Hungary went into the transformation with more market experience, why did it experience the same sort of recession as Poland and the Czech Republic? The answer seems to lie in Hungary's debt crisis. Even though many state-owned companies were profitable and many of the

Hungarian policies toward the transformation were sound, their high debt would hamper their ability to undertake the economic transition without having to accept Western advice.

The tension between the democratic transition and the economic transition became very apparent after the election of 1991, when the democratic dissidents were voted out of office. The blame for the economic downturn was levelled at the new democrats. Similar to Poland and the Czech Republic, the transition project in Hungary seemed to change in nature. During 1989–90 the concentration was on establishing a democratic political process. However, the level of Hungary's debt meant that in order to restructure its economy it would need foreign aid and investment. In order to acquire international credit the Hungarian government had to follow increasingly neo-classical economic policies. This would mean that the ideology of the political party in power would not necessarily dictate the type of domestic policies practised within Hungary. The need for funding and the resulting pressure from international lending institutions would see the left-wing socialist coalition introduce austerity programmes. Similarly the right-wing opposition coalition parties in the run up to the 1998 election would campaign on a ticket of increasing social spending. On the surface this type of political behaviour may seem odd. However, it can be explained through the realization that in a democratic system a population living under austerity programmes will be naturally attracted to campaign promises that claim to improve the living standards of the average person. Similarly, once elected the Hungary party in power will find that they have very little room for making new policies based upon social spending. The phenomenon of debt in the end intensifies the speed and spread of Western economic practices. This is of course at variance with the democratic desires of the majority of Hungarians. Neo-classical economic policies seems to encourage political tensions. There remains an unhappy balance between a functioning democratic political system and economic policies which create public resentment against the transition process as a whole.

7
The EU Effect and the Question of Eastern Enlargement

The relationship between the EU and Central Europe is pivotal. Without a doubt, the EU has massive influence over the future stability and prosperity of Central Europe. If it were not for the EU, it is doubtful that the economic development policies of the early transition period would have been successful. The sheer size and wealth of the European Union could allow it to dominate Central Europe in this post-Cold War world. When we talk about Central Europe in the global political economy we are in effect talking about Central Europe in the EU economy.

Can Central Europe meet the challenge of enlargement? The levels of GNP and GDP have increased in Poland, the Czech Republic and Hungary. This is particularly true if we compare the first years of the transition with the last three years. Economic indicators suggest that these countries have survived the process of transition and are now beginning to reap the benefits of their adherence to a capitalist agenda. However, a strong argument could be made that the American, liberal, 'shock therapy' model of capitalist development has been damaging and that the success of recent years can be attributed to the region's adoption of economic policies similar to that of the EU.

The majority of Central European trade is done with countries of the EU, and this dependency is increasing. The trade figures for 1998 reveals that Germany alone accounts for over a third of export trade in all three countries examined in this study. The economies of Poland, Hungary and the Czech Republic are now tied more strongly to the EU then they once were to the Soviet economy. This has heightened the CEECs' desire for formal integration. Currently, the countries of Central Europe are vulnerable in their dependence on the EU market and yet they have no formal mechanism to affect internal EU policy. In the following section we look at the current state of the integration process.

Table 7.1 Re-orientation of Export Trade of the CEECs

Export Re-orientation of the Central and East European-6, 1989–1994 (%)

Central East Eur. Exports to:	**1989**	**1994**
Former CMEA	41.3	17.1
EU	31.5	57.0
EFTA	7.5	8.4
USA	2.7	3.3
Japan	1.2	0.5
Rest of the world	15.8	13.8

Source: Commission of the EC (1995) *Towards Greater Economic Integration: The European Union's Financial Assistance and Trade Policy for Central and Eastern Europe and the New Independent States*, Brussels: Directorate IA, European Union Document.

7.1 The evolution of the process of integration

It could be said that the process of integration took place from the day that the Soviet Union began to disintegrate. Dissidents and democrats in Central Europe were interested in increasing relations with the West, and for many this meant looking toward the EU. The governments of Poland, Hungary and the Czech Republic believed that integration with Europe was not just necessary, but, inevitable. In a personal interview with Vice Director Stavinoha of the Department for Political Relations to the EU (Ministry for Foreign Affairs, Czech Republic), he clearly articulated that for the Czech Republic, integration with the EU was the only option.[1]

The process began, in an official capacity, with the signing of the Association Agreements. These preliminary agreements were signed in November 1991. The European Commission met with the Governments of Poland, Hungary and the, then still united, Czechoslovakia. They met at Visegrad in Hungary and initialled a series of agreements which became the basis for the Association Agreements. Eventually 10 of the CEECs would sign individual Association Agreements. However, the formal launching of the these agreements did not occur until the Essen European Council in December 1994. The signing at Essen gave birth to the European Agreements, which incorporated the earlier Association agreements and provided for free trade, economic and technical co-operation, financial assistance and the creation of a structured political dialogue. In many cases funding was distributed through the PHARE programme which is the EU's institutional body for transmitting funds and implementing projects in the CEECs. Not dissimilar to some forms of IMF conditionality, the EU insisted that the Agreements incorporate principles of democracy and liberalization before further association would be permitted. The early influence of countries like Poland and Hungary can be seen in the name of this EU funding body for the CEECs, PHARE. The 'P' and the 'H' stood for Poland and Hungary, however, this body now deals with the entire region. The coalescing of various agreements and programmes were part of a general commitment by the EU towards enlargement. The acceptance of the concept of enlargement would be reiterated in various EU summits.

Although the EU would entertain the concept of enlargement, from 1989 to 1993, there seemed to be a reluctance to promise membership to the CEECs. Instead, attention was focused on what changes would be necessary within the CEECs if they wished to join the EU. The issue of the need for internal change within the EU before enlargement, which also meant changes to the EU budget, was side-stepped until 1996–97. The EU's pre-accession strategy had less to do with grand theory and more to do with a series of technical meetings that took place in an *ad hoc* manner. The political vacuum created by the Soviet collapse seemed to suggest that Central Europe would eventually become the responsibility of Western Europe, but the EU was somewhat hesitant, hence the slow start to the enlargement process.

The reluctance towards enlargement is understandable when we consider the difficult task existing member-states have had in adopting the 1992 Maastricht criteria. Many of the EU's summits concentrated on issues of the single currency, the Inter-governmental Conference or other issues of continuing integration between the member-states themselves. Dissent between existing member-states with regards to the future of deeper integration proved as problematic as getting agreement on when to accept new members. In this sense, the pressure to increase the size of the EU came at an awkward time. Despite this, the EU has continued to move in the direction of enlargement.

After the Essen Council of 1994 a pre-accession strategy was discussed. There were calls for a White Paper on the Single Market. European Agreements were given to the Baltic states and Slovenia and a multilateral structured dialogue was put in place. By December 1995, at the Madrid Council meeting, the EU was ready to reiterate its commitment to enlargement. Applicant countries in Central and Eastern Europe were asked to fill out a comprehensive questionnaire which would give the EU information as to their readiness for membership. This questionnaire included everything from current legislation, to debt levels and economic indicators. Organizations such as the WB and the OECD, as well as other organization have been asked for their policy analysis *vis-à-vis* applicant countries' suitability for membership. The EU commission responded to the country questionnaires by giving its opinions to applicant countries. These opinions advised applicants on how they needed to change their political–economic system to make it compatible with EU membership. These opinions were also published by the European Commission. However, the 'Opinions' were not released until July 1997 when the EU had formally agreed to take on new members.

The EU Florence summit in June 1996 and the Dublin summit in December of the same year had, at that time, made no further commitment towards enlargement and indeed made little reference to it. This left the CEECs at a hiatus. Although the EU European Agreements had been taken as a move towards integration, they were still only trade agreements. Similarly the PHARE programme was assumed to prepare the CEECs for membership, but it could also easily be seen as a straight EU aid agency. The CEECs were relieved, therefore, when the EU released its White Paper on the Single Market. Although it was criticised for its lack of coherence it, nevertheless, gave the CEECs a document with which to work with. As a result, many of the countries began to wholeheartedly adopt EU Single Market legislation. Naturally, there is a difference between adopting legislation and using it in practice, however, the CEECs' willingness to take on EU legislation illustrated to the Commission, and others, that the CEEC governments were committed to the idea of joining the EU. The CEECs were disappointed, therefore, when the issue of enlargement was again overwhelmed by the issue of the single currency and EU internal budgetary concerns at the Amsterdam summit in June 1997. The British election in May 1997 had installed the Labour party in government. It was the reluctance of Britain's new government to join the single European currency that dominated much of the Amsterdam summit.

However, an EU Commission document, released in July 1997 helped to clarify the future direction of EU integration. This major EU policy document, *Agenda 2,000,* committed the European Union to taking on new members. Presented in July by the EU Commission President, Jacques Santer, this document detailed proposals from European Monetary Union to that of Common Agricultural Policy reform. It also mentioned the EU's intention of accepting a number of the CEECs.

The procedure regarding who would join and when, was not determined until the European Council meeting in Luxembourg during 12–13 December 1997. The European Council decided to set up a European

Conference which would bring together the Minister's of Foreign Affairs of the existing 15 member states and the 10 Central and East European applicant countries, plus Cyprus (and possibly Malta after its 1998 elections). The first European Conference meeting was held on 30 March 1998.

Although the European Conference includes all applicants, special bilateral negotiations will occur alongside the conference for those countries that are the closest to being able to take on the responsibility of EU membership. Therefore, the European Council convened bilateral intergovernmental conferences in the spring of 1998 with Cyprus, Hungary, Poland, Estonia, the Czech Republic and Slovenia. It is likely that these countries will become members, in some fashion, before the next EU budgetary period ends in 2006. Special meetings will also occur between those applicants who need more time to implement government and structural changes in preparation for future membership: Romania, Slovakia, Latvia, Lithuania and Bulgaria. Cyprus is a case apart and its success will depend on the ability of the Greek and Turkish Cypriot community to co-operate during the negotiation process.

Once accepted the applicants will be full members of the EU. Although some lead-in time may be necessary for the applicant countries. As can be seen from Table 7.2 the level of development and wealth in the CEECs tends to be lower than that of the EU average.

Table 7.2 Key Indicators of Candidate Countries, 1996

	Czech	**Estonia**	**Hungary**	**Poland**	**Slovenia**	**EU15**
Basic Data						
Total area (1,000 sq. km)	79.0	45.0	93.0	313.0	20.0	3236.0
Total population (1,000s)	10,309	1,476	10,174	38,639	1,987	372,654
Population per sq. km	131.0	33.0	109.0	124.0	98.0	115.0
Life expectancy:						
men	70.4	61.7	65.3	67.6	70.3	73.7
women	77.3	74.3	74.5	76.4	77.8	80.1
Deaths per 1,000 inhabitants	10.9	14.1	14.0	10.0	9.5	10.0
Birth's per 1,000 inhabitants	8.8	9.1	10.4	11.1	9.4	10.8

(cont'd)

	Czech	Estonia	Hungary	Poland	Slovenia	EU15
Labour Market						
Economic activity rate (%)	61.3	70.4	56.1	58.8	58.7	55.2
Unemployment rate (%)	3.8	7.6	9.2	12.4	7.3	10.7
Agriculture: % of workers	6.3	13.1	8.0	26.9	7.1	5.3
Economics						
GDP in ecu billion (1995 prices)	37.8	2.8	33.8	91.0	14.3	6,441.5
GDP per person	9,857	3,876	6,390	5,318	10,199	17,264
Gross added value by agriculture (%)	5.2	8.1	6.2	7.6	5.0	2.4
Annual inflation: average (%) rate	8.8	23.1	23.6	19.9	5.8	2.5
Govt (–) deficit/ surplus (+) (ecu million)	–454.5	–52.1	–1,294.2	–1,737.6	+94.9	–
Gross foreign debt (ecu million)	4,909.8	232.5	22,878.6	30,154.9	3,159.9	–
Industrial production (1993 = 100)	119.0	98.8	118.5	135.6	109.6	–
Direct investment abroad (ecu million)	–32.3	–31.6	3.2	–32.1	–5.0	–
FDI in the economy (ecu million)	1,130.8	118.4	1,561.8	2,799.1	146.5	–
External Trade						
Balance of trade (ecu million)	–4,640	–888	–2,414	–10,005	–860	–
EU share of total imports (%)	58.0	64.0	60.0	64.0	37.0	–
EU share of total exports (%)	58.0	50.0	63.0	66.0	41.0	–

Note: (–) data not comparable. *Source*: *European Report*, 1997: 1.

The issue of enlargement of the EU is interconnected with a variety of budgetary and reform concerns. A question mark remains as to how EU funds will be dispersed in the budgetary period from 2000 to 2006. It has, however, already been decided that substantial pre-accession aid will be needed to help the CEECs prepare for EU membership. This type of aid was also given to the Mediterranean countries before they joined in the 1980s. The only difference in the case of the CEECs' enlargement is that there is no plan to increase, on a percentage basis, the amount taken for the overall EU budget. Funds for the enlargement will have to be found from within the existing budget structure, which will mean less money for existing member-states.

The six 'first-wave' candidates (Cyprus, Hungary, Poland, Estonia, the Czech Republic and Slovenia) agreed in July 1998 that each country would put forward at least seven position papers by September 1998 in order to stimulate substantial negotiations with the EU (European Report, Sept. 19, 1998: V, 3). It is proposed that a new round of Inter-Governmental Conferences, at a Foreign Minister level, be held starting November 1998 (European Report, 5 Sept. 1998: V, 5). Poland was the first country to submit its position papers. Its assumed that serious and detailed negotiations will take place during the winter of 1998/99. However, there is no firm dates as to when these candidate countries will become full EU member-states.

7.2 The transition and the effect of the possible integration with the EU: the sectoral example of agriculture

The example of agriculture is chosen here because it is the one sector that was deliberately excluded from the Association Agreements and as such represents an area of great sensitivity with regards to the integration of the CEECs into the EU. The project of enlargement is a daunting one. If all 10 CEECs were taken on over the next 10 years, it would mean an extra 100 million people in the EU. One of the most politically delicate areas is the farming sector, as enlargement would increase agricultural land area by about 50 per cent (Varley, 1997: 4). This in turn would mean a full doubling of the agricultural work force at a time when it is declining in the existing EU. Moreover, the agricultural sector in Central Europe remains a challenge. There was much rhetoric about the superiority of the 'capitalist system of exchange' during and after 1989. However, 8 years after the fall of communism, the farming sector in Central Europe is less productive then under socialism. Moreover, the greater competition of the market system has not brought forth a sleek well-managed agricultural sector, but rather a beleaguered industry riddled with debt and lack of investment, which leaves little money to make the much needed structural changes. Therefore, when the EU accepts these applicants, considerable work remains to be done to make their agricultural sectors viable.

There has been a tremendous amount of speculation as to how the EU CAP will be reformed for the budgetary period of 2000 to 2006. Valid concerns have been raised as the next budgetary period coincides with two major events: (1) the Central European enlargement of the EU and (2) the next WTO round of talks designed to further liberalize international trade.

Reform is developing in a two-pronged manner, which effects the way that CAP and the Structural Funds allocate money. There is a recognition that when the EU starts taking on new members from the East, funds will need to be available to help them during the accession process. The EU strategy document, *Agenda 2,000* (July 1997) sets out a number of reform proposals which will have a noticeable impact on the enlargement process. One of the main thrusts of the aforementioned document is a strategy which will allow for the Central European enlargement of the EU without raising member states budgetary commitments. The current ceiling on the total EU budget is set at 1.27 per cent of EU GDP (*Agenda 2,000*, 1997). Colloquially, known as the Santer proposals (after the then EU Commission President) these *Agenda 2,000* proposals suggest that no specific increase be allowed to finance enlargement.

The Santer proposals do see an increase in the CAP budget from 43.4 billion ecu in 1999 to 44.1 billion ecu in 2000 and 50 billion ecu by 2006. However, the proposals also suggest that at least 6 per cent of this CAP increase should go to the new member states. However, this increase in the CAP budget is rather illusionary, because measures now funded from the Agricultural Structures fund (FEOGA Guidance) will, in the new budgetary period, be funded from the CAP budget. This will include environment programmes, early retirement and forestry schemes (*Agenda 2,000*, 1997).

Agenda 2,000 proposals were conceived with a great awareness of the upcoming GATT/WTO trade negotiations. Throughout the 1990s there has been a move to 'internationalize' agricultural policy. Increasingly, levels of import protection, export subsidies and direct payments are determined by Geneva, not Brussels. With this in mind reform proposals for CAP are based on extending the MacSharry reforms of 1992. In short, this means a greater role for direct compensation, and a reduced or eliminated role for market price support, which pays the producer per unit of produce. The move of 'decoupling' farmer subsidies from the production of food hopes to diminish intervention stocks of produce and put the EU in a stronger negotiating position for the up coming WTO trade negotiations.

The reform to the CAP is but one piece of the puzzle. The Santer proposals are also suggesting changes to the EU Structural and Cohesion Funds. The proposals are actually calling for an increase to the Structural Funds (34.3 billion ecu in 1999, 35.2 billion ecu in 2000, and 42.8 billion ecu by 2006) (*Agenda 2,000*, 1997). The plan is that 1 billion ecu will be allocated in the year 2000 to the joining member-states of Central Europe, but by 2006 this figure will have grown to 12.6 billion ecu. This represents close to a third of the Fund.

Whether we look at either enlargement, CAP/Structural funds reform, or the WTO negotiations, the trend is the same: less subsidization and lower product prices. The attempts at slowing down the process may allow for a certain amount of continued draw on the EU funds, but EU farming policy in general has been changing to be more market oriented. Ironically as Europe and the rest of the world attempts to reform subsidization policy, the countries of Central Europe are actually introducing them. Agricultural policy in Central Europe in the last few years is somewhat like 'shock therapy' in reverse. They are adopting policies similar to the EU as part of the pre-accession process. Of course, there are significant differences between the Central European applicants to the EU. In the case of Poland, agriculture was never properly collectivized. The huge factory farms that are common in Hungary, were not part of the Polish experience. Farms tended to remain small and peasant run. The problem in Central Europe is often one of having farms that are too big or too small with little in between.

For years food prices were subsidized by the Polish government but after 1990 food prices were liberalized and farmers received almost nothing in the way of support. The results were devastating. The industry's importance declined sharply. Total employment in agriculture dropped by 26 per cent and its contribution to Poland's GDP fell from 14 per cent in 1986 to 7 per cent in 1995 (OECD, 1997a). Figures show that Poles spend much of their income on food, but this has little to do with a healthy food sector and more to do with high inflationary food prices coupled with depressed wages. This results in consumer expenditure on agricultural products at almost 40 per cent during 1996 (OECD, 1997a). Those who work on Poland's small farms do not tend to own the land, but lease it from the government. There were over 3 million hectares leased during 1996, with only 324,000 being bought privately during the same period.

As mentioned in chapter four the period of 1989 to 1991 was very difficult for Poland. The early part of Poland's transition resulted in economic stagnation, depression, coupled with high inflation. Added to these problems was the development of a large trade deficit with the EU. Poland, today, remains a net importer of food. The economic crisis brought on by a strongly liberalizing economic policy was counteracted by Poland's desire to retool itself for EU membership. This in turn saw the development of a number of policies designed to offer the agricultural sector some protection.

Protection came in the form of the newly created Agricultural Market Agency (AMA), which similar to its EU counterpart CAP became responsible for intervention purchases. Market intervention tends to occur mostly for meat, sugar, potato, starch, honey, linen and wool. It may interfere in other markets if the internal market requires it to do so. The other main avenue of subsidy is done through market price support, which is done in conjunction with the work of the AMA. As a rule Poland does not tend to use export subsidies. However, it does on occasion provide them for dairy products, sugar, potato starch and pork. Although institutionally unique the AMA's function is identical to that of the CAP.

These protectionist bodies grew out of the recession of 1990–93. They were a response to a lack of investment in agriculture during the transition process. Insufficient capital in this sector was a region-wide problem. The Polish government addressed the problem of a lack of agricultural investment by creating the Agency for Restructuring and Modernisation of Agriculture (ARMA). Its purpose is to provide credit subsidies on loans to farmers. Projects ranged from modernization and restructuring of the farming sector, as well as providing funds to the agro-food processing sectors. The ARMA also provided credit subsidies for basic rural infrastructure.

During the 1989–91 period the price support mechanism that was in place was actually negative and implicitly taxed farmers instead of supporting them. After 1991 a series of border measures and new market support mechanisms were put in place. As a result Poland's Producer Subsidy Equivalent (PSE) has increased substantially since 1991.

The market price support continues to be the main policy instrument and accounts for 85 per cent of the total support given to farmers. By 1996 the PSE had risen by 23 per cent which was a doubling of the market price support. These increases seem substantial, however, Poland's percentage PSE is at 28 per cent which was far below the OECD 1996 average (OECD, 1997a). While these moves have improved the situation for farmers, Poland's domestic prices for agricultural produce were, on average, two-fifths above world prices. The consumer and taxpayer had increased their transfers to the agricultural sector by two-thirds in 1996. Unlike the original intention of the transition process, which was to

Table 7.3 Poland: Transfers Associated with Agricultural Policies

	1989–91	1995	1996	% Change 1995–96
Production Subsidy Equivalent (PSE)				
Total PSE (zloty billion)	–0.15	5.13	8.13	58.0
Total PSE (US$ billion)	0.05	2.11	3.01	43.0
% PSE	0	1.30	28.00	
Consumer Subsidy Equivalent (CSE)				
Total CSE (zloty billion)	0.77	–4.29	–8.27	93.0
Total CSE (US$ billion)	1.37	–1.77	–3.07	73.0
% CSE	19.00	–18.00	–28.00	
Total Transfers*				
(zloty billion)	–0.37	9.51	15.48	63.0
(US$ billion)	–0.40	3.92	5.74	46.0

Note: *Total transfers are not the addition of the PSE and CSE but cover the total value of production and include not only transfers to agriculture, as measured by the PSE and CSE, but also other transfers associated with agricultural policies.
Source: OECD, 1997a: 69.

free prices and markets, the aping of CAP policies has introduced a system of very controlled prices.

Poland's level of agricultural subsidization in the early days of the transition was close to zero. However, its attempt to copy the policies of the EU has seen a marked increase in prices enjoyed by producers. The concentration on introducing EU-style subsidization policies may be no more helpful then the former policies of stark liberalization. This is because the concentration on producer prices maintains the status quo, rather than changing rural and agricultural-processing infrastructure. In particular, the use of border measures are protecting farmers from the world market. This is not to say that some form of protection for farmers was not appropriate. On the contrary, the entire sector is in need of help and attention. However, it is simply putting off the inevitable. There is a strong likelihood of continued reform of the CAP, particularly once the next WTO negotiations begin after the year 2000. Many CEECs could find themselves putting in current EU-style measures only to have to reform them before they become full members in the future.

Hungary is a different case from Poland. The role of agriculture is of extreme importance to Hungary. The value of agricultural exports are triple that of agricultural imports. Much of this success can be attributed to the Hungarian wine industry. Almost 25 per cent of agriculture production goes towards exports, and as such is an extremely important source of attaining foreign currency for the Hungarian government. With these strong figures it is hard to believe that agriculture's importance fell as a share of GDP from 16 per cent in 1989 to 6 per cent in 1995. This was reflected in employment figures as those working in the farming sector dropped from 18 per cent to 8 per cent. Despite this decline agriculture actually increased its output by 5 per cent in 1996 (OECD, 1997a). It is an irony that the farming sector in Central Europe was strongly criticized as being inefficient under communism, because it is only the farms that underwent forced and extensive collectivization that offered the kind of industrial scale that interested foreign buyers. Hungary has some of the best land in the region, but also the farms were collectivized under communism into huge co-operative units, many of which were quickly bought by private industry.

The mimicking of EU agricultural policy is evident in Hungary as it is elsewhere in the region. In 1993 the Agricultural Market Regulation Act was implemented. This Act allows for the direct regulation of markets for milk, feed maize, wheat (for human consumption), live cattle and swine for slaughter. The system used provides a market price support by establishing a minimum guaranteed price, which is paid up to a production quota limit. This system bears a strong resemblance to many national agricultural policies employed in the EU, such as the quota scheme used by the Irish dairy sector. The government will also intervene in the event of market instability. This intervention measure is used in tandem with budgetary support and border measures. Import tariffs and export subsidies are employed for important agricultural products. The agro-industry, in addition, would be eligible for capital grants, and interest-rate support.

The Hungarian government has been undergoing a major review of its agricultural policies since 1997. It wants to establish a rural development programme to be implemented during the next 2 years. The crux of this overview is to bring Hungarian agricultural policy, as well as its legal and institutional structures, into line with that of the European Union, in the hope of eventual membership. Hungary's level of subsidization has been more erratic than that of Poland or the Czech Republic. Its PSE increased dramatically from 1989 to 1995 and experienced a strong decline between 1995 and 1996. As mentioned in our Hungarian chapter, government austerity measures introduced in 1995 saw a general decline in all government spending.

Table 7.4 Hungary: Transfers Associated with Agricultural Policies

	1989–91	1995	1996	% Change 1995–96
Production Subsidy Equivalent (PSE)				
Total PSE (forints billion)	68.48	72.44	69.41	–4.0
Total PSE (US$ billion)	1.17	0.58	0.45	–21.0
% PSE	23.00	16.00	11.00	
Consumer Subsidy Equivalent (CSE)				
Total CSE (forints billion)	–33.80	–24.75	–16.09	–35.0
Total CSE (US$ billion)	–0.57	–0.20	–0.11	–46.0
% CSE	–14.00	–7.00	–3.00	
Total Transfers*				
(forints billion)	n.a.	n.a.	n.a.	n.a.
(US$ billion)	n.a.	n.a.	n.a.	n.a.

Note: *Total transfers are not the addition of the PSE and CSE but cover the total value of production and include not only transfers to agriculture, as measured by the PSE and CSE, but also other transfers associated with agricultural policies.
Source: OECD, 1997a: 69.

The increase in Hungary's PSE during 1989 to 1995 can be explained by the rise in the market price support and subsidies to food production. The drop between 1995 and 1996 saw the PSE drop to pre-1989–91 levels. Again, this was linked to the market price support which in this case fell sharply. The reason that the market price support can effect the overall PSE so drastically is that it forms the largest component of support going to the Hungarian farmer. Direct payments to farmers, for instance, increased by close to 16 per cent during 1996 to the equivalent of US$49 million, however, this still only made up 11 per cent of total support (see Table 7.4). Nevertheless, the percentage PSE estimate for 1996 was 11 per cent and this is one of lowest in the OECD. As a result of the low amount of subsidy, Hungarian prices for agricultural products is close to that of world prices. Subsidies in the form of direct payments go towards programmes designed to protect the environment, the genetic breeding stock and farmers in less-developed areas. Payments are made on a headage or acreage basis. Some of the subsidy figures in the case of Hungary may be slightly misleading in the sense that there was a payout of the equivalent of US$33 million in natural disaster relief due to a severe drought in 1995. The 1995 figures, therefore, are high but this is due to an unusual circumstance.

In terms of trade Hungary has reduced some of its border tariffs. It does have a problem with regards to its export subsidies. Hungary's expenditure on export subsidies is twice the level of its Uruguay Round commitment of 22 billion forints. The United States and a number of other countries have alerted the WTO to Hungary's non-compliance with its commitment, so it will likely have to reduce its subsidy in this area even though its overall level of subsidy is very low. Hungary's agriculture policies seems to have been dually effected by the hope of integration with the EU, while at the same time feeling the constraints place upon its policy-making by virtue of its membership to the WTO.

Hungary has had considerable success in privatizing most of its government owned agricultural holdings. At this stage almost 90 per cent of the agriculturally producing land has been privatized. The same holds true for agro-food companies. Even though 20 per cent of financial capital in the agricultural industry remains in the hands of the government, privatization is continuing. One of the reasons for Hungary's success is the economy of scale afforded by many of its big farms and of course the strength of its wine industry which, very early on, attracted foreign buyers (OECD, 1997a).

The area of concern for the Hungarian agriculture sector is that of trying to meet its international trade commitments. It needs to improve on-farm efficiency rather than using export subsidies to compensate at the point of exit. Hungary's reliance on using export subsidies may sour trade relations with the EU and the US hindering its accession to the EU. It needs, as do all the countries in the region, to concentrate on structural adjustment through training, farm advisory and infrastructure projects.

Similar to Poland and Hungary, the Czech Republic saw a marked decline in the importance of agriculture as a sector. The Czech Republic was a strongly industrialized part of the CEECs. Even in 1989 agriculture only accounted for 6 per cent of GDP. In Ireland, for instance, agriculture accounts for 29 per cent of GNP (Anon, 1996: 29–32). However, the Czech figure managed to drop by half to 3 per cent of GDP by 1996. Those working in agriculture fell from 10 per cent to 4 per cent during the same period. Trade in food products represents less than a tenth of the total trade done in an average year. The Czech Republic tends to be a net importer of food rather than a food producer. The average household would spend about 32 per cent of their income on purchasing food (OECD, 1997a).

The transition to a market economy in agriculture has been completed in the manufacturing sector, but not with regards to land. The Czech state still owns about 900,000 hectares, of which 500,000 are still scheduled to be privatized. The government's Land Fund leases out the land to agricultural producers. Currently about 75 per cent of the arable land is farmed by co-operatives. Only 25 per cent of farms are private.

The State Fund for Market Regulation (SFMR) became responsible for the regulation for bread-wheat and milk. It buys a limited quantity of wheat at a pre-announced price. EU-style quotas are not yet employed, however the quantity of produce that is to be covered by intervention is limited. One of the most common forms of support in Central Europe in general is that of the credit subsidy. In the Czech Republic loan guarantees and credit subsides are dealt with by the Support and Guarantee Fund for Farmers (SGFFF). This body helps in trying to encourage structural adjustment. However, strict criteria are applied before credit subsidies are given. Proposals are given to commercial banks for evaluation before the application for subsidy is considered.

Despite these measures financial transfers to the agricultural sector in the Czech Republic have decreased since the beginning of the transition process (see Table 7.5). The PSE has dropped by 75 per cent between

Table 7.5 Czech Republic: Transfers Associated with Agricultural Policies

	1989–91	1995	1996	% Change 1995–96
Production Subsidy Equivalent (PSE)				
Total PSE (koruna billion)	46.94	11.02	8.76	–21.0
Total PSE (US$ billion)	3.17	0.42	0.32	–24.0
% PSE	52.00	14.00	10.00	
Consumer Subsidy Equivalent (CSE)				
Total CSE (koruna billion)	–19.78	–0.97	2.62	not calculated
Total CSE (US$ billion)	–1.31	–0.04	0.10	not calculated
% CSE	–30.00	–1.00	3.00	–
Total Transfers*				
(Czech koruna billion)	n.a.	10.32	6.60	–36.0
(US$ billion)	n.a.	0.39	0.24	–38.0

Note: *Total transfers are not the addition of the PSE and CSE but cover the total value of production and include not only transfers to agriculture, as measured by the PSE and CSE, but also other transfers associated with agricultural policies.
Source: OECD, 1997a: 41.

1989 and 1995. This can be attributed to the low market price support and a decrease in direct payments.

The figures for 1996 show that there has been a decrease by 4 per cent which brings the Czech Republic PSE down to 10 per cent. This is far lower than the OECD average and makes the Czech Republic level of agricultural subsidization one of the lowest in the OECD.

Lack of investment in the agricultural sector has remained the biggest stumbling block with regards to implementing structural change in the industry. The alternative has been for farmers to borrow heavily. The Czech government has been generous with its credit policy. The difficulty, however, was that the expected prosperity engendered by the transition to Western capitalism did not materialize. As a result, the budgetary cost of agricultural loan guarantees and partial interest subsidies more than doubled during 1996 (OECD, 1997a). Farmers who borrowed during the early years of the transition find that they simply cannot pay back the loans. The amount of matured guaranteed loans that could not be repaid nearly tripled in 1996, but this amount is nothing compared to the amount of loans still outstanding. The Czech government has tried to deal with this growing crisis by forgiving debt, rescheduling repayment of debt and reducing the rents for land leased from the government Land Fund by 90 per cent (ibid.).

Tariff and quotas are used to control the entry of certain goods into the Czech Republic, particularly in the case of cereals and wine. However, in most cases these measures have not contravened the Czech's GATT/WTO commitments. They did use exports subsidies for both bread and dairy products, but again the amounts remained well below the WTO commitments.

Despite the decline in government support to the farming sector, subsidies in the wheat and dairy market remain crucial. The over-riding long-term problem for the agricultural industry in the Czech Republic continues to be that of debt. The burden of debt hamstrings farmers ability to make the structural changes necessary to ensure sustainable development. A major goal of the Czech government is to see that the Czech Republic becomes a member of the EU. As a result, agricultural rules and regulations are being put into place to emulate that of the EU. However, it will take more than legislation to set the agricultural sector right in the Czech Republic, it will also need funds to help with improving agricultural infrastructure as well as coming up with a long-term strategy for solving the crisis of indebtedness of farmers.

In all three cases, the agricultural sector affords an excellent example of the difference between theoretical conception and applied developmental policies. In the beginning of the transition process, Poland, Czechoslovakia and Hungary cut agricultural subsidies and attempted to privatize the farming sector. With the exception of the Hungarian wine industry, the implementation of liberal economic policies that liberalized prices and slashed government subsidies resulted in bankruptcy or increased debt. This may not have been the best policy at a time when most Central Europeans were spending over a third of their salary on buying food. Food shortages, in these areas traditionally known for their agricultural production seems unfortunate. Of course, imported food has been available in all three countries, but locally produced food is more affordable.

The adoption of policies similar to the EU's CAP may seem bizarre in light of the EU's own attempts to reform this costly subsidisation policy. Nevertheless, these policies did offer some form of investment capital into a sector in dire need of structural reform. As inefficient as the CAP is, the Central European emulation of this policy actually resulted in a healthier agricultural sector in each of the three countries than did the liberal policy of simply removing subsidies.

7.3 Why Central European enlargement?

The overview of the agricultural situation in Poland, the Czech Republic and Hungary does raise the question as to why the European Union has decided to take on these Central European countries. It is clear from the Santer Proposals that when these countries become members they will represent not only a developmental challenge but will also seriously divert EU funds away from existing member states. The EU currently has 15 members. EU members from a global point view are wealthy, however many EU countries have problems of rural or inner-city poverty, and this is coupled with high national levels of unemployment. Enlargement is being pursued, despite this, which illustrates how intense the Union's ultimate commitment is to the project of integration. As mentioned earlier in this chapter, by the year 2006 a full third of the Structural Funds will go to the new members of the CEECs at the cost of at least 12.6 billion ecu. The sacrifice is not only monetary. Enlargement will also entail significant changes to the way the EU has internally administered its agricultural and development policies.

Notwithstanding, the difficulties that will undoubtedly present themselves during the enlargement process, the move toward Central European integration with the EU continues. What is a reasonable explanation for this development? When studying the EU it is extremely easy to become distracted by the technocratic nature of research and information disseminated on this organisation. The complexity of the statistical data and the heavy legal material can blind us to the overarching strategy, and desired outcomes of those who influence policy outcomes in the EU. There are important issues here from the point of view of studying the global political economy. The accession agreements that the CEECs are implementing will force these countries to adopt all existing EU legislation. This process will Westernize these countries in a way impossible without integration. Culturally, Central Europe is already European. Enlargement ensures that these countries are locked into the norms of Western capitalism as well. The argument here is not that including Central Europe into the EU is part of a single-minded, simplistic policy orientation based upon old forms of Realist security concerns. While foreign policy objectives (of sphere's of influence amongst existing member-states) has its part to play, the parsimonious concentration on the left versus right divide in politics and International Relations theory has over-simplified our understanding of the contemporary world order. Much of our current thinking is based upon post-war forms of thought. The phenomenon of Central Europe's transition could easily be categorized as the continuing spread of the capitalist mode of production. Responses by the EU and the US could in turn be explained as a pat form of Realist foreign-policy thinking. This could support a convincing academic argument in which the transition of the CEECs is no more than the introduction of an old-fashioned version of liberal economics in combination with Realist attitudes towards enlargement and security concerns. However, this would miss some important trends in globalization and the changing nature of capitalism in general.

In light of the above discussion the difficulty has been revealed, especially in terms of agricultural policy, of introducing pure forms of liberal economics. Such difficulty could be blamed on the former communist regime, or the new government's inexperience of capitalist systems or even on the market failure of out-of-date sectors such as agriculture. However, rather than seeing these conditions as an impediment to pure capitalism it may be wiser to realize that protection of social groups and industrial sectors is an important part of governance in any country. Moreover, increased research should be conducted in this area to help us understand why protectionism continues to be a legitimate part of policy-making, rather than treating the phenomenon as a troublesome hangover of out-moded keynesinism. Although protectionism is often very disruptive and wasteful in a market sense, it could be better understood, and perhaps even managed in such a way as to minimize its effect on the pricing structure of a capitalist system.

The increase of control, yet acceptance, of economic policies that contain an element of social protection is especially pronounced in the legislation of the EU. As illustrated previously in this work, the early days of the CEECs' transition was characterized by policies driven by loan conditionality set down by international financial organizations. Basically, CEECs were encouraged to have a 'new right' attitude, or put differently, a penchant for minimal government control and interference. This was combined with a trade policy that concentrated on trade with countries outside of Central Europe and the former Soviet Union, breaking down trade ties of the former Comecon. However, once the EU decided to seriously prepare these countries for economic integration, the policies required of the CEECs exhibited an about-face. The hub-and-spoke trading pattern suggested during the early part of the transition was substituted by a stipulation within the EU association agreements that the Visegrad countries of Central Europe form a trading bloc of their own. In addition, suggestions of minimal government involvement was replaced by EU criteria that required a reinforcement of the CEECs' institutional and administrative capacity. The questionnaire that each of the prospective applicant countries had to complete is a good example. During an interview with Jiri Zukal of the Czech Department of European Communities, he deliberately emphasized the depth of detail required for the completion of the questionnaire. Every piece of legislation and all administrative practices had to be categorized and listed. Moreover in the EU's reply to the questionnaire all applicant countries were expected to reform their legislation or change their administrative practices to conform to EU standard. The project of integration is, therefore, only partially about the spread of capitalism. It is also about the spread of Western norms and practice. This seems to fit a Gramscian concept of hegemony, but to say that hegemony exists is not enough. It is vital to understand what, in terms of human organization, is contained in a given hegemony. Hegemony in the past has usually been associated with the influence of imperial powers. Obviously, the empire of nineteenth-century Britain is different then the influence of the West in the late twentieth century. The hallmark of the contemporary hegemony is only partially driven by profit and security. The concept of control has become a major concern.

Central Europe is a very important case in terms of understanding where the global political economy is heading. The influence of the West and the EU was profound on the structural changes within the three countries of this study. The success that Poland, the Czech Republic and Hungary have been experiencing under the protection of the EU has given the illusion that the strict liberal policies that were enforced by IMF during the early years of the transition, was actually successful. This misunderstanding has led to a continued belief in the types of developmental policies used in Central Europe. Moreover, the invasiveness of the policies used to reconstruct an entire region to capitalism is now regularly employed with regards to countries that are already capitalist, but happen to be experiencing economic crises. In Chapter 8 the focus returns to the spread of these Western values and the way in which this has effected the project of spreading capitalism.

8
Summary and Conclusions

What trends can be drawn out by looking at the three case-studies considered in this study? When examined individually Poland, the Czech Republic and Hungary are three unique states each with their own history, language and political culture. What they share is a past connected to the communism of the Soviet Union and the subsequent transition to democratic and liberal economic states. The process of their reintegration into the West offers an opportunity to study the major trends in the spread of Western norms and values.

It is important to remember that the collapse of the Soviet Union offered countries in the G7 their greatest opportunity since the Second World War for influencing the political and economic structure of an entire region. Although the structural adjustment programmes of the IMF and the WB were invasive in Latin American and Africa throughout the 1980s, these programmes were but a precursor to the complete transformation of former Soviet bloc countries.

The 1989 collapse of the Eastern bloc, would significantly change the international political economy. It would be the first time that capitalism would be truly global. With the collapse of Soviet communism the last major obstacle to creating a global marketplace had been removed. Even though China would remain undemocratic, it too had begun to adopt market principles for its economy. Poland, the Czech Republic and Hungary were to receive special attention because of their proximity to the EU and their existent level of economic development. They would be the showcase examples of the success of Western principles over the former principals of Soviet communism, which were based on command economies and single party political systems.

Despite a willingness on the part of governments in Poland, Czechoslovakia (later the Czech Republic) and Hungary, the initial transition experiment resulted in a severe recession in each of these Central European countries from 1990 to 1993. The economic hardships experienced by the populations within each of the three countries studied resulted in political disenchantment with the political process in general and the voting in of parties made up of retooled communists.

What can be learned from the Central European experience? Why was the initial transition process in all three countries so troubled with economic failure? The answer can be found by referring back to this study's discussion of imperialism (see Section 1.2). During the 'Age of Empire' the success of the empire was thought to lie with the imperial power itself. The current global political economy is one in which the G7 countries wield an enormous amount of influence through their membership of international financial organizations such as the IMF and the WB. However, the onus of success of policies prescribed by the West to other parts of the world now lies with the recipients of policy advice not its creators. The current global political economy is one in which the West can in effect practice 'imperialism without fault'. In this way, Poland, the Czech Republic and Hungary were on the one hand given specific advice through the medium of loan conditionality and were then criticized for not being able to make the outcome of these policies successful.

It is interesting to note the growing trend of Western policy advice to developing states and countries in transition. Moreover, this trend seems to be coupled with a growing alienation between the West's ability to influence strongly liberal policies in places like Central Europe and the acceptance of responsibility for the outcomes of these policy prescriptions. While these trends are important it raises an even more interesting conundrum. If the West is offering advice through financial organizations which have leverage over transition countries *vis-à-vis* their need for international credit, why is the outcome of this policy advice so often marred by failure?

The main purpose of this study is to show that it is not only the West's ability to influence other countries that may be a problem, but also the very nature of the values it has been transmitting. At the very heart of the 1990–93 recession in Central Europe is the confusion as to what capitalism actually is. Financial lending institutions offered a vehicle for influence and, as seen in the case-study chapters, governments in Central Europe were amenable to adopting Western advice. The question remained as to what these countries should adopt. Very early in the transition process, capitalism was conceived and defined in a neo-classical, economic way. As a result a narrow and highly selective view of capitalism was encouraged in Poland, the Czech Republic and Hungary. This version of capitalism concentrated heavily on the liberalization of prices, the liberalization of markets and the privatization of state-owned firms. While there may not seem to be anything intrinsically wrong with this advice, it does illustrate the strong assumption that the transition in Central Europe was first and foremost the transition to capitalism.

The transition, however, was social and political in addition to economic. The strong concentration on the economic and the austerity programmes it fostered may have made sense from a purely macro-economic sense, but it would create much disillusionment with the other part of the transition process, democratization. The disenchant with the political process in Poland, the Czech Republic and Hungary was born out of the confusion between the project of political emancipation and the other project of fostering global capitalism.

It can be argued that the neo-classical economic policies prescribed to Central Europe caused significant tension between the political and economic transition. This was particularly evident in Poland were the neo-classical 'shock therapy' model of economic transition was most willingly embraced. Under the stewardship of Deputy Prime Minister, Leszek Balcerowicz, Poland attempted to 'leap' to the market by lifting price controls, making the zloty a fully convertible currency, removing trade barriers to imports and eliminating most government subsidies to state-controlled enterprises. These measures, combined with the privatization of state-owned companies, were intended to cut government expenditure and attract foreign direct investment. These economic measures adopted by the Polish government would cause a trade deficit, a fall in economic output, and create high unemployment (see case-study chapter for details).

Poland's experience, however, was not unique. Although, the other two countries had their own specific conditions in which the transition occurred, the outcome of adopting neo-classical economic policies would result in similar problems. Hungary, for instance, had allowed a certain amount of autonomy to managers of state-owned companies and had partially liberalized prices before 1989. Despite Hungary's greater experience with market mechanisms it ran into similar difficulties as Poland. One of the more serious problems for Hungary was its trade deficit. Western advice suggesting that Central European countries reduce their trade barriers resulted in an import/export trade imbalance as foreign goods became widely available. The trade deficit eroded revenue that was needed by the Hungarian government to repay loans it had received from the West. In order for Hungary to remain internationally creditworthy it found itself introducing austerity programmes in 1995 that bore a striking resemblance to Poland's 'shock therapy' of the early 1990s.

The Czech Republic, had neither the Polish government's commitment to implementing neo-classical economic policies nor Hungary's level of debt. By 1998, however, it found itself having to introduce similar policies which the governments of the other two countries had at different times implemented. The Czech Republic of the early 1990s had low debt and low unemployment. How then did strict neo-classical economic policies become mainstream in a country which had made an attempt to introduce capitalism under its own terms during the early 1990s? The answer lies in the liberalization of Czech financial markets. The Prague stock market and the young national investment funds had been tolerating corruption which was found to be linked to the government and this in turn would cause financial instability and threaten a collapse of the Czech koruna. In order to re-establish international faith in its currency the government had to request funding from international financial organizations for a rescue package that ultimately did not stop the koruna from slipping. Problems with the koruna spilled over into cross-border trade and the Czech Republic found itself suffering from a serious trade deficit. The government during 1997 adopted strong neo-classical measures in the form of two austerity programmes.

The implementation of austerity programmes caused a rise in prices, a cap on wages and a decrease in social spending. This in turn would cause disenchantment amongst the voting population in Poland, the Czech Republic and Hungary. In this way a growing tension was created between the democratic process and the process of economic transition. Economic policy as it has been manifested in Central Europe conceived of capitalism as only the exchange of goods and services. However, capitalism in the Western world rests upon a wide base of social norms and legal institutions which allows the process of economic exchange to occur in a climate of regulated business behaviour.

Economic policies encouraged by Western advice through the medium of loan conditionality assumed that the societies of Central Europe would perform the same role as those in the West. However, privatization and recession in Europe or North America occurs in democracies that are already well established. Presenting Poland, the Czech Republic and Hungary with strict neo-classical economic advice during the 1990s has often resulted in economic recession. Therefore, Western policy advice has ignored the fact that much social legislation and social norms associated with capitalism still had to be developed in transition countries.

As a result of placing strict economic policy guidelines on Poland, the Czech Republic and Hungary the national populations of these countries have reacted to economic hardship by questioning the transition process as a whole. Most of the pre-1989 dissidents in Central Europe helped engineer the collapse of single party rule in their countries in the hope of establishing a democratic system. Without exception, however, the Central European political parties which had brought about the introduction of democracy in 1989–90 were voted out of office in reaction to the economic hardships experienced by people as a result of the introduction of capitalism. As mentioned above (see Section 1.2), E.M. Wood (1997) suggests that there continues to be a strong confusion between the project of enlightenment and the development of capitalism. Wood maintains that the enlightenment is based on ideas of civil equality and an attack on privilege. This is in contrast to ideas of modernity that are tied to the ideals of improvement which are technocratic in nature and in the past have been tied to the spread of industrial capitalism.

Western institutions and policy makers have been quick to use the language of the enlightenment and human emancipation when discussing the need for the transition in Central Europe. However, at this specific point in time it seems that the democratic process has been somewhat hamstrung by Central Europe's integration into global capitalism. Since 1990, Poland, the Czech Republic and Hungary have experienced a number of elections, and, regardless of whether the political party in office is right-wing or left-wing, each governments' commitment to foreign lenders and its need for foreign investment has resulted in similar economic policies. Unfortunately, this seems to suggest that the spread of liberal democratic principles, for which many people in Central Europe have made considerable sacrifices, is being sidelined in favour of policies which facilitate an integrated global capitalist system. It is important to point out that the populations within Poland, the Czech Republic and Hungary have consistently voted against the types of economic policies that are practised in the region. Lack of domestic funds and international pressure encourages the government in power to adopt strict neo-classical economic policies. Sadly, in spite of the West's confidence in the economic advice being given, the policy outcomes have not been particularly positive.

Although neo-classical economic policies seem to be synonymous with economic austerity, there has been an assumption that the relative stability recently experienced by the three countries in this study is due to the Western economic policy advice given after 1989. This assumption is not only incorrect, but fosters an undeserved confidence in the types of policies encouraged by international financial institutions like the IMF. As discussed in Chapter 7 of this book, the increase in foreign investment and its relative stability is more appropriately ascribed to the region's relationship with the EU. The process of integration is only partially about the spread of capitalism. The EU is, of course, made up of states which engage in a capitalist form of exchange. However, the process of EU integration is a much wider project which requires the adoption of an enormous amount of existing EU legislation, which encompasses politics, economics, social policy, the environment, health and safety standards, etc. Where the neo-classical economic advice given to Central Europe in the early years assumed that capitalism was largely economic, the project of EU integration has a tacit acceptance that economic integration between states can only occur if a high level of social and political norms are also shared. This does not make the EU's policies less capitalist than that of the IMF or other international financial institutions, just more comprehensive and, therefore, more likely to be successful in the transmission of values which encompass capitalism and democracy.

How does the transition in Poland, the Czech Republic and Hungary shed light on growing trends in the global political economy? The collapse of the Soviet Union and the subsequent transition in areas like Central Europe should be viewed as a watershed with regards to the way in which theory is translated into policy, particularly the way in which it is translated into developmental theory constructed in the West for the developing world. Of course, the spread of norms by the powerful to those less powerful is not new. What, however, makes twentieth-century hegemony different from nineteenth-century imperialism? Today the Western world is left in a curious situation in which its institutions have not lost their desire for proscribing solutions to the rest of the world yet seem unwilling to consider that their role carries an assumption of superiority. The holding of foreign territory may have become *passé*, but the holding of foreign assets remains fashionable. Despite the coyness of current policies, the 'civilizing' mission remains intact. The question remains: where are these current policy trends in the global political economy taking us?

Despite evidence to the contrary there remains a deep-seated belief, particularly in the West, that the world is constantly improving. Part of this faith in linear progress springs from a confidence in the benefits of technological advance. Therefore, even though problems of economic development continue to plague us, an assumption exists that technological progress will eventually overcome our current difficulties. However, our understanding of the role of technology in economic development is often limited or muddled (see above, Chapter 2). That global capitalism as a phenomenon is changing is widely accepted. However, the nature of the modification is often ascribed to technology. Technological advancement is often heralded as having a revolutionary influence. Though technology may facilitate the way we already do things it rarely changes the structure of the global system. Just as the industrial revolution facilitated the spread of Western norms and values in the form of imperialism and adventure capitalism, a case could be made that our current technological revolution, rather than being a force for positive change, could be seen as a powerful tool in the hands of those who have no interest in promoting global equality. Further study needs to be conducted, but early results suggest that our current technologies have done much to increase global inequality. It is not a lone causal factor creating inequality, but technology plays a part in transmitting those values discussed in our section on Western norms and values. Similarly, it is critical to the functioning of the financial sector and allows for the level of monitoring desired by organizations such as the IMF.

Since the beginning of the computer age during the 1970s, there has been a marked growth in income inequality. The expansion of communication and computer-related technologies coincided with the rise of the new-right in the 1980s and helped transmit the distorted Western version of the Enlightenment project. With regards to the Central European transition, the availability of fax, email and internet access was essential for maintaining contact with the West and the transmission of Western norms. But the solidity of the ideas that the West is transmitting is still problematic. Unlike Western countries, access to and use of computer technology follows an old-fashioned core-periphery pattern in which governments and other crucial centres in Central Europe have access to technology, but its existence is not widespread. This pattern can be found globally. Internet access and access to computers in Brazil, China, India and Russia is negligible whereas in the United States there is almost 400 computers for every 1,000 people (Birdsall, 1998: 85). The technological revolution and its unequal distribution has coincided with trends of global income inequality. The argument made here is *not* that technology is solely responsible for inequality. It needs to be emphasized, however, that technology *enhances* the speed and invasiveness of the transmission of Western norms and values, but not its *effectiveness*. The point, therefore, is that the West is becoming increasingly better at transmitting ideas and solutions which are not only flawed but also are often damaging for those in receipt of them.

During the last 20 years there has been an ever widening gap between the ideals of the Enlightenment project (which are now strongly identified with democracy), and the development of globalized capitalism. Moreover, although democratic principles are undoubtedly Western in origin, countries adopting these principles do so with consent. The question of consent and legitimacy with regards to the type of capitalism dictated to Central Europe and other countries outside the Western world remains an important one. Increasingly these norms are economic in nature and pressed upon non-Western countries. International Organizations, particularly financial ones such as the WB and the IMF, graft democratic conditions onto the economic conditionality of their loans. However, encouraging forms of democratic governance in states whose governments are then required to play an ever decreasing role in the economy makes one wonder about the effectiveness of the democracy being offered. In the case of Central Europe it was almost a case of the post-1989 CEECs having to adhere to a strict form of neoclassical economic reforms, directly after 1989, in order to be 'allowed' to practice democracy. This study is interested in how the economic transition in Central Europe can be fitted into wider trends of global capitalism. The side-lining of democracy and the human emancipatory aspect it contains should become an issue of concern. In the past nation-states controlled most aspects of life within their boundaries. Recent developments, particularly during the last 15 years, have seen the breakdown between local, national and international policy-making so that most aspects of life have some form of international/global component. International governance has increased, but not international democracy. International organizations and private capital have been gaining greater control over peoples lives, but have not acquired greater responsibility. States have much less control than in the past, but somehow they have been left with the burden of responsibility and the level of politics where democracy can occur. It could be said that the state is assumed to be the only place where the Enlightenment project of human emancipation is suitable. However, tension has continued to grow between economic policies that support global capitalism and political projects supporting national democracies. International Organizations (WTO, WB and the IMF) are continuing to support programmes that increase income inequality in a decision-making process that lacks democratic legitimacy. As the business of states, corporations, and international organizations continue to collapse into each other, solutions to the democratic deficit will have to be found. It may be that the capitalist project is unsustainable without the modifying influence of the Enlightenment's goals for improving the lot of all people.

The Central European transition, and the other post-Soviet transitions, were the catalyst for changing the behaviour of the IMF. As mentioned in the Introduction (Chapter 1), the transition period for Central Europe and other parts of the former Soviet bloc would lay the ground work for how international financial organizations would deal with all other post-1989 crises. After the collapse of the Soviet Union organizations such as the IMF suggested policies that went beyond prescribing desirable targets for economic indicators. They began to stipulate, through loan conditionality, the complete restructuring of the government and private sector institutions. This trend has continued and in both the Mexican peso crisis of 1994 and the Asian crisis of 1997, global financial organizations have tied bail-out capital to institutional restructuring (see Section 1.2). The policy orientation of the suggested restructuring has tended to be strongly driven by the desire to transmit Western standards. However, as mentioned above, the achievement of Central Europe's transition has had more to do with its relationship with the EU than with the success of the neo-classical economic policies prescribed by the IMF. Despite the obvious role of the EU in Central Europe's success, the IMF appears to strongly believe in its own policies. As a result the IMF transmits policies to other parts of the non-Western world which are similar to the policies given to Central Europe after 1989. Much of their economic advice has been based upon financial and price liberalization. In defence of the IMF, they are often called in when a country is in serious financial difficulty and therefore there are no easy solutions. However, Western policy-makers in general may have misinterpreted the ingredients necessary to promote economic stability. For instance, the call for financial market deregulation throughout the 1990s was to have highly volatile results. Since April 1998 the world economy and international capital markets have suffered. Even wealthy well developed countries have seen a drop in economic growth. In response to the spreading crisis, the Board of Governors of the IMF dedicated much of their 4 October 1998 meeting to the problems and challenges of the global economy and its capital markets. In the IMF's communiqué it recognized the difficulties experienced by transition economies during this time of global economic instability (IMF, 1998a). The IMF conceded that the current instability is caused by large capital movements often precipitated by the flight of investment capital. This is particularly the case with regards to investment in non-G7 countries. Under the current international financial system if foreign direct investors become nervous about the performance of a host country's economy it can quickly return its investment capital to markets within the G7. Known as the 'flight to quality', this phenomenon has been responsible for exacerbating economic crises. Capital investment is becoming increasingly short term. Moreover, the large-scale movement of financial capital is beginning to cause instability in the traditionally more stable markets of the United States and Western Europe.

The cost of financial bailouts and the continuing problem of global economic instability has seen the IMF recognize the importance of issues like social safety nets. Similarly there is a growing recognition that individual state institution building is important in creating states that can withstand the pressure of international economic shocks. Despite a new interest in social policy and institution building, the IMF's main policy thrust in regards to solving the current crisis is identical to the policies suggested to Central Europe in 1989. They feel the solution lies in implementing strong economic adjustment programs (IMF, 1998a).

Western advice to transition and developing countries remains concentrated on restructuring at a state level. However, it could be argued that the problem lies not at the level of the state but at the level of global institutions and with the behaviour of global private capital. However, the tightening of global capital controls is the one policy that international organisations like the IMF are not willing to entertain (IMF, 1998a).

As illustrated in the case of Central Europe the enforcement of strict neo-classical economic development policies are unlikely to work without financial and institutional support from a wealthy trading partner, in this case the EU. Moreover, the continuing concentration on financial liberalization when constructing development/aid packages for non-western countries can plant the seed for financial instability which can often not be contained in an individual nation state.

Maintaining stability in the global political economy will be an onerous task in the current climate. The IMF and the WB may possibly have to look more closely at the functioning of their sister organization, the WTO. There is no weighted voting in the WTO and its rounds of trade negotiations rely heavily on the concept of trade management.

The WTO is still an organization that is interested in supporting capitalism and transmitting Western norms and values. It is also committed to trade liberalization in the same way that the IMF is committed to financial deregulation. However, where the two organizations differ is that WTO has had to recognize the importance of enlightenment issues of social equality and fair treatment when dealing with trade negotiations. Business behaviour through the WTO is also more strongly regulated. If there are compliance problems with WTO trade regulations it is dealt with by legal action through trade tribunals. By contrast, if a recipient country of an IMF loan does not meet its loan conditionality it can have its funding suspended. This alone illustrates how the operating procedures of the two organizations are considerably different.

Ultimately the question has to be asked: what is the purpose of current policies and are their objectives being fulfilled? The ideals of the post-war era was meant to embody the principles of emancipation and equality in the international organizations that were created. Intertwined with these objectives was the assumption that sound economic policies would enhance the overall project of human emancipation by achieving growth and stability in the global political economy. During the 1970s the concern became less a question of changing the world into a better place and more a question of just trying to keep the international political economy working. Now in the 1990s, without even the threat of Soviet-style Communism to distract the Western world, the global political economy is characterized by crisis management. It need not be necessary to dismantle our current international organizations, but perhaps we should ask ourselves whether the policies being prescribed are leading the global system in a direction that will be beneficial for the world at large?

Notes

Introduction

1 *Newsweek*, 14 September 1998.
2 Russia has now been largely accepted as a member of this organization which is often referred to as the G8. However, it remains financially fragile and politically weak and for our argument here we wish to concentrate specifically on the original G7 members whose power and influence dominates the Western world.
3 The term 'liberalism' can cause confusion, particularly in the United States where it has entered the language as a popular term meaning the enhancing of not just individual rights but rights of social groups as well, usually through the medium of government programmes.
4 Wood suggests that the Enlightenment is often seen, wrongly in her view, as being characterized by a 'totalizing' view of the world, with a proclivity for the standardization of knowledge, a belief in universal truths and values, and a belief in linear progress.
5 Named after the then US Secretary of State, George C. Marshall, the Marshall Plan was a European recovery programme conceived in 1947. The Plan was based on the US providing raw materials, goods and capital, in the form of credits or even subsidies in the hopes of stimulating Europe's economy.
6 The formal name of the WB is the International Bank for Reconstruction and Development.
7 The IMF formally ratified a second amendment to its charter in 1978. This formally ratified the change to floating exchange rates, making the IMF's past role defunct. Although OECD countries rarely use the IMF, Britain did suffer a liquidity crisis caused by a balance of payments problem in 1976. The crisis was short term but the UK did rely on IMF funds.
8 On 23 September 1998 the American Long-Term Capital Management hedge fund almost collapsed due to systemic instability caused by over-extension into Russia's financial sector. It was exposed to US$900 billion of liabilities and had only US$4 billion in capital stock. The Clinton Administration worked with the US Treasury and heads of several American banks to furnish a US$3.5 billion rescue package (Watson, 1998: 3).
9 Wade and Veneroso claim that since the 1997 Asian financial crisis, Japanese and American companies have gone from being minority to majority owners of Southeast Asian firms in exchange for writing down debt. Added to this trend is the devaluation of Asian companies making them a bargain for foreign companies (Wade and Veneroso, 1998: 14).

2 Western Developmental Approaches

1 Fox took Bull's quote from 'Force in Contemporary International Relations', *Survival*, X (Sept. 1968), 300–2, at 302. The book was David Vital's (1967), *The Inequality of States* (Oxford, Clarendon Press).

2 Sachs' transition model (Sachs, 1990; 1994) was based upon a rapid transition from communism to capitalism in which the type of capitalism that would be encouraged would be starkly liberal. This policy quickly became dubbed by others as 'shock therapy' a term that Sachs is reputed to dislike.
3 Alice Amsden is a Professor of Political Economy at the Massachusetts Institute of Technology.
4 Dr Ghia Nodia is the Chairman of the Board of the Caucasian Institute for Peace, Democracy and Development. He is also the head of the Political Philosophy Department at the Institute of Philosophy at the Academy of Sciences in Georgia, and a professor in the Department of Sociology at Tbilisi State University. He conducted the research cited above when a visiting fellow at the International Forum for Democratic Studies which is part of the National Endowment for Democracy in Washington, DC. Dr Nodia's research focuses on democracy and nationalism, and the post-communist transitions in the former Soviet Union.
5 Poland as a new republic was in crises during 1919 to 1922 when the 'legionaires' who supported the Chairman, Pilsudski, were in conflict with the National Democrats. With military backing Pilsudski was set up as head of state. However, in 1921 there was a ratification of the parliamentary constitution and a 1922 election saw the victory of the National Democrats and the resignation of Pilsudski.

3 Central Europe: Introduction to the Case-Studies

1 Neo-classical economics, as discussed in Chapter 1, is built on the theoretical foundations of classical liberal economics. The mainstay of this school of thought is that governments should not intervene in markets because free-markets are assumed to be self-regulating. Countries involved in free trade need not benefit equally in order for a liberal market system to be a success. All that is required is that individual states accrue some benefit. The goal of this form of economics is that political impediments to the free movement of capital, goods and labour are eliminated.
2 China's transition has been taking place for over 15 years. Unlike the CEECs, China concentrated on privatizing its agriculture sector first. Liberalization of prices was delayed. Exchange rates were maintained on a multi-tier basis and imports remain restricted. Also privatization of industry has been slow (Adams, 1993).

4 Poland

1 Kosciuszko, Tadeusz (1746–1817). Know predominantly as a Polish national hero, he also went to America and served with colonial forces in the American Revolution (1775–83), contributing to the decisive American victory at the Battle of Saratoga in 1777. In 1784 he returned to Poland to become a major general in the Polish Army.
2 The Curzon Line, name after the British politician, Lord Curzon (1859–1925), was established as the Eastern boundary to Poland by the First World War allies in 1919. The Curzon Line was an attempt to demarcate the Polish

boundary according to the geographical location of existing populations of ethnic minorities.

3 Balcerowicz was brought into the government because of his foreign experience and economic expertise. He graduated (1970) from the Central School of Planning and Statistics (now Warsaw School of Economics) where he specialized in foreign trade. He received an MBA from St John's University in New York in 1974. In 1975 he was awarded his doctorate from the Warsaw School of Economics. During 1981–82 he was deputy Chairman of the Polish Economic Association. Before the transition Balcerowicz had been awarded two foreign research fellowships, at the Universities of Sussex (1985) and Marburg (1988).

4 *Nomenklatura* is a term used to refer to people in the post-1989 period who held positions within government but who had also held bureaucratic or party positions during the communist regime.

5 Zbigniew Bujak is the legendary Leader of Solidarity's Warsaw section and was proposed at one stage as leader of the legalized Solidarity party. During 1990 a serious split in the party occurred. Bujak worked to create the new party (ROAD) which was the political foundation for Mazowiecki's government (Kowalik, 1995).

6 In actual fact there are very few Jews in Poland. Of the total population 75 per cent are practising Roman Catholics, but a full 95 per cent describe themselves as being Catholic. The remaining 5 per cent are made up of Eastern Orthodox, Protestants and Jews.

7 Throughout the post-war recovery Britain's economy was heavily dependent on the US. Its trade deficit with the US was extensive and caused currency problems. The British chancellor of the exchequer, Sir Stafford Cripps, confided to his cabinet during June 1949 that a complete collapse of sterling within the year was a possibility. This crisis made the US State Department realize reluctantly that additional long-term aid would be needed after 1952 when the US had originally hoped it would no longer have to contribute funds to the post-war recovery.

8 Many figures on the Polish economy are derived from either the Polish Central Statistical Office or the Gdansk Institute who often have close, but not identical figures.

9 A hub-and-spoke trade regime is a term used by trade analysts when referring to an asymmetrical trading relationship. An example could be made using the United States as the hub with Canada and Mexico acting as satellite economies. The hub economy has diverse trading relationships, but the satellite economies find their economies strongly dependent on the export trade to the larger hub economy. For transition countries such as Poland, Hungary and the Czech Republic trade dependence remains a concernz *vis-à-vis* their relationship with the EU.

10 A *voivodship* is a government administrative area similar to a county but can also contain rural towns.

11 Information received from the Polish Statistical Office, 1995.

5 Czech Republic

1 Unlike many other currencies in Central Europe the exchange rate of the Czech koruna has been quite stable. In 1990, 29 koruna = US$1, by 1994, 30 koruna = US$1, and its exchange in 1998 was 35 koruna = US$1.

2 Literature on privatization tends not to give a fixed number of employees for 'small' versus 'big' firms. In practice, privatized 'small' firms tend to be below 50 employees. 'Big' firms, however, is a much wider category and may refer to state-owned firms with a few hundred employees or as many as a few thousand full-time workers.

6 Hungary

1 Janos Kadar was premier of Hungary from 1956 to 1958, and from 1961 to 1965 and First Secretary of the Hungarian Communist Party from 1956 to 1988.

7 The EU Effect and the Question of Eastern Enlargement

1 Mr Stavinoha's interview was one of a series conducted in Prague as part of a research award given by the Seed Foundation, University of Limerick, to the present author.

Bibliography

Unpublished sources

Adams, F. G. (1993), 'Transition patterns: China versus Eastern Europe'.
Site address http://www.ssc.upenn.edu/east/fall94/Transition Patterns.html

Boote, A. R. (1992), 'Assessing Eastern Europe's capital needs', Working Paper Series, WP/92/12, IMF document.
Site address: http://www.imf.org/external/pubs/cat/brcat.cfm?brletter=A&type=Title

Calvo, G. A. *et al.* (1995), 'Capital flows in Central and Eastern Europe: evidence and policy options', Working Paper Series, WP/95/57, IMF document.
Site address: http://www.imf.org/external/pubs/cat/brcat.cfm?brletter=C&type=Title

Gupta, S. (1998), 'Economic transition and social protection – issues and agenda for Reform', *Papers on Policy Analysis and Assessment* P,PAA/98/14, IMF document.
Site address: http://www.imf.org/external/pubs/cat/date.cfm

IMF (1998a), 'Communique of the Interim Committee of the Board of Governors of the International Monetary Fund', Press Release No. 98/47, 4 Oct., IMF document.
Site address: http://www.imf.org/external/np/sec/pr/1998/PR9847.htm

IMF (1998b), 'Annual Report of the Executive Board for the Financial year Ended April 30, 1998', IMF document.
Site address: http://www.imf.org/external/pubs/ft/ar/98/index.htm

Haque, N. Ul and K. Moshins (1998), 'Do IMF-supported programs work?: a survey of the cross-country empirical evidence', Working Paper Series, WP/98/169.
Site address: http://www.imf.org/external/pubs/cat/date.cfm

Hussain, Qaizar and E. Nivorozhkin (1997), 'The capital structure of listed companies in Poland', Working Paper Series, WP/97/175, IMF document.
Site address: http://www.imf.org/external/pubs/cat/brcat.cfm?brletter=C&type=Title

Pazsgay, I. (1987), 'Turn and reform'.
This paper was a policy document for the Hungarian political party, the PPF, later the HDF.

Quirk, P. (1994), 'Adopting currency convertibility – experiences and monetary policy considerations for advanced developing countries', Working Paper Series, WP/94/96, IMF document.
Site address: http://www.imf.org/external/pubs/cat/brcat.cfm?brletter=A&brtype=Title

Sachs, J. D. (1999), 'Biography', in Jeffrey Sachs' homepage at the Harvard Institute for International Development.
Site address: http://www.hiid.harvard.edu/about/peopl e/sachs/biograph.html

Siklos, P. L. (1996), 'Capital flows in a transitional economy and the sterilization dilemma – the Hungarian case', Working Paper Series, WP/96/86, IMF document.

Site address: http://www.imf.org/external/pubs/cat/brcat.cfm?brletter=C&type=Title

Stanislaw, G. (1994), 'The role of international financial institutions: the Polish and Russian experience 1989–93', Paper to Conference on the Role of International Financial Institutions in Eastern Europe, Munich, Apr.

Varley, M. (1997), 'Presentation on the Santer Package and the CAP Reform Proposals', presentation prepared by Martin Varley, the Director of Policy Development for the Irish Co-operative Organisation Society (ICOS), Aug.

Watson, M. (1998), 'The "common-sense" of "market rationality": neo-liberal lock-in effects and the "privatisation" of debt-financed growth regimes', paper presented to the Annual Conference of the British International Studies Association, University of Sussex, Brighton, 14–16 Dec.

Published primary sources

Commission of the EC (1994), *European Economy, Supplement A*, no. 3, Mar., DG for Economic and Financial Affairs.

Commission of the EC (1995), *Towards Greater Economic Integration: The European Union's Financial Assistance and Trade Policy for Central and Eastern Europe and the New Independent States*, Brussels: Directorate IA, European Union Document.

Commission of the EC (1997), *Agenda 2,000*, EU Strategy Document.

Czech Republic (1999), *Factbook*.

EIU Country Report (1995), *Country Report, 4th quarter 1995, Poland*, London: The Economist Intelligence Unit.

EIU Country Profile (1996), *EIU Country Profile 1995–96, Hungary*, London: The Economist Intelligence Unit.

EIU Country Profile (1996), *EIU Country Profile 1996–97, Czech Republic and Slovakia 1996–97*, London: The Economist Intelligence Unit.

EIU Country Report (1996), *EIU Country Report, 1st quarter 1996, Czech Republic*, London: The Economist Intelligence Unit.

EIU Country Report (1998), *EIU Country Report, 3rd quarter 1998, Hungary*, London: The Economist Intelligence Unit.

EIU Country Report (1998), *EIU Country Report, 3rd quarter 1998, Poland*, London: The Economist Intelligence Unit.

European Bank for Reconstruction and Development (EBRD) (1994), *Transition Report*, London: EBRD.

European Report (1997), Economic and Monetary affairs, no. 2277, Dec.

European Report (1998), External Relations, no. 2339, 5 Sept.

European Report (1998), External Relations, no. 2341, 12 Sept.

OECD (1994), *Integrating Emerging Market Economies into the International Trading System*, Paris: OECD.

OECD (1997a), *Agricultural Policies in OECD Countries: Monitoring and Evaluation 1997*, Paris: OECD.

OECD (1997b), *Agricultural Policies in OECD Countries: Monitoring and Evaluation 1997*, 10th edn, Annual Report, Paris: OECD publication.

UN, Economic Commission for Europe (1988), *Economic Survey of Europe*, New York: UN.

UNCTAD (1994), *World Investment Report*. Geneva and New York: UN Conference of Trade and Development.

UNICEF (1994), *Economies in Transition Studies, Regional Monitoring Report, 1994: Crisis in Mortality, Health and Nutrition*, Florence: UN International Children's Emergency Fund.

World Bank (WB) (1987), *Poland: Reform, Adjustment, and Growth*. vol I. Washington, DC: World Bank.

Published secondary sources

Books

Amsden, A., J. Kochanowicz and L. Taylor (1994), *The Market Meets Its Match: Restructuring the Economies of Eastern Europe*, Cambridge, Mass.: Harvard University Press.

Augelli, E. and C. Murphy (1988), *America's Quest for Supremacy and the Third World: An Essay in Gramscian Analysis*, London: Pinter.

Axilrod, S. H. (1996), *Transformations to Open Market Operations: Developing Countries and Emerging Markets*, Economic Issues No. 5, Washington, DC: IMF.

Bardhan, P. (1997), *The Role of Governance in Economic Development: A Political Economy Approach*, Development Centre Studies: Development Centre OECD, Paris.

Bossak, J. W. (ed.) (1995), *Poland, International Economic Report, 1994/95*, Warsaw: Warsaw School of Economics; World Economy Research Institute.

Brown, C. (1997), *Understanding International Relations*, London: Macmillan.

Butterfield, H. (1931), *The Whig Interpretation of History* (new edn 1965), London: W. W. Norton.

Cox, R. W. (1987), *Production, Power, and World Order: Social Forces in the Making of History* (New York: Columbia University Press).

Crouch, C. and Wolfgang Streeck (eds) (1997), *Political Economy of Modern Capitalism: Mapping Convergence and Diversity*, London: Sage.

Dziewanowski, M. K. (1959), *The Communist Party of Poland: An Outline of History*, Cambridge, Mass.: Harvard University Press.

Epstein, F. T. (1973), *Germany and the East*, Don Mills, Ontaio: Fitzhenry & Whiteside.

Europa Publishers (1994), *Eastern Europe and the Commonwealth of Independent States 1994: A Political and Economic Survey*, 2nd edn, London: Europa.

Frydman, R. *et al.* (1993), *The Privatization Process in Central Europe*, vol. I, Budapest: Central European University Press.

Galbraith, J. K. (1973), *The Great Crash of 1929*, London: H. Hamilton.

Garton Ash, T. (1990), *We the people: The Revolution of '89*, London: Granta Books.

Gelb, A. and C. W. Gray (1991), *The Transformation of Economies in Central and Eastern Europe*, Policy Research Series, no. 17, Washington, DC: World Bank.

Gerner, K. (1985), *The Soviet Union and Central Europe in the Post War Era*, Aldershot: Gower.

Gill, S. (ed.) (1993), *Gramsci, Historical Materialism and International Relations*, Cambridge: Cambridge University Press.

Grabbe, H. and Kirsty Hughes (1997), *Eastward Enlargement of the European Union*, London: The Royal Institute of International Affairs, European Programme.

Grabiec, J. (1974), *Wspolczesna Polska w cyfrach I faktach* (Contemporary Poland in Figures and Facts), Cracow.

Hasib, A. (1957–58), *Monetary Negotiations in the World Economic Conference 1933*, Aligarh, India: Faculty of Arts Muslim University.
Hill, R. J. (1985), *Soviet Union, Politics, Economics and Society*, Boulder, Col.: Lynne Rienner Publishers.
Hobsbawm, E. (1987), *The Age of Empire 1875–1914*, London: Orion Publishing.
Hobson, J. A. (1902, rev. edn 1948), *Imperialism: A Study*, London: Allen & Unwin.
Hutton, W. (1996), *The State We're In*, London: Vintage Press.
Keegan, W. (1993), *The Spectre of Capitalism: The Future of the World Economy After the Fall of Communism*, London: Vintage.
Kinder, H. and Werner Hilgemann (1978), *The Atlas of World History, Vol. II: From the French Revolution to the Present*, Harmondsworth: Penguin.
Kinder, H. and Werner Hilgemann (1979), *The Atlas of World History, Vol. I: From the Beginning to the Eve of the French Revolution*, Harmondsworth: Penguin.
Kindleberger, C. P. (1973), *The World in Depression 1929–1939*, London: Penguin Press.
Kovrig, B. (1979), *Communism in Hungary: From Kun to Kadar*, Stanford: Hoover Institution Press.
Kubiak Report, The (1982), *Survey*, 26(3).
Landesmann, M. A. and Istvan P. Szekely (eds) (1995), *Industrial Restructuring and Trade Reorientation in Eastern Europe*, Cambridge: Cambridge University Press.
Lichtheim, G. (1977), *Imperialism*, Harmondsworth: Penguin.
Macartney, C. A. and A. W. Palmer (1972), *Independent Eastern Europe: A History*, London: Macmillan.
Maurer, P. and Wlodzimierz Siwinski (eds) (1988), *Creditworthiness and Reform in Poland*, Bloomington, IN: Indiana University Press.
Mendell, M. and Klaus Nielson (eds) (1995), *Europe: Central and East*, Montreal: Black Rose Books.
Molnar, Miklos (1978), *A Short History of the Hungarian Communist Party*, Folkeston: Dawson Press.
Morawetz, R. (1991), *Recent Foreign Direct Investment in Eastern Europe: Towards a Possible Role for the Tripartite Declaration of Principles Concerning Multinational Enterprises and Social Policy*, Geneva: International Labour Office, Multinational Enterprises Programme, Working Paper 71.
Morgenthan, Hans J. and Kenneth W. Thompson (1985), *Politics Among Nations: The Struggle for Power and Peace*, 6th edn. New York: Knopf.
Murphy, C. N. and Roger Tooze (eds) (1991), *The New International Political Economy*, Boulder, Col.: Lynne Rienner Publishers.
Pettman, R. (1991), *International Politics, Balance of Power, Balance of Productivity, Balance of Ideologies*, Boulder, Col.: Lynne Rienner Publishers.
Polanyi, K. (1994), *The Great Transformation*, New York: Farrar & Rinehart.
Rose, R. (1998), *Elections in Central and Eastern Europe Since 1990*, University of Strathclyde, Glasgow: CSPP Publications.
Rosenberg, T. (1995), *The Haunted Land: Facing Europe's Ghosts After Communism*, London: Vintage.
Rostow, W. W. (1960), *The Stages of Economic Growth: A Non-Communist Manifesto*, Cambridge: Cambridge University Press.
Russett, B. and Harvey Starr (1996), *World Politics*, 5th edn, New York: W. H. Freeman.
Sachs, J. (1994), *Understanding Shock Therapy*, Washington, DC: Social Market Foundation.

Saunders, C. T. (ed.) (1995), *Eastern Europe in Crisis and the Way Out*, London: Macmillan, in association with the Vienna Institute for Comparative Economic Studies.

Spero, J. E. (1981), *The Politics of International Economic Relations*, New York: St. Martins.

Suda, Z. L. (1980), *Zealots and Rebels: A History of the Communist Party of Czechoslovakia*, Stanford, Calif.: Hoover Institution Press.

Swain, Nigel (1992), *Hungary: The Rise and Fall of Feasible Socialism*, London: Verso.

Talalay, M., C. Farrands and R. Tooze (eds) (1997), *Technology, Culture and Competitiveness: Change and the World Political Economy*, London: Routledge.

Tausch, A. with Fred Prager (1993), *Towards a Socio-Liberal Theory of World Development*, Basingstoke: Macmillan.

Toma, P. A. and Volgyes, I. (1977), *Politics in Hungary*, San Francisco: Freeman.

Vital, D. (1967), *The Inequality of States*, Oxford: Clarendon Press.

Wallerstein, I. (1974), *Das Moderne Weltsystem – Die Anfaenge Kapitalistischer landwirtschaft und die europaeische Weltoekonomie in 16 Jahrhundert: Aus dem Amerikanischen von Angelika Schweikhart*, Frankfurt: Syndikat: English edn, 1974, *The Modern World-system: Capitalist Agriculture and the Origins of the European World-economy in the Sixteenth Century*, London: Academic Press.

Weidenfeld, W. (ed.) (1995), *Central and Eastern Europe on the Way into the European Union*, Gutersloh: Bertelsmann Foundation.

Weisskopf, W. A. (1973), *Alienation and Economics*, New York: Dell Publishing.

White, S., Judy Batt and Paul G. Lewis (eds) (1993), *Developments in East European Politics*, London: Macmillan.

WIIW (Wiener Institut fur Internationale Wirtschaftsvergleiche) (1996), *Countries in Transition 1996, WIIW Handbook of Statistics*, Vienna: WIIW publishers.

World Economy Research Institute (1995), *Poland, International Economic Report 1994/1995*, Warsaw :Warsaw School of Economic, 1995, p. 32.

Chapters in books

Berry, Richard Ross (1994), 'Hungary, the economy', in *Eastern Europe and the Commonwealth of Independent States 1994: A Political and Economic Survey*. 2nd edn, London: Europa, pp. 330–7.

Bozoki, Andras and Bill Lomax (1996), 'The revenge of history: the Portuguese, Spanish and Hungarian transitions – some comparisons', in Geoffrey Pridham and Paul G. Lewis (eds), *Stabilising Fragile Democracies: Comparing New Party Systems in Southern and Eastern Europe*, London: Routledge, pp. 186–206.

Brown, A. and G. Wightman (1977), 'Czechoslovakia: revival and retreat', in Brown, A. and J. Gray (eds), *Political Culture and Political Change Communist States*, London: Mamillan, pp. 80–123.

Dyba, K. and J. Svejnar (1994) 'Stabilization and transition in Czechoslovakia', in Olivier Jean Blanchard, Kenneth A. Froot and Jeffrey D. Sachs (eds), *The Transition in Eastern Europe, Volume 1: Country Studies*, Chicago: University of Chicago Press, pp. 35–57.

Fallenbuchl, Z. (1980), 'The Polish economy at the beginning of the 1980s', in *US Congress, Joint Economic Committee: East European Economic Assessment*, Washington, DC: Government Printing Office, pp. 43–57.

Farrands, C. (1997), 'Interpretations of the diffusion and absorption of technology: change in the global political economy', in Michael Talalay, Chris Farrands and Roger Tooze (eds), *Technology, Culture and Competitiveness: Change and the World Political Economy,* London: Routledge, pp. 75–90.

Fitoussi, J. (1997), 'Following the collapse of communism, is there still a middle way?', in Colin Crouch and Wolfgang Streeck (eds), *Political Economy of Modern Capitalism: Mapping Convergence and Diversity,* London: Sage, pp. 148–61.

Gill, S. (1991), 'Historical materialism, Gramsci, and international political economy', in Craig N. Murphy and Roger Tooze (eds), *The New International Political Economy,* Boulder, Col.: Lynne Rienner Publishers, pp. 50–74.

Gill, S. (1993), 'Epistemology, ontology and the "Italian School"', in Stephen Gill (ed.), *Gramsci, Historical Materialism and International Relations,* Cambridge: Cambridge University Press, pp. 21–48.

Gill, S. and D. Law (1993), 'Global hegemony and the structural power of capital', in Stephen Gill (ed.), *Gramsci, Historical Materialsim and International Relations,* Cambridge: Cambridge University Press, pp. 93–124.

Handl, V., Cestmir Konecny and Josef Poeschl (1995), 'Czech Republic', in Werner Weidenfeld (ed.), *Central and Eastern Europe on the Way into the European Union,* Gutersloh: Bertelsmann Foundation Publishers, pp. 49–69.

Kowalik, T. (1995), 'From self-governing republic to capitalism: Polish workers and Intellectuals', in Marguerite Mendell and Klaus Nielson (eds), *Europe: Central and East,* Montreal: Black Rose Books, pp. 92–111.

Lewis, P. G. (1993), 'History, Europe and the politics of the east', in Stephen White, Judy Batt and Paul G. Lewis (eds), *Developments in East European Politics,* London: Macmillan, pp. 262–74.

Mason, D. S. (1993), 'Poland' in Stephen White, Judy Batt and Paul G. Lewis (eds), *Developments in East European Politics,* London: Macmillan, pp. 36–50.

Messerlin, P. A. (1995), 'Trade relations of the Eastern European countries', in Christopher T. Saunders (ed.), *Eastern Europe in Crisis and the Way Out,* London: Macmillan, in association with The Vienna Institute for Comparative Economic Studies, pp. 202–25.

Nesporova, A. (1995), 'Industrial restructuring in Czechoslovakia after 1989', in Michael A. Landesmann and Istvan P. Szekely (eds), *Industrial Restructuring and Trade Reorientation in Eastern Europe,* Cambridge: Cambridge University Press, pp. 21–42.

Pontusson, J. (1997), 'Between neo-liberalism and the German model: Swedish capitalism in transition', in Colin Crouch and Wolfgang Streek (eds), *Political Economy of Modern Capitalism: Mapping Convergence and Diversity,* London: Sage, pp. 55–70.

Prust, J. (1988), 'Partial recovery from the economic crisis', in Paul Maurer and Wlodzimierz Siwinski (eds), *Creditworthiness and Reform in Poland,* Bloomington, Ind: Indiana University Press, pp. 18–31.

Rady, Martyn (1994), 'Hungary: history', in *Eastern Europe and the Commonwealth of Independent States 1994: A Political and Economic Survey,* 2nd edn, London: Europa, pp. 326–30.

Richter, Sandor (1996), 'Hungary: successful stabilization', in Leon Podkaminer (eds), *Transition Countries: Economic Developments in 1995 and Outlook for 1996,* Research Reports, The Vienna Institute for Comparative Economic Studies, no. 225, Feb., pp. 60–8.

Ritchet, X. (1981), 'Is there an 'Hungarian' model of Planning?', in P. G. Hare (eds), *Hungary: A Decade of Economic Reform*, London: Allen & Unwin, pp. 70–83.

Rostworowski, E. (1979), 'Czasy Saskie: Oswiecenie' in J. Tazbir (ed.), *Zarys Historii Polski*, Warsaw: Panstwowy Instytut Wydawniczy, pp. 295–370.

Rutland, P. (1994), 'The Czech Republic: the economy', in *Eastern Europe and the Commonwealth of Independent States 1994: A Political and Economic Survey*, 2nd edn, London: Europa, pp. 264–9.

Smolik, J. E. (1995), 'The Transformation of East-West Trade Relations', in Christopher T. Saunders (ed.), *Eastern Europe in Crisis and the Way Out*, London: Macmillan, in association with the Vienna Institute for Comparative Economic Studies, pp. 240–52.

Strange, S. (1991), 'An Eclectic Approach', in Craig N. Murphy and Roger Tooze (eds), *The New International Political Economy*, Boulder: Lynne Rienner Publishers, pp. 33–49.

Swain, Nigel (1993), 'Hungary', in Stephen White, Judy Batt and Paul G. Lewis (eds), *Developments in East European Politics*, Houndsmills, UK: Macmillan, pp. 66–80.

Talalay, M., C. Farrands and R. Tooze (1997), 'Technology, culture and competitiveness: Change and the world political economy', in M. Talalay, C. Farrands and R. Tooze (eds), *Technology, Culture and Competitiveness: Change and the World Political Economy*, London: Routledge, pp. 1–9.

Wightman, Gordon (1993), 'The Czech and Slovak Republics', in Stephen White, Judy Batt and Paul G. Lewis (eds), *Developments in East European Politics*, London: Macmillan, pp. 51–65.

Wightman, Gordon (1994), 'The Czech Republic: History', in *Eastern Europe and the Commonwealth of Independent States 1994: A Political and Economic Survey*, 2nd edn, London: Europa Publishers Limited, pp. 255–63.

Journal Articles

Balazs, Katalin (1994), 'Transition crisis in the Hungarian R&D sector', *Economic Systems*, 18(3), Sept.: 281–306.

Bartlett, D. and Anna Seleny (1998) 'The political enforcement of liberalism: bargaining, institutions, and auto multinationals in Hungary', *International Studies Quarterly*, 42: 319–38.

Bartlett, D. L. (1997), 'Has the East really become the South?: ownership structure and economic policy in Eastern Europe and Latin America', *Politics and Society*, 25(2): 202–33.

Birdsall, N. (1998), 'Life is unfair: inequality in the world', *Foreign Policy*, 111, summer: 76–93.

Bognar, J. (1982), 'Hungary's progress in a world economic context', *The New Hungarian Quarterly*, 23: 87.

Bjork, J. (1995), 'The uses of conditionality: Poland and the IMF', *East European Quarterly*, 29(1): 89–124.

Bossanyi, Katlin (1995), 'Taking stock of the economic transition', *The Hungarian Quarterly*, 36, summer: 92–9.

Brenner, R. (1977), 'The origins of capitalist development: a critique of neo-Smithian Marxism', *New Left Review*, 104: 25–92.

Brokl, K. and Mansfeldova, Z. (1995), 'Czech Republic', *European Journal of Political Research*, 28: 305–12.

Burant, S. (1993), 'International relations in a regional context: Poland and its Eastern neighbours – Lithuania, Belarus, Ukraine', *Europe–Asia Studies*, 45(3): 395–418.

Campbell, J. L. (1996), 'An institutional analysis of fiscal reform in postcommunist europe', *Theory and Society: Renewal and Critique in Social Theory*, 25(1): 45–84.

Fallenbuchl, Z. (1982), 'Poland's economic crisis', *Problems of Communism*, 31(2): 35–49.

Fox, A. B. (1969), 'The small states in the international system, 1919–1969', *International Journal, Canadian Institute of International Affairs*, 24(4), autumn: 751–64.

Gowan, P. (1995), 'Neo-liberal theory and practice for Eastern Europe', *New Left Review*, 213, Sept./Oct.: 3–61.

Grieve, M. J. (1995), 'Buying security after the Cold War: what price peace?', *International Insights*, 11(2), autumn: 81–95.

Hettne, B. (1994), 'The political economy of post-communist development', *The European Journal of Development Research*, 6(1), June: 39–60.

Huntington, S. (1993), 'The clash of civilizations', *Foreign Affairs*, 72(3), summer: 22–49.

Kapur, D. (1998), 'The IMF: a curse or a cure?', *Foreign Policy*, 111, summer: 114–29.

Lane, Sarah J. (1995), 'Business starts during the transition in Hungary', *Journal of Business Venturing*, 10: 181–94.

Mayall, J. (1998), 'Globalization and international relations', *Review of International Studies*, 24: 239–50.

Meaney, C. S. (1995), 'Foreign experts, capitalists and competing agendas; privatization in Poland, Czech Republic and Hungary', *Comparative Political Studies*, 28(2): 275–305.

Mladek, J. (1995), 'Privatizing the Czech Republic', *World Policy Journal*, 12(3), autumn: 124–8.

Nodia, G. (1996), 'How different are postcommunist transitions?', *Journal of Democracy*, 7(4), Oct.: 15–29.

Palda, K. (1997), 'Czech privatization and corporate governance', *Communist and Post-Communist Studies*, 30(1): 83–93.

Puja, F. (1983), 'Hungary's part in East–West relations', *The New Hungarian Quarterly*, 24: 90.

Rotte, R. (1997), 'The political reorganisation of the international economy', *Aussenpolitik*, 47(1): 43–52.

Sachs, J. (1995), 'Consolidating capitalism', *Foreign Policy*, spring, 98: 50.

Sanford, G. (1995), 'The Polish road from communism', *The Slavonic and East European Review*, 73(1), Jan.: 106–10.

Simai, M. (1992), 'Hungarian problems', *Government and Opposition*, 27(1), winter: 52.

Schmieding, H. (1993), 'From plan to market: on the nature of the transformation crisis', *Weltwirtschaftliches Archiv. (Review of World economics)*, 129(2): 216.

Sojka, M. (1994), 'The transformation of the Czech economy – present and future developments', *Czech Sociological Review*, 2(1): 35–51.

Staniskis, J. (1991), 'Political capitalism in Poland', *Eastern European Politics and Societies*, 5: 127–41.

Stanislaw, G. (1992), 'Polish economic reform, 1990–1991: principles, policies and outcomes', *Journal of Comparative Economics*, June: 338–72.

Tranholm-Mikkelsen, Jeppe (1991), 'Neo-functionalism: obstinate or obsolete?: a reappraisal in the light of the new dynamism of the EC', *Millennium*, 20(1), spring: 1–22.

Ulc, Otto (1996), 'Czechoslovakia's velvet divorce', *East European Quarterly*, 30(3), Sept.: 331.
Wade, R. and Frank Veneroso (1998), 'The Asian crisis: the high debt model versus the Wall Street-Treasury-IMF complex', *New Left Review*, 228: 3–23.
Wallerstein, I. (1997), 'Eurocentrism and its avatars: the dilemmas of social science', *New Left Review*, 226, Nov.: 93.
Wollner, Ernest J. (1995), 'Focus: Hungary', *European Current Law*, Aug.: 5–13.
Wood, E. M. (1997), 'Modernity, postmodernity or capitalism?', *Review of International Political Economy*, 4(3), autumn: 539–60.

Newspaper and periodical articles

Anon. (1994), *The Economist*, 3 Dec.: 24.
Anon. (1996), 'Food's uncertain future', *Business & Finance*, 17 Oct.: 29–32.
Barany, Zoltan (1994), 'Socialist–Liberal Government stumbles through its first year', *Transition*, 28 July, 1(13): 64–9.
Engelberg. S. (1990), 'Polish workers yield new power', *New York Times*, 28 Dec.: 10.
Friedrich, A. (1998), 'Czechs drag feet in race to join EU', *Prague Post*, 21 Oct.: 1.
Klee, K. and R. Thomas (1998), 'Defending the one true faith', *Newsweek*, 14 Sep.: 26–7.
Sachs, J. (1990), 'What is to be done?', *The Economist*, 13 Jan.: 19–22.
Shirong, Wan (1994), 'Economic rehabilitation in Czech Republic', *Beijing Review*, 26 Sept., 37(39): 18–19.
Steiger, S. (1996), 'Miracle of low unemployment', *Economic and Political Weekly*, 27 Jan.: 204.

Internet websites

Sites used for current affairs information:

Central Europe Today.
Site address: http://www.transition@omri.cz.
Business Europa Briefing (Central Europe).
Site address: http//www.business-europa.co.uk/
The Hungary Report.
Site address: http://www.isys.hu/hrep/
CTK Czech News Agency Praha.
Site address: http://www.ctknews.com/thuctk.html

Sites used to verify parliamentary election results

British Helsinki Human Rights Group (parliamentary elections, Poland, Czech Republic and Hungary).
Site address: http://www.bhhrg.org/
Area Studies
Site address: http://www.psr.keele.ac.uk/area.htm

Index